Archaeological Cultures of the Sheyenne Bend

Archaeological Cultures of the Sheyenne Bend

Michael G. Michlovic
George R. Holley

The Digital Press at the University of North Dakota
Grand Forks, ND

2022 The Digital Press @ The University of North Dakota

Library of Congress Control Number: 2922930800
The Digital Press at the University of North Dakota, Grand Forks, North Dakota

ISBN-13: 978-1-7364986-7-5 (paperback)
ISBN-13: 978-1-7364986-6-8 (Ebook/PDF)

Table of Contents

Acknowledgements

Long-term support for the authors' work in the Sheyenne Bend was provided by Minnesota State University Moorhead (MSUM), which included maintaining an Archaeology Lab and providing summer salaries and travel funds for fieldwork. Other funding sources over the years included the National Science Foundation (grant SRB-9408735) for work at the Rustad site, the State Historical Society of North Dakota for support of the Shea excavations, the Cass County Joint Water District for the Maple River archaeological survey, and the National Park Service Midwest Archaeological Center for study of the Biesterfeldt site. We are especially grateful to the many landowners and collectors in the Sheyenne Valley who allowed us to access their property, or view their artifact collections over the years. We especially recognize the late Roger Shea, Dean Sprunk, Charles Rotenberger, Lynn and Marcia Utke, Charles Wall, the Solhjem family, Elsie Peterson, the Rustad family of Kindred, and the Archaeological Conservancy. Dr. Dick Herring, Lisbon, made his private collections available for study, and Dr. Frank Zeck provided airplane service for aerial photographs, along with much appreciated advice about the location of sites. Elgin Crows Breast served as a consultant prior to and during excavations the authors conducted in the Sheyenne Bend, and we are grateful for his guidance. Our thanks also to Bill Caraher and reviewers for The Digital Press at the University of North Dakota, and to Fern Swenson of the State Historical Society of North Dakota for suggested improvements to our manuscript, and to Jackson Carr for the base map of many of the figures in this volume. We wish to express our appreciation to Fred Schneider, whose continuing interest in the Sheyenne Valley stimulated much of the work described here, and to Cherie Haury and Garry Running, our colleagues and contributors to our understanding of the Sheyenne Bend. Most of all, we acknowledge and thank the many archaeology students from MSUM who filled out our field crews and took up lab assignments to complete the tedious work that archaeological projects require. Their devotion and work ethic, their enthusiasm and camaraderie, are largely responsible for the discoveries made during our work in the Sheyenne Valley.

Preface

This account of the archaeology of the southern part of the Sheyenne River Valley in eastern North Dakota is based largely on work performed by one or both authors, and also by archaeologists from an earlier day who worked sporadically in the Sheyenne Bend. We acknowledge the earlier field studies of W.D. Strong, Elden Johnson, Rain Vehik, and Cherie Haury-Artz. We note especially the work of Fred Schneider, who initiated interest in several hamlet-size settlements enclosed by dry moats or ditches in the Sheyenne and Maple River regions. Garry Running discovered very old, buried archaeological deposits exposed in industrial cuts into Sheyenne delta in the 1990s. Important work was also conducted by Rinita Dalan, who began remote sensing at several important sites discussed here, adding to our understanding of larger portions of sites than were available from excavations.

The two authors of this volume have spent over 20 field seasons of study in the Sheyenne Bend area of North Dakota. Some of this work was reconnaissance, that is, looking for places of archaeological interest; some of it was excavation, or the intensive study of a single archaeological site. The result is uneven, and some places are better known than others, since sites in those places were quite rich. Other areas are less well understood, either because no work has yet been undertaken, or nothing was found there, or what was found was an impoverished remnant of the past. Yet even if the record we present here is spotty, it is worth remembering that without the archaeological record, we would know far less than we do.

Archaeological fieldwork, the basis for this book, is highly enjoyable, but unavoidably messy. It's not only the rain, or the heat, or the insects that interfere with the tidy plans laid out in offices and labs for how field projects are supposed to proceed. Not knowing what might be found, how it will be scattered through the soil, what won't be there that was expected, and what will be there that wasn't—all these normally mean that projects take us two steps forward and one step sideways.

Keep in mind that the site descriptions and discussions that follow are presently our best estimate of what these materials mean, but they will undoubtedly be modified by future work. Besides this, these labors were not completed as part of any long-term, well-funded, and thought-out research program. Some of this was done as part of field school exercises at our university, with the belief that it was a waste of time and effort to teach students archaeology by having them dig at pretend archaeological sites, when there were actual cultural deposits that would otherwise be lost to some damaging impact. Some of this was done as part of cultural resource management projects, required by law prior to the destruction of cultural sites by needed construction or development projects. Other work was done at the request of state or federal agencies. For this reason, some of the work described here was completed in well-funded projects, while some was done with little in the way of funding. Sometimes, even without enough money to do everything we would have liked, it was necessary to excavate at a site simply because it was being destroyed, and any study at all, however poorly funded, was better than nothing.

Throughout we use the term Native American, indigenous peoples, and American Indian interchangeably. We hope that this is not offensive to any reader. Our experience interacting with native students, and with native consultants whose advice was asked prior to many of the projects reported here, usually referred to themselves as Indians. On the other hand, we are aware that not everyone feels the same about this issue. Given the history of oppression and discrimination that Native American peoples have faced over the centuries, we understand that it is not always possible to satisfy the feelings of all those whose past is touched on here. If we knew the term of reference that would satisfy everyone, we would certainly use it.

On a related matter, there has been a field tradition among archaeologists of excavating indigenous burial sites in North America, including in the Sheyenne Valley. Native peoples have been active for many years in opposing this intrusion into ancient burials by archaeologists and physical anthropologists. Such projects mostly came to an end in the 1970s, at least in this part of the country, although occasionally the imminent destruction of a prehistoric burial will still require excavation and removal of human remains. Today, though, this is done under the direction of Native authorities and the burials are re-interred on reservation land. None of the work done in the Sheyenne Bend by the two of us involved burial excavations. However, some of the materials used in interpretations offered here did come from burial sites. Out of respect for the dead, and for the descendent communities, we do not illustrate any human remains from the prehistoric sites discussed here, nor will we present pictures of any of the excavations conducted into burial sites. We also note that disturbing burial mounds in North Dakota is against the law, whether they are on private or public land. They are to be treated the same as cemeteries.

Archaeological sites may be on public land or on private property. In either case removing artifacts from a site requires the permission of the property owner, or the appropriate government agency. Archaeologists discourage unregulated collection of artifacts, even if private landowners agree to allow it, for the simple reason that private artifact collecting disturbs a site and erodes the remaining evidence of the past. Over time, the collection of artifacts, even from a disturbed surface site, makes it less and less likely that the site, if ever recorded by an archaeologist, will retain any potential for a proper interpretation. Of course, many farmers pick up artifacts in their fields during the course of planting, cultivating and harvesting. This normal practice is different from the intensive collecting activity of the "artifact hunter." Most farmers that we have met in our research have been generous in showing us their collections and pointing out where they were found. From this, a good deal of archaeological information has come to light. Also, some collectors carefully record what they find, and are willing to share their finds with archaeologists, allowing us to photograph and record the find locations of their collections. As the reader will see later in these pages, some of these private collections have been instrumental in the interpretation of certain periods in Sheyenne Bend prehistory.

In what follows here there are descriptions of stone artifacts and pottery sherds that may be confusing, or difficult to visualize. We have tried to provide explanations for the terms used in these descriptions when they are introduced, but we realize that these may be hard to keep in mind throughout the text. We hope that the overviews and discussion sections at the beginning and end of the main chapters will alleviate this problem, and give the reader a broad understanding of the importance of the finds reported here. We also understand that for some readers, archaeology brings to mind pyramids, temples, palaces, gold and silver art objects, and buried cities. In some places that is what archaeologists have to deal with, but in our study domain, there are bits and pieces of ancient life left by people who are entirely unknown by the general public. Here, we try to bring to our audience some small appreciation of these people, who have been forgotten by society at large. They, too, have a story to tell, and the fragments from the ground that we present here, when carefully interpreted, make up a chapter in that story.

The indigenous peoples who once lived in the Sheyenne Bend—whether they were Dakota, Cheyenne, Hidatsa, or some other, have stories about their past handed down through the generations. These stories have historical content and significance, and readers may expect that they will be recounted here as a complement to the archaeological record. In this regard, we must disappoint any such expectation. This volume is offered as an archaeology of the Sheyenne Bend. We believe that the traditional history of the land is best left in the hands of Native scholars and elders. Perhaps they will be able to take what we offer here and make use of it in combination with their own interpretations of the past. As we see it, our job was to take what the earth offered to us and make sense of it as one version of this region's past. We hope we have achieved that modest goal.

For all we have learned about the Sheyenne Bend, there is much that we do not understand, and we hope that future archaeologists will return to this intriguing region to continue uncovering the prehistoric past, which annually diminishes under the impact of natural forces and human activity. We leave it to those who succeed us to carry on, to correct our mistakes, and to add to our collective understanding of this fascinating past.

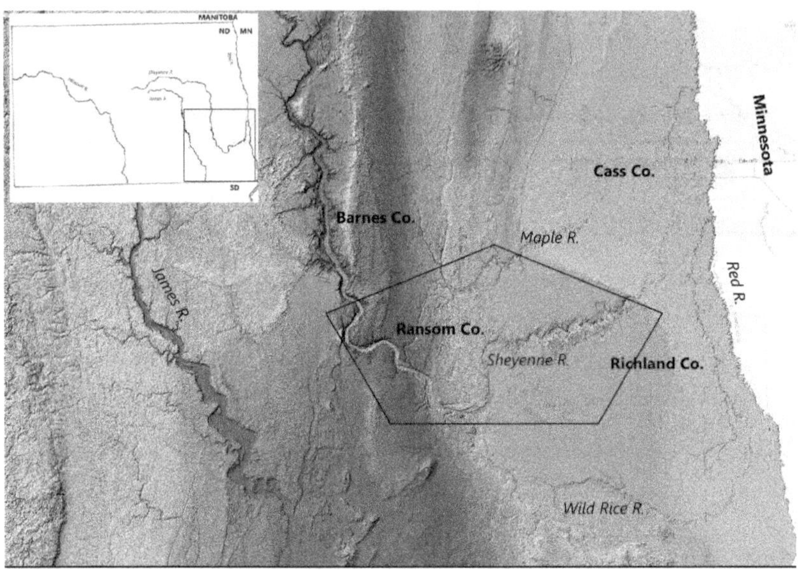

Figure 1. North Dakota showing the Sheyenne River Bend. Insert shows map area in the State of North Dakota. Northern extension of the outlined area includes the Maple River Bend.

Chapter 1
Introduction

The Sheyenne Bend region is the southernmost portion of the Sheyenne Valley, and is almost entirely within Ransom County. The Sheyenne itself is the longest of all the rivers encompassed entirely within North Dakota, being somewhat over 500 miles in length. It originates in central North Dakota to the southwest of the Devils Lake basin. Following a ragged course mostly eastward, the river turns south near McVille, from there flowing through Valley City in Barnes County, and the town of Fort Ransom in Ransom County. The river runs southeast from Fort Ransom to Lisbon, where it describes a dramatic "elbow" south and east of the city. Then it meanders east, and from the vicinity of Kindred begins a northeasterly course, eventually joining the Red River north of Fargo. It is just north of Fort Ransom that we define the western edge of the Sheyenne Bend area, since from here the river begins a great and zig-zagging curve south and east. We identify the eastern edge of the Sheyenne Bend where the river begins its northward course near Kindred, cutting through the Lake Agassiz lowlands (Figure 1).

This is a roughly defined study area, since we here include a portion of the Maple River Valley as well. This tributary stream follows a course like that of the Sheyenne about ten miles to the north, and describing a smaller, but similar bend. Overall, the entire Bend region as we define it here comprises roughly 400 mi^2, mostly in Ransom, but with small portions of Cass and Richland counties as well.

The Sheyenne gets its name from the Dakota language. It means the river where the Cheyenne people planted their gardens. In the name of the river itself we have a hint of its human history, since the name is Dakota in origin, and the reference is to the Cheyenne people. In fact, as we will explain later, the place where the Dakota meant to indicate the Cheyenne planted their fields was about in the middle of the Sheyenne Bend, near the southernmost part of the region. But there were other peoples as well. Some, who lived there before the European intrusion and settlement, we know by name; and they appear in historical documents as the Cheyenne and Yanktonai Dakota. Others have oral traditions of having lived here, such as the Hidatsa, although they are more commonly associated with the northern part of the Valley around Devils Lake. There are still many more who preceded these peoples whose names we cannot say since they are lost to history, but their presence is revealed nonetheless by the testimony of the spade.

While the Sheyenne River is in North Dakota, the boundaries of the state have no relevance to the prehistoric past. It is more appropriate in archaeological terms to refer to our region as part of the North American Plains. In this case, we may further delineate our study area as a sub-region of the Great Plains known as the Northeastern Plains. This is an area that encompasses several major river valleys besides the Sheyenne: the Assiniboine, James, Red, Souris, Big Sioux, Des Moines, and Minnesota rivers. While our attention here is on the Sheyenne, we will need to occasionally refer to finds made in these other areas, which in prehistory were interrelated to the events and cultural processes occurring in the Sheyenne Valley.

The history of this region stretches back in time thousands of years. For some this may seem a strange claim, since most people think of regional history as the period beginning with Lewis and Clark in the early 1800s, or the visit of La Verendrye to the villages of the Missouri River peoples in the 1730s. But the Missouri River peoples, the Mandan, the Hidatsa and their southern neighbors, the Arikara, now known as the Three Affiliated Tribes, had by the time of the first European explorers a very deep past that extended back hundreds of years. And besides the peoples of the Missouri River, there were the many other cultures on the Northern Plains; Lakota, Cheyenne, Arapahoe, Blackfoot, Cree, Crow, Yanktonai, Yankton and Sisseton, Assiniboine, and Plains Ojibwa. Here, we hope to make a contribution to understanding the ancestors of at least some of these people.

Part of the problem with discussing history is that different people use the term in different ways. For some, history is the documented account of past times, and by documented they normally mean through written records such as journals of explorers, government records, newspaper stories, letters from the frontier and the like. If we expand our conception of history to include other types of evidence, such as traditional narratives or oral "history," the past becomes filled with new stories and different perspectives. Every people on the Northeastern Plains had their own traditions, often handed down by word of mouth. Sometimes these oral histories were supplemented with Winter Counts, normally paintings on buffalo hides in which a figure represented a mnemonic aid, reminding the storyteller about an important event that was tied to the full narrative for that year. Sometimes traditional accounts are as accurate as official

Figure 2. Pyramid Hill, Fort Ransom. This natural hill was mistaken by some as manmade and evidence of an ancient culture. The Viking statue atop the hill reflects the regional belief that Norse explorers lived in this area prior to the arrival of Columbus. Here is a reflection of two separate versions of ancient times in the Sheyenne Bend, neither of which have archaeological substance.

(written) histories. Other times they may confuse. Ruth Landes (1968:20-21). recorded an origin story claiming that the Dakota came on four great arks across the ocean and moved westward. Howard (1984:37-39) recounts origin stories of the Canadian Sioux, mostly Santee, that some of the Sioux originated around Quebec 400–500 years ago, then helped the English defeat the French, moved to Ohio and eventually to Minnesota. A standard tradition among the Dakota is that their origin was around Mille Lacs, in central Minnesota, but a recent controversy arose when a claim was made that the Dakota originated near the juncture of the Mississippi and Minnesota Rivers around present-day St. Paul (Dahlheimer 2003; National Park Service 2006). Recounting traditional origin stories among the Mandan, Fenn (2015) describes two versions of Mandan beginnings. One involves a migration from the Gulf of Mexico up the Mississippi River eventually ending on the Missouri in North Dakota. A second tradition recounts the creation of the Mandan in the region where they lived in the Historic Period, with no migration. Using traditional stories to track ethnic history is often difficult and filled with missteps, particularly for outsiders. Our feeling is that these accounts are best presented by Native insiders who have a deeper appreciation for the cultural meaning and religious significance of these various origin stories.

The most unusual tale of the regional past in the Sheyenne Bend region is about pre-Columbian Scandinavian explorers. The story is at once demonstrably false and obviously ethnocentric. It is a narrative centering around a popular regional idea that medieval Norse explorers traveled through and used this land hundreds of years before the French, the English, or the Americans. This notion traces back to the Kensington Runestone, discovered in Minnesota's Douglas County in 1898, an area of heavy Scandinavian settlement. Although the Kensington Stone is regarded as a fake by scholars—linguists, historians, archaeologists—many local enthusiasts still regard it and other finds from the Minnesota-North Dakota region as authentic proof of a pre-Columbian Norse presence. Boulders with holes drilled in them, including some in the Bend region, have been called "mooring stones" and attributed to Norse sailors who used them to moor their boats, although more recently they have been re-identified as Norse property markers. In Fort Ransom, a large, pyramid-shaped hill is believed by some to have been, perhaps, related to this Norse visit. On top of the hill today is the statue of a Viking, complete with horned helmet and sword (Figure 2). Unrelated to the "Viking" story, others have suggested that the pyramid, along with a petroglyph covered rock near old Fort Ransom, were the work of a people known as "Tewaukonians" who lived here 5,000–9,000 years ago (Thorfinnson 1975:19-22). This sounds very much like long-discredited nineteenth century notions of a lost race of "civilized" peoples who lived in America before the arrival of the American Indians. How widespread this particular notion is today we cannot say, but it was clearly in circulation when our archaeological studies of the Bend region began.

There are also histories based on various types of scientific and scholarly methods. In the nineteenth and twentieth centuries many anthropologists compared shared cultural traits found among different Native American groups which they reasoned could only have come about as a result of contact and interaction between different peoples in past times. This process of contact between peoples and the associated sharing of features is known in anthropology as diffusion, and although diffusion studies do not provide a continuous narrative of what happened in the past, they do illustrate past episodes of interaction between peoples, and in that sense, are of historical significance. More recently, genetics has been used to determine the spread of human populations around the globe, although this sort of study requires the analysis of human remains, something that is often unacceptable to contemporary American Indian groups.

Oral history and traditions, genetics and diffusion are not, however, the subject of this book. Here we take a different approach to the past—not the same as the historian or ethnographer, and different from oral tradition as well. We offer a narrative of the past in the Sheyenne Bend focused on the "archaeological past;" that is, a past based on physical evidence left in the ground by earlier cultures. Archaeology is a way of making sense of all these objects found in the ground and left by past peoples. For the archaeologist, history, or the past, encompasses a great deal more than the written record. Our focus in this volume, therefore, will be on this physical evidence in the soil, the raw material of archaeology. Sometimes this archaeological record dovetails with historical accounts, or with oral traditions. Sometimes it does not. Our intent is not to offer archaeology as a superior point of view, but as another way of learning about the past using evidence not taken up by other approaches. Archaeology has its shortcomings. Seldom do we know the names of the people we deal with in the distant past. It is one of the reasons for referring to much of the archaeological past as prehistory. Some people take offense at this term, arguing that it diminishes the past of the people who lived then. Nothing could be more mistaken. In fact, without archaeology we would frankly not even know the existence of many periods in the ancient past, nor would we know anything about the people who lived then.

It is true that archaeologists rarely know the actual names of the people they study; we are forced by the scanty evidence available to refer to them by the artifacts they made. So, sometimes we discuss the people who made such-and-such artifacts as, for example, Sandy Lake peoples, who made that particular type of pottery known as Sandy Lake ware. Or we call Northeastern Plains Villagers the people who lived in the small villages and hamlets in eastern Dakota known to archaeologists as the Northeastern Plains Village culture. If we knew the names of these peoples, we would certainly use them. Sometimes it's possible to connect an archaeological "culture" with a modern group. This has been done with the people who lived in the large villages along the Missouri River in North Dakota: the Mandan and Hidatsa. We can link the Cheyenne people with at least one site in the Sheyenne River Valley, and we believe there is pretty good evidence that some group of the Dakota used our study area in prehistoric times as well. Unfortunately, with most prehistoric sites and cultures it is simply not clear which modern group to associate with them.

So, archaeology makes use of cultural remnants in the soil to help us understand the past. In so doing, it also provides a means of taking us far back into the distant past; thousands of years ago, to the time of the Ice Age itself. Archaeology helps us understand how cultures changed over extended periods of time, time spans that dwarf the written records. Aside from this, archaeology is a very democratic study. Since it is concerned with the debris left behind by past peoples, archaeology studies everyone who created garbage: powerful and poor, people in populous towns and cities, or sparsely settled hunters.

Archaeologists often refer to periods in the past not as "history," but as culture-history. This is because what we find in the archaeological remains are bits and pieces of past life-ways, or cultures. Implements of stone, bone, or fired clay are a fraction of a past technology. The ecofacts, or natural objects found at sites, tell us something about the subsistence habits of ancient people. The distribution of sites over the landscape reflects past preferences for where to live, while the presence of mounds and earthworks is an indicator of people's ceremonial habits. When we find evidence of house structures we learn about their architecture, while the presence of fortifications gives us a pretty good idea that warfare was practiced on a scale large enough to require special structures for protection. All of these—technology, subsistence, patterns of settlement, ceremonialism, conflict—are elements or sub-parts of larger cultures, or ways of life. As we mentioned, the archaeological record does not inform us about everything of interest of past cultures, but we take what we can get. We trace the presence or absence of cultural elements in the archaeological record, and how they changed through time. Thus, the preferred term for archaeological reconstructions of the past is culture-history to distinguish it from the history garnered from written records.

We feel that the Sheyenne Bend has a significant part to play in a fuller understanding of Great Plains prehistory. In a technical sense, the Bend region is part of the so-called Prairie–Plains. This means it was part of the North American Grassland, but received more rainfall, and had a more abundant vegetation cover than the High Plains farther west. The Sheyenne Valley is also near the Eastern Woodland borderlands, and has clearly been influenced by multiple cultural impulses from that direction. Even so, the Bend is a grassland environment, and sustains a Plains flora and fauna.

Over the entire course of prehistory, the Plains illustrates a fundamental continuity in lifestyle: one focused on large game hunting, mostly bison, small game hunting and trapping, gathering wild plants, and eventually, in some areas, household-level farming (Wood 1998). The engagement in this combination of subsistence activities varied over space and time on the Plains, since various resources were more abundant in some areas than in others, or were enhanced or diminished over time. This temporal variability was due in part to the fluctuations in climate that influenced the grasslands of the North American interior. Climatic changes were prominent on the Great Plains. As the glaciers retreated at the end of the Ice Age, the climate warmed and grasslands spread. Eventually, arid conditions characterized much of the Plains, this being the case sporadically from about 8000–5000 years ago. Then more mesic conditions were established which continued into the Historic Period when European traders and settlers intruded.

Sometime around AD 900 a warm period lasting until about 1300, saw the spread of farming. This occurred in the major river valleys extending into the Plains from the east and south. These river valleys had been significant avenues of travel and locations for settlements from the beginning of Plains prehistory, but by this later date, the wooded river floodplains became the focus of garden plots managed by families belonging to larger communities than were typical of earlier periods. Up to this time almost all Plains settlements had been occupations of hunting-gathering people, consisting, we believe, of families or small groups of related families. Once domestic plants were added to the subsistence routine settlements grew in size as more people could be sustained by gardening or small-scale farming, and the longer-term occupations probably encouraged somewhat larger families, since mobility tends to discourage too many children. With small-scale farming, larger families, and longer occupations, more substantial houses were used, and archaeologists begin at this time to speak of villages on the Plains. Naturally, these villages were confined to the perimeters of the river valleys where the forests along the river banks (gallery forests) provided lumber for houses and floodplain soils for gardens. Archaeologists refer collectively to these domestic-farming communities as the Plains Village cultures.

Bison hunting and gathering wild foods continued for these village groups; however, their annual routine was changed to accommodate the preparation and care of gardens, and of course, the harvesting of their plantings. Since gardens produce far more than most patches of wild plants not everything harvested could be used immediately. This led to the development of storage facilities, often consisting of deep pits featuring protective linings so that garden produce could be used during the subsequent winter and spring seasons. During times when the gardens did not require attention, villagers would leave their settlements to travel onto the grasslands to hunt the bison. In this way was born the life-style archaeologists have long termed the "dual economy" of the Plains Villagers—domestic-scale farming and hunting/gathering, and the hunting mostly involved bison. On the Great Plains these societies were known from the Historic Period and included, among others, the Wichita and related peoples on the Southern Plains, Pawnee and Omaha on the Central Plains, and to the north and west, along the Missouri River in South and North Dakota, the Arikara, the Mandan and the Hidatsa.

The dual economy villagers of the Plains have been much studied and discussed in the archaeological literature; however, until recently there was little to be said about such cultures on the Northeastern Plains. Southern Minnesota and Northwest Iowa did have Late Prehistoric expressions of such adaptations, including the Cambria culture of the lower Minnesota River Valley, and Oneota of southern Minnesota, parts of Nebraska, Kansas and South Dakota. But for eastern North Dakota generally, and the Sheyenne Bend in particular, the later portion of prehistoric times was regarded simply as a continuing adaptation of sparsely settled hunter-gatherers. In the 1960s a village culture was described in the James River Valley, just west of the Bend region. It was named the Stutsman focus. More work in that region since the 1970s expanded our understanding of these village sites in eastern North Dakota. The work we describe here for the Sheyenne Bend concludes with a description of sites discovered to the east of the James Valley that illustrate a complex interplay between Plains Villagers and the peoples and cultures of the Minnesota forest and lake country.

The Sheyenne River valley in the Bend area is relatively well defined with prominent bluffs bordering a broad, flat floodplain. Although mostly agricultural today, remnants of woodland, which once covered the valley floor, still survive. The Sheyenne Bend was chosen as the focus of this volume because a lot of archaeological work was done here, and because it is particularly rich in prehistoric sites reflecting different aspects of life in ancient times. There are archaeological sites spanning over 8000 years of North Dakota's past, and places where ancient people hunted bison or elk, others where they buried the dead and honored their ancestors, and some where they lived in compact farming communities. In these pages we hope to place the Sheyenne Bend within a broader framework of Plains and Upper Midwest prehistory. For some time periods this will be pretty easy, for others, not so much. Also, as we approach the later part of the prehistoric period our vision of the past will come to be more focused and complete. This is to be expected in the archaeological world, where older sites are sometimes more deeply buried and hidden from view, and are more likely to have experienced the ravages of time. By the later periods we consider here it will be possible to remark on the presence of known ethnic groups which were present in the Bend region, including the Cheyenne, Dakota, and Hidatsa.

Our account begins with some background information about regional prehistory, along with the natural environment, including descriptions of the land and resources. Some of these were composed by early European visitors in the eighteenth and nineteenth centuries. Most of the information for our presentation comes from archaeological work done over the past century. Much of this work the authors conducted from the 1980's to the present, some of it was done by archaeologists from the University of North Dakota and the State Historical Society of North Dakota. The table below, along with Figure 3, is a rough outline of the culture history of the Bend region based on the evidence we present here. We feel this best represents the division of prehistoric time in the Sheyenne Bend, but caution that it is not necessarily appropriate for all of the Great Plains. We offer it here since the terms in the left-hand column will be used repeatedly throughout this volume.

The dates that we offer in the text are mostly based on radiocarbon assays. This dating method requires organic substances, such as charcoal, wood, bone, and the like. Radiocarbon dating is based on the decay of carbon-14, which diminishes by half every 5,730 years or so. We know how much of this carbon isotope is present in the atmosphere today, and in plants and animals, so if half as much is present in charcoal from a fire hearth at an archaeological site, that fire probably burned around 5700 or so years ago. The method is very good, but not without its problems. Sometimes dated samples are contaminated with younger or older material, thus giving an inaccurate date. We try as much as possible to rely on multiple radiocarbon dates rather than on single assays. Another problem is that carbon-14 in the atmosphere is created by cosmic radiation, which varies over time. For this reason, radiocarbon dates have been calibrated to match calendar, or "real" years. Here, we use the CALIB-8.2 calibration for dates to give what we hope is a more accurate presentation of the age of the sites and cultural complexes discussed in the text. We offer most dates here in terms of standard calendar dates, or as years ago, rather than quoting actual radiocarbon dates with one or two standard deviations. It is important to remember that in archaeology, ages reckoned in years ago are calculated from the year 1950 (when radiocarbon dating began). Our dates in "years ago" should be understood to be years before 1950.

Period	Approximate Date	Cultural Features
Northeastern Plains Village (NEP)	800–300 years ago	Settled, small villages, regular use of domesticates, widespread mound burial
Late Prehistoric	900–300 years ago	Contemporaneous with NEP Villages; little evidence of villages or domestic plants
Woodland	2,300–900 years ago	Limited use of domestic plants, burial in mounds begins, pottery
Archaic	8,500–2,200 years ago	Various wild resources, notched and stemmed points
Paleoindian	11,000–8,500 years ago	Use of megafauna early, lanceolate points, hunting and gathering

Table 1. Sheyenne Bend Region Chronology

Figure 3. Chronology of projectile point types. Illustrated points are from the Sheyenne Bend region.

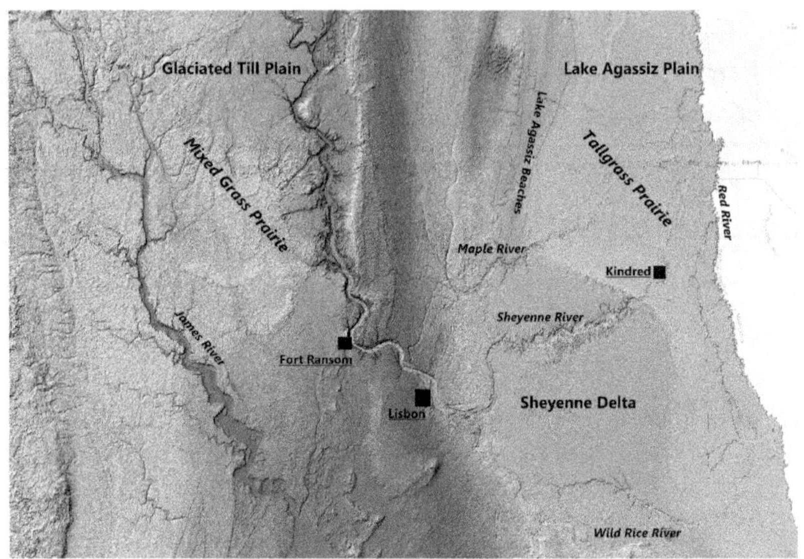

Figure 4. Map showing the Sheyenne and Maple Rivers in eastern North Dakota, and major vegetation and physiographic regions.

Chapter 2
Natural Setting

The Sheyenne Bend and its environs is remarkably varied, largely a product of geomorphic processes. These are the natural forces that shape the near surface and surface features of the landscape. The far eastern perimeter of our study area is the flat lowland of old glacial Lake Agassiz, which probably receded to the north between 10,000–9,000 years ago. Abutting these lowlands to the west are the sandhills of the Sheyenne Delta, formed when the glacially fed waters of the Sheyenne River flowed into Lake Agassiz. And west of the sandhills is the glacial till plain, a moderately undulating terrain formed by the debris laid down by melting glaciers. Meandering through all of these landscapes is the Sheyenne River itself, with its incised trench, natural levees, and wide floodplain (Figure 4).

Ancient people were very close to the land they used for their livelihood. For this reason, the landscape, the vegetation and soils, the water resources and animal life are important for the archaeological understanding of this study area. The types of plants and animals ancient people used were products of the climate, and the surface geology. Before discussing the archaeological record, let's briefly review the Sheyenne Bend as an environment that sustained humans in the past (Figure 5).

In the middle of the Bend region near Lisbon, the Sheyenne is about 45 meters wide. The river gauge in Lisbon records significant variation in discharge. Over the past 60 years it has ranged from a recorded low of 8 ft^3/sec to a high of 488 ft^3/sec (USGS 2017). The floodplain of the river here is bounded by well-defined bluffs and uplands and is about one kilometer in width. Today, the river bottom land is farmed all along the course of the floodplain. The steep bluffs and associated ravines dissecting the perimeter of the uplands are dotted with springs and seeps, and these provide water for lush but circumscribed plant communities, and fresh water for human use. Most of these bluff tops are cultivated as well, although some areas remain in pasture. Gravel and sand pits are common.

Figure 5. View of the Sheyenne Bend from Inyan Bosndata (Standing Rock), on the northwest side of the Bend area. View is to the southeast.

Geology

The geological deposits in the Bend area are important for understanding the archaeology of the region because archaeological sites are buried in deposits of different ages, and these deposits were laid down by different natural agencies. The nature of the processes responsible for encasing cultural materials helps the archaeologist in several ways. First, it provides a better understanding of how the archaeological sites were buried and whether or not the cultural materials might have been disturbed by the action of natural forces that buried them. Second, understanding the kind of process involved in site burial often gives us clues about the environmental conditions that existed when the enclosing sediment was created, and thus under what type of environment ancient people lived. Finally, sometimes understanding the natural deposits that contain archaeological materials helps us understand the age of the site.

The Bend area is part of the Glaciated Plain physiographic region of northern and east central North Dakota. It is in the Hudson Bay drainage (Artz 1995:67-68). This is an area of rolling to more or less flat topography created by deposits from the Wisconsin glacial advance of the Pleistocene epoch, or in ordinary terms, the late Ice Age. In North

American archaeology, interest in the Pleistocene or last ice age is normally concerned with the final Glacial Maximum, or that part of the Pleistocene occurring during the time the first Americans appeared in the archaeological record. This was probably about 20,000–15,000 years ago.

The most deeply buried geological strata in the region are Precambrian gneiss, schist and granite. Overlying these are a variety of shales belonging to the Greenhorn, Carlile, Pierre, and Niobrara formations, all of Mesozoic age. Geologists from North Dakota State University recovered a mosasaur fossil, the most complete find of this marine reptile ever found in North Dakota, from Niobrara formation deposits in northwest Ransom County (Bluemle 1979:4-9). Only very limited exposures of any of these Mesozoic rocks are found in the Sheyenne Bend. The few exposures that are mapped in the region are along the perimeter of the Sheyenne River trench over a stretch of about ten miles in the vicinity of Fort Ransom (Bluemle 1979: Plate 1).

Overlying the bedrock are between 100-300 feet of glacial deposits, mostly unsorted debris of boulders, cobbles, gravel, sand, silt, and clay, collectively called till. This till was laid down by the melting of glaciers after about 14,000 years ago. Glaciers move over the land as a result of pressure created by massive amounts of ice and snow deforming the ice at the bottom of the glacier. Ice at the glacier's base melts under pressure, seeps into the earth or into cracks in the bedrock. Here, the ice re-freezes, expands, breaks up the bedrock and incorporates it into the base of the glacier. On the upper surface of the glacier dust from the wind is captured by the ice and snow in much the same way that wintertime snow today, if it does not melt quickly, begins to look dirty. In glaciers, particulate matter accumulates this way for centuries. So, while dust and dirt accumulate on the surface of the glacier, the base of the ice is breaking up rock and incorporating it, and anything else it happens to move over, into the ice. When the ice melts, the till is left to blanket the land surface. The dimensions of the ice sheet that once covered this part of North Dakota may be imagined based on the hundreds of feet of glacial till dropped by the melted ice.

The glacial debris in the Bend area consists of a number of sediment types or facies. On the far northwestern margin of the Bend are layers of till that cover earlier glacial deposits and include large rocks thrust up near the margin of the glacier. Standing Rock, a state monument near Little Yellowstone Park in the northwestern part of the Bend, is regarded by geologists as one such rock thrust. This particular rock feature had special meaning to the native people of the region. The great majority of the

Bend area consists of rocks and cobbles in a sandy and silty matrix that includes both glacial till and lake sediment laid down in standing water left behind as the glaciers melted. The topography of the central and western portion of the Bend is generally rolling or somewhat flat. In the middle of the Bend area, in a linear north-south deposit to the north of Lisbon is a flat deposit of sand, gravel and some boulders deposited by an early stream or possibly lake-shore wave action. Farther to the east in the vicinity of Sheldon is an area of about 20 square miles of rolling to level plains, also consisting of glacial till (Bluemle 1979:plate 1). Much of the Bend also has near surface sub-glacial stream channel deposits known as eskers. These are linear deposits of sandy and gravelly material within the surrounding matrix of glacial till (Harris 1987).

When the glaciers began melting, massive amounts of water began ponding at the perimeter of the ice. This ponded water became a gigantic body of water known as Lake Agassiz, which covered the present-day Red River Valley and some surrounding areas in Minnesota, North Dakota, northwestern Ontario, southern Manitoba and portions of eastern Saskatchewan. The Sheyenne River carried glacial meltwater into Lake Agassiz. At the time of the ice melting the Sheyenne in the vicinity of Lisbon was probably about one-mile-wide and 100 feet deep (Blumele 1988:31). In the area where the glacial Sheyenne River flowed into the lake it lost much of its energy and dropped its sediment load. This largely sandy deposit is the modern Sheyenne Delta. Large portions of the Delta today feature knobby, sandy hills. In fact, some simply refer to the Sheyenne Delta as the sandhills. These hills today are actually stabilized dunes that formed in the period after Lake Agassiz dried out. These deposits are found from near the village of Anselm and extend in a great bulge eastward to the vicinity of Walcott.

The Sheyenne River probably assumed its present-day course as a result of glacial meltwater running along the western perimeter of the ice in a southeasterly direction. Surface geological materials south of the Bend extending toward and past Milnor indicate that water once flowed in a broad, shallow channel toward the Big Stone area (on the Minnesota-South Dakota border). This channel apparently clogged up and the Sheyenne diverted to the north (Harris 1987). The present course of the river in the Bend is simply that area where the river, for reasons of local topography, began to flow east and north and east again as the glaciers continued to recede. The smaller Maple River, to the north, followed a similar course most likely for similar reasons.

As the glaciers retreated and the Sheyenne River carved its valley along the western edge of the ice sheet, the region witnessed the last phase in the life of what paleoecologists call the "mammoth steppe." Various grasses, sedges, and forbs comprised the vegetation in the Bend region giving it the appearance of a Plains environment, although different in floral composition from the prairie of more recent times. In fact, pollen samples from cores in the Fargo area, and farther to the west on the Missouri Coteau, contain spruce fossils from the Late Glacial period down to the time when Lake Agassiz drained. The environment at the end of the Ice Age and during the time of Lake Agassiz was a mosaic of species perhaps not replicated in North America today. And add to the fossil plant assemblages, the occasional find of mammoth and giant bison (*Bison antiquus*) teeth, we have ample evidence about the differences between that time and the recent period (Ashworth 1999). At the end of the Ice Age, we may imagine the southern Sheyenne Valley inhabited by bison larger by half than modern bison, although perhaps not as gregarious. There were also mammoth, probably living in family groups much like modern elephants. Horse, reindeer, musk ox, wolf, bear and other Ice Age mammals would have flourished here.

The post-Pleistocene (or post-Ice Age) time period is known geologically as the Holocene Epoch. It represents the last 11,700 years of geological history. During the earliest phase of the Holocene the glaciers continued to melt as global climate warmed, and Lake Agassiz changed its configuration as the ice withdrew to positions farther and farther north. Geological deposits in North Dakota laid down during the Holocene are often referred to as the Oahe Formation, layers of near-surface gravel, sand, silt, and clay found over large portions of North Dakota and adjacent areas (Bluemle et.al. 1986). In some places it is up to six meters thick. Soils formed on the surface of this accumulating Holocene sediment, and these soils themselves were buried by additional sedimentation, becoming what are known as paleosols. A couple of these paleosols are fairly widespread in North Dakota's Holocene deposits and may reflect periods when stable land surfaces existed with ample plant cover to prevent erosion (Artz 1995). During droughty periods wind erosion would be more likely and would mask or erase the evidence of any soil development in the geological profile.

The Holocene was itself a time of changing climate. This epoch is normally divided into three phases. The Early Holocene spans a period from over 11,000 years ago to 8,000 years, when the climate in North America was cool, but warming. During the Early Holocene prairie conditions were established in eastern North Dakota and within the Sheyenne Bend, although in some areas there were patches of spruce woodlands.

During the Middle Holocene, from 8,000–4,000 years ago, climatic warming continued and led to occasional severe droughts in the Plains region. This period is sometimes called the Altithermal by archaeologists. The idea of a hot, dry period, or Altithermal, during the Middle Holocene was introduced in the late 1940s and many saw the warming trend responsible for the end of the Ice Age as a process that continued unabated until parts of North America were turned into an expansive desert. Archaeologists once used this idea to suggest that the Great Plains did not support even grassland vegetation, but rather gave way to a parched landscape uninhabited by humans. Today, paleo-climatologists have more or less abandoned the Altithermal term, even though archaeologists continue to use it with the understanding that the notion of a drought-like heat wave lasting over the entire central portion of North America is no longer what Altithermal means. Many prefer the term Middle Holocene, which was, nevertheless, climatically distinct from modern times. The Plains region was subjected to drought conditions more frequently than today and average annual temperatures may have been higher than typical for more recent centuries. At times, however, conditions during the Middle Holocene probably approximated our own climate. That conditions were overall drier, and possibly warmer, is evident in some major environmental shifts documented at this time (Running 2005:41). Evidence from pollen in sediment taken from lake bottoms show that the forest border in Minnesota and southeastern Manitoba was shifted as much as 100 miles to the east, as prairie grasses expanded into areas now wooded (Gibbon 2012:66).

These Middle Holocene arid conditions had a severe impact on the Sheyenne Delta region. The sandy matrix of the Delta, being coarse, holds little water. During dry periods these sandy sediments would have rapidly lost any potential to support plant growth and the ground surface would have become denuded. Wind would blow the exposed sand into dunes. We believe that the knobby topography of the sandhills is a result of dune formation during the middle portion of the Holocene. Later, when conditions turned more mesic vegetation returned and the dunes stabilized with grass and some trees growing on the now stationary dunes, so that the conditions we see today in the sandhills represent a landscape that probably dates to the end of the Middle Holocene and perhaps the beginning of the Late Holocene (Running 2005) (Figure 6).

Figure 6. Aerial view of dune formations in the Sheyenne delta. These are parabolic dunes that form often in semi-arid and sub-humid conditions rather than in true deserts. These probably formed at the end of the Middle Holocene and perhaps somewhat later.

Information derived from a variety of climatic proxies at Moon Lake, located in Barnes County, North Dakota (immediately north of the Bend), indicate that more mesic periods alternated with episodes of rather severe aridity between 6,600–6,200, 5,400–5,200 and 4,800–4,600 years ago. This is indicated by sediment stratigraphy, carbon isotopes and carbonates, diatoms, and pollen (Valero-Garces et.al. 1997:368).

Rivers in eastern North Dakota, the Sheyenne for example, migrated laterally during more arid times. This was the result of eroded sediment from uplands washing downslope into streams and clogging river channels. During droughty times the Sheyenne did not have enough flow to move the sediment load, so the river channel filled in and the river itself found another, usually adjacent course. This process is indicated in the river stratigraphy from Middle Holocene times, where point bar deposits allow geomorphologists to track the migration of the river back and forth across its floodplain (Artz 1995:81). Many Middle Holocene sites, and those that might be present from the Early Holocene as well, may have been destroyed by the erosional forces of the dynamic river systems of this time period. Ancient peoples, just as more modern populations, concentrated many of their more substantial settlements near rivers and lakes. Migrating rivers may have moved over sites that had once been situated on their banks, washing away the evidence of the once existing settlements.

The Late Holocene, roughly the past 4,000 years, has been a time of more or less modern conditions in the Northern Plains. However, even during this period it is possible to distinguish a number of climatic and environmental shifts. The Moon Lake climatic sequence indicates continuing episodes of aridity even after the Middle Holocene ends, particularly between 3,500–2,000 years ago; however, by this time climate was becoming slightly cooler and wetter in eastern North Dakota. Cool wet periods alternated with centuries-long warmer periods, including what is often referred to as the Medieval Warm period, from about AD 950–1250. This was a time when agricultural productivity in Europe grew dramatically, sea ice disappeared in the North Atlantic, and Norse settlers established a colony in Greenland. After this, during the fourteenth century the climate began to cool during a climatic episode called the Little Ice Age. Rather significant growth and movement of glaciers occurred in the northern hemisphere, and these glacial advances did not subside until the end of the nineteenth century.

The variability of the eastern North Dakota climate is clearly visible in the growth rings of oak trees that provide a dendrochronological (tracking time by counting tree rings of trees that add a growth ring each year) record of climate. Thick growth rings indicate mesic or moist conditions, narrow rings more arid periods. From AD 1400–1750 tree ring data shows that there were 14 periods of significant drought in eastern North Dakota. These droughty periods lasted from three years up to 30 years, and some of them are believed to have been more severe than the 1930s' "Dust Bowl." About 50% of the years in this 350-year period were dry (Severson and Sieg 2006:25). Historic period travelers, explorers and naturalists also provide some indication of modern climatic conditions. For instance, in 1862 the Wild Rice and Maple rivers were flowing, yet the next year they are described as having only standing pools of water in their stream beds. Lake Traverse was not discharging into the Bois de Sioux (on the Minnesota–South Dakota border) in 1835, yet in 1839

Nicollet described the Sheyenne Valley as thick and rich with prairie grasses. In 1849 John Pope, traveling from the Sheyenne north to the Maple River, stated the ground was covered with water between two inches and two feet deep. But in 1864 General Sibley's soldiers found the Maple River dry (Severson and Sieg 2006:29-32). Such climatic shifts must have had a real impact on the ancient peoples of the Sheyenne Bend, who depended more or less directly on the naturally occurring resources found on the Northern Plains.

Soils

The soils of the Sheyenne Bend are mostly classified as mollisols, being soils with well-developed topsoil, or A-horizons. This soil A-horizon is rich in organic material and is the medium in which plants grow. Below the A-horizon is the B-horizon, usually a lighter color than the soil above. The brighter color is the product of the downward leaching of minerals from the A-horizon as water passes through the profile. Iron, calcium, aluminum, silica, and other minerals accumulate in the B-horizon along with clay particles. The longer a soil develops, the more the B-horizon achieves its characteristic features. For example, over time as water percolates through the soil more and more clay particles, the tiniest of sediments (smaller than 0.002 mm), move from the A- to the B-horizon. Sometimes the clay content of the B-horizon may be used to estimate the age of the soil, that is, how long the soil has been a stable weathering surface. This has been useful in estimating the age of more than one archaeological site.

The soils in the region are developed in glacial sediment that was eroded from shale deposits, which gives the regional soils some of their distinctive coloration and texture. Soils were also formed in glacial materials reworked by rivers and deposited as alluvium, or river sediment. They are generally characterized as loams, that is, containing sub-equal amounts of sand, silt, and clay. These soils are relatively susceptible to erosion and used today as both cropland and as pasture, with heavier water retaining soils (silty and clayey) more often used for crops, and sandier soils more for pasture. To the east in the Sheyenne Delta soils are sands and loamy sands and generally used for pasture. Much of the Sheyenne Delta area today is part of the Sheyenne National Grassland (Omodt et al. 1968:23, 28, and map).

Mollisols are found throughout the temperate grasslands. The prairie grasses that grow here form a dense root mat that extends deep below the surface; many feet in some cases. In fact, prairie grasses have far more biomass below the ground surface than above. The soils in prairie

Figure 7. Soil profile from upland along the Maple River. Note the very thick A-horizon, or topsoil, typical of prairie mollisols. White staining is calcium carbonate enriched B-horizon. Depth is 70 cm.

environments support a wide array of nematodes, microbes, and fungi that break down the root material creating a thick layer of organic matter (Chapman, et.al 1998:25,58). This is an important part of the process by which the rich prairie top soils are formed. It also has a lot to do with the way Native groups on the prairies farmed the way that they did (Figure 7).

An in-depth description of the soil at an archaeological site is normally required for a full understanding of the human occupation. For one, understanding the soil often provides a clue about the age of the site, often before anything else is known about it. The simple task of taking a core sample of the soil may tell whether there have been multiple episodes of deposition at the site. For example, if a core shows that below the B-horizon is another dark colored, organic rich horizon, it is likely that an earlier landscape existed here. The old land surface weathered and developed a topsoil. This was later buried with sediment that in turn weathered into the modern soil. If the buried soil, or paleosol, was relatively short-lived and did not remain as an exposed and weathering surface long enough to form a recognizable B-horizon, it is known simply as a "buried A-horizon," and not a full paleosol.

Inspection of the soil profile helps the archaeologist understand whether or not the site has been heavily disturbed. A natural soil profile is fairly easy to identify, and a disturbed profile may mean that any cultural materials will have far less interpretive value. Because rivers flood frequently, the natural levees along the perimeter will accumulate sediment on an irregular basis. Every time there is a flood, as the overflowing water spreads out over its floodplain, it loses much of its energy and drops sediment. This sediment builds up over time, burying earlier land surfaces. For this reason, it is not uncommon for archaeologists to find buried soils along the course of larger streams like the Sheyenne. Since the banks of larger streams are also preferred locations for human occupation, buried sites are common in these contexts.

It takes time for newly deposited sediment to form into a soil. To create an A- and B-horizon, there must be plant growth and animal life in the sediment to add organic matter. As this happens an A-horizon develops at the surface of the newly deposited sediment. The parent material—say, flood sediment—is called the C-horizon, and its top surface weathers over time into the A-horizon. The leaching of minerals into the layer below the A-horizon as water from precipitation moves through the profile creates a B-horizon. Thus, the presence or absence of a B-horizon can be useful to the archaeologist in interpreting the geomorphic processes that shaped the context of the archaeological deposit. It is also a pretty good indicator of the passage of time, since many years may be involved in the development of an A-C soil profile into an A-B-C soil profile.

The nature of the soil at an archaeological site has a lot to do with the visibility of some cultural materials. For instance, if people drive posts into the ground to serve as braces for the wall of a house, the posts penetrate into the lighter colored subsoil. Over time the posts rot away leaving a tell-tale blackened circular stain in the subsoil. These old wall posts are called post molds by archaeologists and they are signatures of the structure that once stood there, indicating the size and shape or outline of the building. In some of the rich mollisols of the Bend region the dark topsoil is so thick that the black, organic staining of post molds are invisible because they never penetrated all the way through the thickness of the topsoil. This problem arose repeatedly in our work over the years as we worked at archaeological sites in the prairie soils of the Sheyenne Bend.

Figure 8. Prairie grasses in midsummer.

Vegetation

Today the Sheyenne Bend area is a mix of farmland, pasture for cattle, and some sand and gravel quarries. Before the introduction of Euro-American style agriculture and ranching in the nineteenth century the Bend region would have been a grassland environment with copses of trees scattered in the Sheyenne Delta, or sandhills area, and a substantial gallery forest along the Sheyenne River itself. To the north the Maple River was probably wooded along portions of its course in the small bend area described by that stream in extreme southwestern Cass County.

The natural beauty of the region has led to the creation of several parks, preserves and scenic attractions. The eastern portion of the region, or the Sheyenne Delta, is part of the Sheyenne National Grasslands, controlled by the U.S. Forest Service. This includes the H.R. Morgan State Nature Preserve (also called Mirror Pool), on the Ransom–Richland County border. Here, oxbow lakes formed by the Sheyenne River on the edge of the sandhills sustain a unique community of plants. On the western side of the Bend is Fort Ransom State Park and the nearby Fort Ransom Historic site, and on the Barnes-Ransom County border, Little

Yellowstone Park. East of Little Yellowstone is the Standing Rock Historic site. The entire western perimeter of the Bend to the City of Lisbon is part of the Sheyenne River Valley National Scenic Byway.

The potential natural environment of the Bend region is North American Grassland (Figure 8). The part of this grassland that includes the Bend is often referred to in the archaeological literature as the Northeastern Plains. This is a mesic grassland with tall, lush grasses, sedges, forbs, and brush usually referred to as prairie. In more specific terms, the Bend area is a wheatgrass-bluestem-needlegrass prairie (Severson and Sieg 2006:13). Many of the typical prairie grasses send roots to a depth of 2–6 feet, while some non-grass plants, such as Blazing Star or Prairie Dock have root systems penetrating to as much as 12–14 feet below ground level. The thick mat of grasses shades the surface of the ground and prevents parching, the root system holds the soil in place, while the great variety of species diminishes the likelihood of epidemic diseases sweeping through the grassland community (Chapman et.al. 1998:22). For such reasons the prairie is a well-established and stable ecosystem. This prairie floral community is more diverse than might appear on casual inspection. A quarter section (160 acres) of prairie may contain up to 30 species of grasses and sedges. One study of the Sheyenne Delta region documented over 800 species of plants and animals. Common grass species are western wheatgrass, prairie junegrass, green needlegrass, needle-and-thread, blue grama, little bluestem, and needleleaf sedge. The Eastern North Dakota mixed-grass prairie supports forbs such as pasque flower, western wall-flower, prairie smoke, purple coneflower, and yarrow (Anonymous 2012). The vegetation community would provide forage for about 1/3–1.0 animal unit/acre, with an animal unit defined as a bison cow weighing 1000 lbs. (Sedivec and Printz 2012:3, 6-7). Other animals such as elk would compete for some of these resources, so counting acres and projecting animal populations can only be approximate; even so, the prairie biomass would have been considerable, and the number of game animals useful to humans comparably significant. The over 200,000 acres of prairie in the Bend area might have supported tens of thousands of bison, elk, and perhaps pronghorn.

The North American prairie is the product of several natural forces. The amount of rain and snowfall in the prairie, along with the natural and human induced incidence of fire keep trees from becoming established. The diversity of plant life in the prairie is partly a product of fire and the feeding behavior of herbivores (Helzer 2010:1-2). Prairie grasses grow from a point on the plant very near ground level, and low temperature fires, which are typical in grasslands, fail to impair the grasses' ability to re-grow. Trees are more likely to be seriously damaged by fires. Grazing animals such as bison pick up prairie plant seeds on their hair and move them across the landscape, while large animals disturb the ground by their activities, creating micro-niches for the growth of a variety of plant species by opening new microhabitats.

Some prairie grasses produce seeds that may be processed for eating; however, the seeds are very small and large quantities would be needed for even a single meal. Besides that, the seeds are encased in tough, adhering, and indigestible hulls. Getting the seeds free from the hulls would have been a major chore. It is probably for this reason that we have little ethnographic or archaeological evidence for the use of prairie grasses for food, although occasional use among some groups has been documented (Kindscher 1987:4, 229 ff). There are edible forbs, such as the prairie turnip, and shrubs, such as chokecherry, that were commonly used for food. Kindscher (1987:4) points out that some prairie peoples determined their early summer route to the bison hunting grounds not by where the bison would most likely be found along the way, but by where they might find the prairie turnip (*Psoralea esculenta*). The point here is that it is important not to underestimate the significance of plant foods to the peoples of the Sheyenne Bend. Some of the more common plants used as food by the prairie Indian peoples are listed here (Kindscher 1987):

- Pigweed (*Amaranthus graecizans*), seeds
- Serviceberry or Saskatoon (*Amelanchier alnifolia*), fruit used raw or cooked; leaves for tea; also used in making pemmican
- Hackberry (*Celtis occidentalis*), the soft parts of the berries may be eaten raw, the pits are hard and difficult to chew, but they may be ground into a nutritious paste. The berries were also used for medicinal purposes.
- Milkweed (*Asclepias syriaca*), young shoots eaten after cooking
- Ground plum (*Astragalus crassicarpus*), also known as buffalo pea; pods used raw or pickled
- Lamb's Quarter or goosefoot (*Chenopodium berlandieri*), seeds were dried and pounded to meal, or greens could be eaten fresh. In some parts of North America this plant was domesticated, and it may have been so used in the prehistoric Bend region.
- Prairie clover (*Dalea candida*), used for tea
- Wild strawberry (*Frageria virginiana*), eaten fresh
- Jerusalem artichoke (*Helianthus tuberosus*), roots used raw or cooked

- Wild plum (*Prunus americana*), fruits eaten raw, cooked, jellied, or dried
- Chokecherry (*Prunus virginiana*), cooked or dried, used in pemmican
- American licorice (*Glychirrhiza lepidota*), used in tea; roots could be eaten raw or cooked; also used as a medicine
- Prairie turnip (*Psoralea esculenta*), roots used fresh, dried, or cooked; one of the most desired plant foods, often used to thicken soups and stews
- Prairie wild rose (*Rosa arkansana*), fruit could be eaten raw while leaves and stalks boiled for tea and the petals used in salads
- Buffalo berry (*Shepherdia argentea*), eaten raw, dried, or cooked

Along the Sheyenne River there were gallery forests, or woodlands, fringing the river floodplain and the adjacent slopes. This woodland would have been similar to the Sheyenne Forest today, with a variety of deciduous trees and shrubs, including bur oak, cottonwood, elm, ash, hackberry, basswood, and various bushes. The woodland provided much needed resources to the people of ancient times, including fuel, lumber for building, and a variety of other materials useful for manufactures: bark for plates or platters, fiber for weaving and cordage, and wood for any number of artifacts. The gallery forest was also a habitat for many game animals (Barker and Nelson 1974).

Several domestic plants were used by peoples in eastern North Dakota, and in the Sheyenne Bend specifically. The most important of these was maize or corn. This is a tropical plant originally brought under domestication in Mexico sometime before 7,000 years ago. Maize is a genetically pliable plant and it was adapted through selective breeding to grow outside of the tropic and subtropics. It is found several thousand years ago in the southwestern part of the United States and began to make its way up the Mississippi drainage by 2,000 years ago. It was certainly being grown as a domestic plant by people in the Missouri Valley before 1,000 years ago and appears in the Sheyenne Bend area by 500–600 years ago. Basing their claims on starch granules and phytoliths from archaeological sites, Boyd et al. (2006) believe maize was being used, at least occasionally, as far north as the Canadian prairie after AD 1000. Other plants known to be domesticated in the region include squash and tobacco. It is likely that some local plants, such as *Chenopodium* were also purposely grown rather than simply collected wild.

While we do have the physical remains of domestic plants from archaeological sites in the Bend area, we are not aware of documented

Figure 9. The Sheyenne Valley showing gallery woods on the eastern side of the Bend, the most likely area for Native farm plots. Courtesy Google Earth.

descriptions of Indian peoples using agriculture in the Sheyenne Bend. The Cheyenne planted their gardens here in the eighteenth century, but we have no accounts outlining their actual farming practices at that time. For this reason, we are not able to use written accounts of native lifeways to fill in details of precisely how the peoples of the later part of the prehistoric past in this region managed their domestic plant production. There are many good descriptions of the farming habits of the Native groups of the Missouri Valley. Gardens were situated in the lowlands of the river valleys (Figure 9). Trees were cleared and perhaps burned off. Women would use modified bison scapulae as hoes to mound the topsoil, into which they planted their seeds of maize, squash, sunflower, and perhaps beans. The upland grasses formed a root mat too thick to easily break up with hand tools, and the plow was not known. This gardening was successful enough to permit the formation of large villages that were occupied for decades at a time, at least along the Missouri River, and as we will show here, to some extent in the Sheyenne Bend as well. Farming made possible larger populations than allowed by hunting and gathering only wild resources.

Game Animals

In the Sheyenne Valley it is likely that animals provided a more abundant food source than plants. This is because only modest nutritional returns can be gotten from prairie grasses, sedges, and forbs, while those same plants form the diet of large game animals that convert the prairie plants into a usable package of protein-rich food. Prior to the introduction of farming in the region, after 1,000 years ago, hunting was the major subsistence pursuit in the Sheyenne Bend, and in the Plains generally.

Both large and small game were used by the prehistoric peoples of the region, although except for dogs none of these were domesticated. Animals were important as a food source, but also for hides and pelts used for clothing, foot and headgear, lodge coverings, ceremonial and decorative items, along with bone, horn, and antler, which were used as tools. Beaver, muskrat, skunk, squirrel, and raccoon, for instance, all provided usable fur or pelts for a range of clothing. Bone from large animals was used for tools and utensils. Elk antler might be trimmed to a shape useful for some aspects of fashioning stone tools, large animal bones were used for utensils such as scoops, ladles and spoons. Bird bones were sharpened and used as needles. And the scapula, or shoulder blade, from bison and elk was used in later prehistoric times for hoes. The articular joint was attached to a handle, while the spine of the bone was broken off, forming a wide-bladed implement for gardening. Bone might also be used as a handle for inserting stone tools, particularly for scraping wood and hide. Porcupine quills could be bundled together to form a brush. The long bones from larger birds, being hollow, were often cut and strung together as elongate beads. Feathers, particularly from raptors like hawks and eagles were used as decorative items and often had a place in ceremonies and religious rituals. We are not providing an exhaustive list of uses to which animal products were put by the peoples of the Bend area, but do wish to note the variety of uses realized for animal resources (Lowie 1982:55ff).

Naturally, game animals were most important for their food value. For example, an 1100-pound bison might yield about 600 lbs. of meat, a larger animal somewhat more (Hauer nd); a bull elk, in excess of perhaps 900 lbs. about the same as a small bison, while a whitetail deer might provide over 50 lbs.; a little more for a mule deer. These figures are somewhat higher than modern hunters take from the same animals, since in pre-modern times people used more of the carcass, including marrow from the larger bones. Small game, such as rabbit, turkey, or duck would yield only a few pounds of usable meat. The prehistoric people in the Sheyenne Valley would have been well acquainted with the resources of their environment and had their preferences for meat sources. Bison was clearly a target for hunters throughout the prehistoric period, but at some sites it is clear that other game resources were targeted; sometimes ducks, sometimes mussels from the river, or fish and rabbit, and occasionally, elk.

Bison were the prime game animal for the Plains peoples. Bison, or American buffalo, are taxonomically classified today as *Bison bison* or sometimes as *Bos bison.* The latter term is a taxonomic change recognizing a closer relationship with cattle, placing the two as separate species of the same genus (Tesky 1995). Indeed, cattle, introduced by Europeans have more or less taken over the niche previously occupied by bison in North America, and their dietary preferences and feeding habits are quite similar (Helzer 2014). The bison is regarded as a keystone species throughout the North American Grassland, meaning that bison herds were an integral part of the prairie biome, aiding in the maintenance of the prairie itself (Knapp et al. 1999). Bison droppings fertilized the soil, their pathways and wallows provided an opportunity for a variety of plants to establish themselves, often seeds were carried on their hide, and their feeding constantly cropped the mature grasses and created openings for younger plants.

McHugh (1972:16) estimated that tallgrass prairie could support about 26 bison on each square mile of land. The Sheyenne Bend, as we define it here, comprises about 400 square miles. This allows us to suppose that up to about 10,000 bison might be supported in the Bend area. Bison were sometimes observed in the region in large herds. Nathaniel Langford traveled through North Dakota in 1862 and claims to have seen herds in the hundreds of thousands; one even estimated at a million animals! Other herds were smaller numbering from 5,000–10,000 animals (McHugh 1972:15). By the middle of the nineteenth century bison in the eastern part of North Dakota were much reduced in number; however, we have the account of Alexander Henry in 1800 describing massive herds of bison in the nearby Red River Valley (Coues 1897). Some authorities argue that bison was more abundant west of the Missouri River, since the short grass species of that region are felt to be preferred by bison (cf. Isenberg 2000:22). But the historical documents and the archaeological record clearly show that prior to the Euro-American settlement the bison were the dominant large game species in the Bend area.

Bison prefer grasses with tender blades and will graze on plants in the earlier stages of maturation. The herds would move from place to place seeking out the freshest growth, so the variety of grasses growing in the prairie would have been used by the bison based on the schedule of their growth (Severson and Sieg 2006:206,215). They prefer high quality regrowth after a burn, and in the early spring prefer cool season forage in wooded areas or lowlands. During this time warm season grasses are still dormant, but as the seasons progress, the bison shift to the warm season grasses. Because of this, bison in mixed grass prairies may graze year-round without having to migrate long distances in search of forage (Steuter and Hindinger 1999:335-337). In the Sheyenne Bend region, there was a mixed prairie with various species that would grow at different rates. Furthermore, the Sheyenne Delta on the eastern side of the Bend had sandier soils and would have supported a somewhat different array of grasses and sedges. Finally, a day's travel east of the Bend area was the vast lowland of the Lake Agassiz plain with thick, heavy clay rich soils. Here was the Bluestem prairie, a grassland featuring tall grasses and lush growth, and able to support a good ground cover even during droughty times when the sandier soils of the Bend area and the Sheyenne Delta might only support a sparse growth. Considering the floristic diversity of the Bend area and its regional environs, along with the historical records, there is good reason to suspect that bison populations were substantial throughout prehistoric times.

Fire was an important factor in bison feeding habits. Areas burned in a previous season would feature a fresh crop of grass that would be attractive to bison. There are many reports in the historic literature that native groups would burn areas in the fall, for instance, so that in the spring they might expect to find the buffalo grazing on the fresh growth in the burned area. Sometimes, fire was also used to funnel the bison toward a trap, or even to surround them so that the animals could be more easily killed. When fire was started by lightning, burned areas would be visited by hunters who could expect the buffalo to be there when the fresh growth emerged (McHugh 1972:69-70).

For the peoples of the prairie the bison was the most important resource. Their flesh provided sustenance; their bones, tools; their hides, clothing and shelter. Bison hides were prepared by women for robes and for tipi or lodge coverings, and parts of the bison, skulls for instance, were even used in ceremonies. The bison also figured prominently in the religion of the Plains Indian peoples, and as with many elements of American Indian life, everyday activities were surrounded by spiritual belief and ceremony. Among the Lakota there are references to Buffalo Dreamers, Buffalo Maidens, Buffalo Braves, and even the Buffalo Nation; that is, the bison themselves (Hassrick 1964:277-293).

The native groups on the Plains hunted bison using several methods. Sometimes the animal was stalked by one or a few hunters who approached stealthily, sometimes covered in skins or hides, trying to get close enough to shoot an arrow. In winter, bison might be hunted in snow where the animal could be trapped in deep drifts and killed. Of course, individual hunting was used on other animals as well, such as deer and elk. More elaborate techniques were employed for the group hunts where entire communities might join together in an effort to take a large number of bison at a single kill event. Lowie (1982:13-14) describes several communal methods for buffalo hunting. One involved the use of fire to trap a group of bison in an area causing them to mill in a circle. Another was to build a corral. Using members of the community to form a V-shaped drive line, the bison were enticed to enter the wide side of the drive and were moved or stampeded to the vertex, where a wooden corral was constructed. Here, the bison entered the corral and moved around in a confused state, where they were speared or shot with arrows by surrounding hunters. The drive line set-up could also be used to stampede bison over a cliff, gully, or even an artificial embankment, in the expectation that some of them would be hurt by the unexpected drop, perhaps breaking a leg. Wounded in this way, the animals were easy prey for the hunters (McHugh 1972:62).

Several aspects of Native American bison hunting are worth keeping in mind. First, communal hunts required a major cooperative effort among the members of a community, or even with people from more than one community. Women, men, and even children might be involved in taking up positions along the arms of a V-shaped driveline in order to keep the buffalo moving ahead toward the trap. Young hunters might be behind the herd trying to frighten the animals to move deeper into the trap. Seasoned hunters would be stationed at the prepared kill site. It was also important that the herd be managed by the scouts and enticed in the right direction, that is, toward the drive line. This meant that no one could alarm the animals by trying to make a premature kill, causing the herd to run off and away from the trap. Thus, there were rules of behavior, a division of labor, and a coordinated and timed effort. However, the payoff was impressive. If only 10 or 15 animals were killed, this might represent several tons of meat, marrow, bone and hide (see Brink 2008 for an extended discussion of communal bison hunts).

When a kill was made butchery had to take place immediately. A buffalo carcass was too heavy to transport, and if it were not cut open and dressed quickly it would begin to bloat and the meat spoil. At a bison kill site initial butchery probably took place where the kill was made. Meat from the animal would be transported back to a campsite. The spinal column, perhaps the pelvis, and maybe the skull would be left. Sometimes the lower jaw was removed with the tongue for transport to camp, along with meat from the ribs, and the legs with the meat from the haunches. At archaeological sites we often find only portions of the bison skeleton;

namely, those parts of the animal that were removed from the kill site. These include lower jaws (mandibles), leg bones and rib fragments. Vertebrae, pelvic bones and skull parts are often not present at campsites or are represented in only small quantities (Brink 2008).

Elk are another large game animal found on the plains and prairies. Elk, sometimes known as wapiti, are mainly grazers but do shift to browsing woody plants if grasses are too dry or unavailable (Severson and Sieg 2006:203-204). They may be described as habitat generalists and are found in grasslands, steppes, and forests. Elk live in groups of bulls with harems of females. Elk herds may number upward of 100 individuals. Although elk inhabit a territory throughout the year, they may migrate from a few to nearly 100 miles, usually in spring or fall (Innes 2011).

Elk were common in the Red River Valley and presumably in the Sheyenne Bend as well. Early travelers commonly report elk, sometimes in considerable numbers. Elk meat is certainly regarded as tasty, the hide is usable, and elk antler was used for tools among the Plains Indians. Elk also figured into Plains peoples' ideology as a powerful masculine figure, and elk teeth were commonly used in jewelry such as necklaces and sewn into women's tunics (Lowie 1982:49).

Elk are typically active near dawn and dusk. They prefer forest edge habitats and might have been most common in the Bend area near the Sheyenne River itself. In the woods, elk may be quite noisy but they are alert to scents, so hunters must be careful to approach from a direction that the elk will not be likely to detect their scent. Yet even though elk are not the most difficult animal to hunt, and they were abundant in the region, elk are remarkably rare in regional archaeological sites, whether in the Sheyenne, James or Red River valleys. In the sites discussed below, bison are more or less ubiquitous, but elk are documented in only a few locales.

Deer and pronghorn were probably also hunted occasionally by the people of the Sheyenne Bend area, although evidence of their presence at archaeological sites is not common. White-tailed deer would have been present in the gallery woodlands along the Sheyenne and Maple rivers in the past, just as they are today. Their numbers may have been lower due to the presence of elk, but nevertheless, their range did extend into this region. Pronghorn are reported in eastern North Dakota as recently as 1879, where they are described as abundant in western Cass County (just northeast of the Bend area) (Bailey 1926:28) but they are absent from archaeological sites excavated so far. It is possible that evidence of these animals may turn up in future studies.

Other large animals potentially hunted by the people of eastern North Dakota include wolf, coyote, grizzly, and black bear. This, however, is based on the assumption that their presence in the area in the Historic Period, and evidence of their being hunted in other portions of the Plains means that they were probably also hunted in the Sheyenne Valley. At this point, as is the case with deer and pronghorn, such conclusions are speculative.

While large game was the focus of hunting activities throughout the Plains, and undoubtedly in the Sheyenne River Valley, smaller animals were also taken, and for many of these we do find evidence at archaeological sites. Beaver, muskrat, groundhog, rabbit, squirrel, skunk, and other small animals are often recorded as present in the bone samples from archaeological sites. They would have provided an important source of food that could be locally hunted, snared or trapped. Besides the meat from the animal, the furs of beaver, muskrat, rabbit, and various mustelids, like skunk and weasel, were used for some types of clothing. Waterfowl are common at some sites and include a variety of duck species. The Sheyenne Bend was on or near one of the flyways that migrating birds took during their annual migrations. The many prairie potholes in and near the Bend region were attractive to these birds. Occasionally bones from raptors are also found. They were probably hunted for their feathers rather than for their flesh. An eagle trapping pit was even found at one of the sites north of Fort Ransom. Fish are sometimes present in small numbers, bottom feeders such as catfish being common when fish are present. Mussels from the Sheyenne and Maple rivers are frequent finds at archaeological sites, and these would have been used for food, and their shells used as occasional utensils, beads, and other ornaments. In the later part of the prehistoric period crushed mussel shells were also used to temper pottery.

The only domestic animal used by the Indians of the Plains, and by the peoples in the Sheyenne Bend, were dogs. We know that dogs were already domesticated when the first Americans arrived in North America during the last Ice Age (Little Wolf nd; Olsen 1974). Some tribes kept dogs as pets, many as hunting companions. Dogs were used to pull the travois, a device with two poles tied together at one end and expanded outward at the other in a V-shape. Between the poles would be a hide or webbed frame or platform on which burdens were placed. Sometimes the elderly or children on travois were pulled by dogs. On other occasions packs were simply tied to a dog's back. Some groups kept large numbers of dogs, as many as a dozen for a family. Among the Hidatsa, twenty dogs were regarded as a large number for a family. The Assiniboine were reported to have more dogs than the Mandan and Hidatsa (Lowie 1982: 39-40). At certain times among some of the tribes, dogs might also be eaten.

Chapter 3
Archaeological and Ethnographic Background

One of the archaeologist's jobs in areas where non-native people settled in the Historic Period, areas like North America, is to determine who traditionally lived there prior to the spread of colonial European powers or the introduction of industrial production and capitalist economies. Here, we will remark on the people who lived in the Bend when the first historical, or written, documents were composed. This is the time when the first European explorers and traders entered the region and left written accounts. For the Bend area one of the first reliable and useful reports of the native peoples is from an account by a Canadian explorer, mapmaker, and fur trader. David Thompson, around 1800, provides a narrative by an Ojibwa from Red Lake that his people attacked a village of the Cheyenne on the Sheyenne River. Many scholars estimate that this happened sometime between 1720–1780 (see Wood 1971 for an extended discussion). It is at about this time, then, that the Sheyenne Bend enters written history.

Ethnography

The Cheyenne spoke an Algonquian language related to Ojibwa, Ottawa, Cree, and the languages of other peoples who lived around the Great Lakes area. How long the Cheyenne may have been in the Sheyenne Bend area is a matter of some controversy. According to historical sources the Cheyenne migrated from the forested lands in Minnesota or Wisconsin to the Minnesota River Valley around the seventeenth or early eighteenth century. From here they moved to the west and north until they came to the Sheyenne River Bend, where they built a substantial village of pit houses surrounded by a fortification ditch. The site was big enough to accommodate over 600 people, possibly many more (Grinnell 1918). We will have more to say about the site where the Cheyenne lived later on.

The Cheyenne are known from historic times as bison hunting nomadic people of the High Plains (Moore, Liberty, and Straus 2001). They were described in the nineteenth century living west of the Missouri where they often traded with the village–farmers on the Missouri River in the Dakotas, particularly with the Arikara. The lifestyle of the people is taken both from Cheyenne informants and from the descriptions written about them by outsiders. Cheyenne subsistence revolved around the buffalo hunt, although pronghorn and elk were also important. They gathered a variety of wild plants such as the prairie turnip and Jerusalem artichoke. Most sources agree that formerly the Cheyenne were village-living people who practiced a traditional form of farming involving the planting of gardens in river floodplains, growing maize, squash, beans, and a few other crops.

The Cheyenne people were divided into ten or so different bands, each of which operated for most of the year as an independent unit. Each band might include several hundred people. The bands chose chiefs who acted together with chiefs from the other bands to regulate the people as a whole (Moore, Liberty, and Straus 2001). However, most of what we know about the Cheyenne comes from their own descriptions and from ethnographic studies of their culture in the nineteenth century. What their society might have been like before the arrival of the Europeans and the introduction of guns, horses, metal tools, and Euro-American trade is something that must be reconstructed from several lines of evidence. These include Cheyenne traditions, the archaeological record, and analogies with more recent cultures whose life-ways are assumed to be like that of the Cheyenne when they lived in sedentary villages and farmed rather than living as hunters in a nomadic subsistence system. For now, we only note that most sources say that the Cheyenne were only present in the Sheyenne Bend region for a short period, perhaps a generation or so. In any case, the claim that they were driven out by the Ojibwa indicates that the Ojibwa as well made at least occasional use of the area.

The native people most commonly associated with the Sheyenne Bend in the historical documents is the Yanktonai. They are a division of the Sioux or Dakota, who are often divided into the Eastern or Santee Dakota, and the Western Sioux or Lakota, also known as the Teton. There is a third group of Dakota people known as the Yankton and Yanktonai. The territory of these two groups included much of eastern South and North Dakota. The Yankton tended to use the area of eastern South Dakota and far western Minnesota south of the Minnesota River. This included the famous Pipestone Quarry at Pipestone, Minnesota.

The Yanktonai Dakota used the eastern half of North Dakota south of Devils Lake, east of the Missouri, and approximately to the Red River of the North. They were one of the largest sub-groups of the Sioux and dominated much of the Northern Plains east of the Missouri River in the eighteenth and nineteenth centuries (Galler 2008:468). The territory of

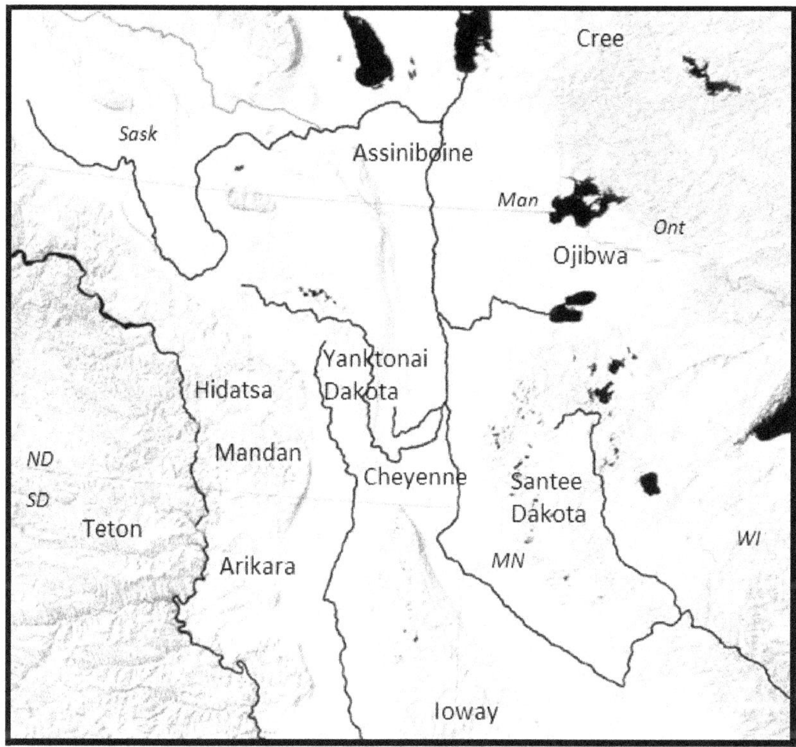

Figure 10. Northern Midwest and Northeastern Plains ethnic groups, 18th-19th centuries. Ethnic groups moved location during the Historic period and were not all present in these positions simultaneously. Political divisions in italics.

the Yanktonai included the Sheyenne Bend region, and indeed the entire Sheyenne Valley, as well as the James Valley and a large portion of the Red River Valley in North Dakota. The Yanktonai were hunters and gatherers and their major food was buffalo. In the middle of the nineteenth century, one Yanktonai band on the Missouri River established a permanent village of earth lodges, similar to those of the Mandan or Hidatsa. Here they planted gardens and farmed. They claimed this was their first attempt at agriculture (DeMallie 2001: 777-780). Prior to this they lived a more mobile life and depended on hunting rather than on growing crops.

According to some historical records and maps it seems that the Yankton and Yanktonai formerly lived in Minnesota, and by the eighteenth century some of them were located along the course of the Minnesota River (Figure 10). Who might have been using the eastern part of North Dakota and the Sheyenne Bend area at this time is not clear.

Old maps from the late seventeenth century and early eighteenth century show the Teton (Lakota) living west of the Minnesota River in the general area of the Sheyenne Bend. It is possible that the Teton were only one of several groups to use the Sheyenne Bend area. Europeans tended to place Indian peoples in discrete territories based on where one or another observer found them at the time of a visit. However, the presence of a group of people in one area does not mean that in other seasons or years they might not have used another area as well. For example, the Ojibwa attack on the Cheyenne mentioned above suggests that the Ojibwa were occasionally in the Sheyenne Bend area. As for the Yanktonai, they have been described as living in central Minnesota around 1680, and being in the Minnesota River Valley during the eighteenth century. By the late eighteenth and early nineteenth century they were reported in eastern North and South Dakota (see Galler 2008 for a discussion of their locations). European reports are normally interpreted to mean that as Europeans moved into the region, the Indian peoples migrated westward. But this may tell only a part of the story. The Yanktonai may certainly have been present in central Minnesota in 1680, and their presence in the Minnesota River Valley several decades later may also be accurate, but not because they moved or migrated, but because this was part of their use area, and possibly had been for a long time. In other words, it was the Europeans moving west, not the Native people.

The Yanktonai Dakota were heavily involved in the Northern Plains trade system. They participated in the large trade fair held on the James River during the eighteenth century; a rendezvous that could attract up to a thousand lodges, possibly 10,000 or more people! In fact, even into the nineteenth century the Yanktonai were still trapping smaller fur-bearing animals in the river valleys of eastern North Dakota, since their pelts were somewhat more valuable than buffalo hides (Galler 2008:473–475).

There are also accounts of the Hidatsa living in the Sheyenne and adjacent Red River valleys in Late Prehistoric times. Bowers (1965:23) notes that there were groups of Hidatsa living in both agricultural and nonagricultural settlements on the lower Sheyenne River and in the Red River region prior to their move to the Missouri River. Some early archaeology in the Sheyenne Bend led researchers such as Wheeler (1963) and Bowers (1965:213) to conclude that Hidatsa were living on the Sheyenne River at a site not many miles east of the Cheyenne village already mentioned, but at an earlier time period.

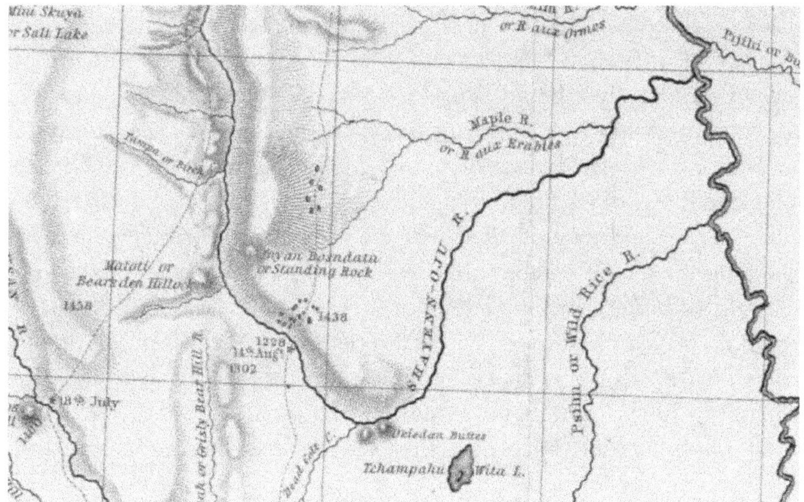

Figure 11. Portion of the Nicollet Map, showing the Sheyenne Bend region. Note depiction of Okiedan Buttes, Matoti (Bear's Den), and Inyan Bosndata (Standing Rock). Use of Dakota terms for locations clearly illustrates the affiliation of the people who lived in the area. Taken from http://hdl.loc.gov/loc.gmd/g4042m.ct001419.

One of the features of Native life in eastern North Dakota before the European settlement is that both farming and hunting/gathering are mentioned in the historical accounts. The Cheyenne, during their tenure in the area, had a settled village and planted their corn along the Sheyenne River. The Yanktonai, though bison hunters, were also willing to experiment with farming and settled village life, and the Hidatsa are believed by many to also have hunted and farmed in the Sheyenne Valley. This pattern that we see reflected in the Historic Period, of peoples who sometimes tilled the soil and at other times hunted and gathered wild foods, will be important in helping us understand some of the later portions of the prehistoric record as indicated by the archaeological materials recovered in the Bend region.

Early Explorations

Historical records mention places in the Sheyenne Valley used by early peoples. David Thompson and Alexander Henry (Coues 1897) mention a village of the Cheyenne people on the Sheyenne River. An early nineteenth century map by William Clark shows the Bend area of the Sheyenne River with a place name of "Old Trading Fort" (Tucker

1942:Plate XXXI). Joseph Nicollet's 1839 manuscript map of the Sheyenne River names an "ancient village of the Cheyenne" on the eastern side of the Sheyenne Bend (Wood 1993:Plate 75A), that is, the same spot as the old trading fort noted on the Clark map. Today we know this location as Biesterfeldt, a well-studied archaeological site. The Nicollet Map mentions other areas of interest in the Bend area. Around three miles to the southwest of the Cheyenne village he records an area called "*Okiedan Buttes*." We believe this term means something approximating "mourning buttes," making reference to the many burial mounds situated upon them. On the western side of the Bend area Nicollet makes note of *Matoti* or "Bear's Den Hillock," and northeast of there is *Inyan Bosndata*, "Standing Rock." The Bend region was obviously of considerable cultural significance and Nicollet reflected this in recording native names for these special places (Figure 11).

These locales are still known today in the Bend area. Standing Rock is a State Historical Site on the western edge of the Bend. There is an up-thrust gneiss boulder at the site today, stabilized by a concrete collar. Geologists claim that the hill on which the rock is situated was thrust up by glacial action. The State Historical Society suggests that the rock itself is atop an artificial burial mound, and that other adjacent prominences include two additional round mounds connected by a massive lineal mound. In any case, whether natural or cultural in origin, this high place provides a magnificent view of the Sheyenne Valley below and was of some ritual significance to the Dakota people.

South of Standing Rock is the town of Fort Ransom in the plain of the Sheyenne. The bluffs on the west side of the town feature a number of burial mounds from the prehistoric period. The most prominent of these mounds are located along a bluff top known as Bear's Den Hillock. The Dakota referred to this location as Matoti. It probably had a ritual significance similar to the Okiedan Buttes on the southern perimeter of the Bend region and was the site of significant funerary activities (Figure 12). And besides the burial structures here there are also reports of tipi rings in the same general location (Arnold 1918:8). These reports are from the early part of the twentieth century, and the tipi rings have not been identified in any formal archaeological work. Even so, it would not be surprising to find such features in an area so heavily used by Native peoples.

Just below Bear's Den Hillock are some of the most enigmatic archaeological remains in the Sheyenne Valley. These comprise numerous petroglyphs, including one boulder locally known as the "Fort Ransom Writing Rock" (Figure 13). T.H. Lewis (1891) described it as a "cupstone"

Figure 12. Large burial mound in the Sheyenne Bend area.

Figure 13. The Fort Ransom Writing Rock.

with long grooves and other undecipherable figures (at least to non-Native Americans). Nearby there are over a dozen inscribed boulders with petroglyphs on their surfaces, most barely visible. Callahan (1999) believes that the Writing Rock was possibly used in shamanic rituals and refers to what he calls the "amphitheater acoustics" of this area. He suggests that it is possible to project the human voice eastward from the hillside on which the Writing Rock is situated quite effectively to the other side of the valley.

Burials and Mound Sites

During prehistoric times many burials in the Sheyenne Valley were placed beneath and in earthen mounds, and in the past, these were normally defined as archaeological sites. In the nineteenth and for much of the twentieth centuries these mounds were sometimes dug into by looters, as well as by amateur and professional archaeologists. Even though this practice is discontinued today, it would be negligent of us to ignore some of what was found in this earlier work. We refrain here from any detailed description of the deceased buried in these cemeteries, but will treat the finds in abstract fashion and only as a means of shedding some light on the past of the Sheyenne Valley.

During the nineteenth century archaeology was a relatively new scholarly field and sometimes those involved in the serious study of the distant past were known as antiquarians. Some of these antiquarians believed that the earthworks and mounds throughout the Midwest were traces of a lost race, commonly called the Moundbuilders. For example, in Manitoba George Bryce (1884, 1904) argued that the mounds were built by 'civilized' Toltecs around the eleventh century and later, or perhaps by pre-Columbian north Europeans. While this sort of speculation mostly died out by 1900, they were the stimulus for a great deal of effort to study the mounds and earthworks. Such ideas were apparently current in Ransom County as late as the 1970s. Thorfinnson (1975:18-23) suggested that the Moundbuilders of the region used a writing system displayed on the Writing Rock, near historic Fort Ransom, and that this undeciphered glyph showed some relationship with Sino-Tibetan, and even Mayan languages. He also felt the authors of the Writing Rock script probably built Pyramid Hill in the town of Fort Ransom, which Thorfinnson felt is an artificial mound built as long as 9,000 years ago! Pyramid Hill is, of course, a natural feature and not an artificial mound, and there is no evidence of Moundbuilders with Sino-Tibetan or Mayan affiliations in the Sheyenne Bend region. Still, the speculations about the several features in the Fort Ransom vicinity highlight the popularity of this 200-year-old Moundbuilder myth, and the importance of mounds and earthworks in the development of the prehistory of the Bend region.

Much of the work directed at the excavation of mounds was not only because they were believed to be remnants of a lost race, but the mounds were mostly grave sites, and they often contained exotic and ornate grave offerings such as decorated ceramic vessels, inscribed tablets, carved pipes, and well-made stone artifacts. After the demise of the nineteenth century Moundbuilder, or "lost race" theory, and recognition that ancient Indian peoples built the mounds, these sites still attracted a great deal of attention both because of the richness of the artifact assemblages found in them, and because they contained human skeletons. For archaeologists, study of the human skeletons provided information on the physical relationships and health status of ancient populations.

One of the most productive of these pioneer archaeologists focused on mound study was T.H. Lewis, employed by Alfred J. Hill, a well-to-do St. Paul civil engineer. In 1890 Lewis came to North Dakota and surveyed earthwork sites in the Sheyenne Bend between Fort Ransom and Scoville Township (on the western and eastern sides of the Bend respectively). Lewis described, but did not dig into the mounds. Most of the pre-modern earthworks are conical mounds on the bluffs overlooking the Sheyenne River. It is worth making note of the fact that Lewis did not survey in river floodplains (Haury 1990:74). He believed that mounds were always located on high ground where they could be easily seen. There are mounds known from lowlands of the Upper Midwest, but we know of only one on the floodplain of the Sheyenne River in the Bend area.

The majority of these are single structures, although nearly half of these have two or more mounds. Groups of three or more are relatively rare. The mounds were described as being generally between 0.3–1.0-meter-high, although the Lucas and Ranes mounds on the Okiedan Buttes include individual mounds that are almost two meters in height. Most are circular in shape with diameters ranging from 10 to 25 meters. At least one mound is associated with a rock cairn, a few have flat tops that may have served a purpose different than that of the other, conical mounds.

Today, most of the mounds have been farmed over; many have been obliterated and others are only faintly visible. A large number of these mounds have depressions in their tops. These are remnant looting pits which were dug into the mounds to remove skeletons or artifacts. The result of farming and uncontrolled digging into the mounds resulted in the loss of a great deal of historical and scientific information; even so, the large number of mounds remaining is as impressive as the loss to local history is regrettable.

An examination of Lewis' survey results relevant to the Bend Region (Copy of field notes at the State Historical Society, Bismarck, ND) reveals a total of 164 mounds stretching about 20 miles from the western side of the Sheyenne National Grassland on the eastern margins, west to Bear's Den Hillock at Fort Ransom. Many of these mounds are no longer present (Haury 1990); nevertheless, there are a remarkable number of mounds for a relatively small area. Examining the distribution of mounds reveals a nearly continuous scattering of mounds, with clusters about every 4-6 miles. These clusters comprised from 7 to 50 mounds. The densest clustering of mounds is in the Okiedan Buttes area where a total of 50 mounds were identified. These include the Lucas Complex and the Ranes Mound Complex.

In 1989 Cherie Haury retraced the travels of T.H. Lewis, visited the sites recorded by him in North Dakota, and recognized five categories of mound and earthwork sites (Haury 1990:149).

1. Single, conical, elliptical or linear mounds unassociated with other earthworks. This category made up 53% of the sites Lewis mapped in the Bend region.
2. Paired mounds that are not connected to each other but are in close proximity.
3. Patterned features, or mounds with conical and linear features that are interconnected.
4. Mound groups, including three or more earthen features in proximity but not interconnected.
5. Mound complexes, which are groups of three or more mounds in which some features are interconnected, and others are in close proximity.

Linear mounds attached to conical mounds appear to be diagnostic of the Northeastern Plains (Chomko and Wood 1973; Wedel 1961). Conical shapes are the most common (n=128), followed by linear mounds (n=24) and ovals (n=12). Within the Bend Region there are seven separate instances of linear mounds attached to conical mounds based on the Lewis 1890 survey.

Lewis was not able to interpret the meaning of the mounds and earthworks he recorded, and his work came at the end of the popular interest in the mounds as evidence of pre-Indian, or moundbuilder, civilizations in America. This interest ended decidedly for professional archaeologists with the publication of Cyrus Thomas' Smithsonian Institution volume on the North American mound phenomenon. In this work (Thomas 1894) the mounds were recognized as having been built by the ancient American Indians, not by a lost race of mound building peoples. So, in the end, Lewis' survey stands not as a testament to a "lost race," but as an important contribution to the history of regional native peoples.

Rain Vehik (1979) completed an archaeological survey in the lower Sheyenne that included a one-mile stretch along the river in the Okiedan Buttes Locality. It yielded evidence for 15 mounds, while another one-mile stretch to the immediate west of this locality (Dead Colt Creek) also along the Sheyenne, yielded three mounds per one-mile stretch of survey. Survey blocks to the north along the Sheyenne River, and outside the Bend Region, yielded only about one mound per mile of survey. No mounds were recorded in the section of the Sheyenne Valley that entered the Red River lowlands.

Historic Period Indian peoples did not usually bury their dead in mounds. David Bushnell (1927) reviewed the burial practices of many American Indian people of the Plains as reported to him, or garnered from various historical accounts. He argued that funerary customs were partly dependent on the environment in which members of one or another culture found themselves. For instance, people such as the Osage, living near rocky cliffs, buried their dead under heaps of stone, while groups like the Ojibwa, who occupied forested regions, used log covered graves, and those living on the prairies raised the dead above the ground on scaffolds. Several of the groups known to have used the Bend region, such as the Cheyenne and Yanktonai, are described as having used scaffold burial (Bushnell 1927:8, 27-29). As for the construction of mounds, none of the native peoples west of the Mississippi built substantial mounds, but Bushnell (1927: 61, 79) describes both the Oto and the Pawnee as building small mounds over the graves of the deceased.

While some groups still maintained the practice of mound burial in a modest fashion, we are not familiar with any such evidence from groups in the eastern Dakotas. Ella Deloria (2007:65-68) provides some detail that she retrieved from Dakota elders about the burial practices of the Teton or Lakota. In death, she reports, the corpse was elaborately attired with specially made clothing, including richly decorated moccasins and favorite implements to accompany the deceased. The person was then wrapped in a buffalo hide and laid in the boughs of a tree, or on the open prairie. If a scaffold was used, it would be built on a knoll in sight of the camp. Cremation was never practiced. Oneroad and Skinner (2003:99-102) report that the Sisseton also placed the deceased on scaffolds, or arranged them in the branches of trees, with the corpse wrapped in a buffalo hide. Some elders stated that it would be offensive to throw dirt on the bodies of the departed. Of interest, however, is Deloria's statement that a Santee survivor of the 1862 Dakota Conflict said that they would return to Minnesota to visit the graves of their relatives which they referred to as "makapahas" or earth hills, a seeming reference to the mounds. And Amos Oneroad, a Dakota man, told the story that once many people lived in this country, many of whom were killed in fighting. The survivors of the fighting heaped up dirt to cover the corpses. But wolves dug into the graves, so relatives returned and placed more dirt on the graves, this happening repeatedly so that over time large mounds were formed (Oneroad and Skinner 2003:102).

We may suppose that the many mounds found in the Bend region were built in the prehistoric past when the burial customs of the regional cultural groups were considerably different from those of the historic past. The limited mound construction among the Oto or Pawnee was clearly a cultural survival of a previous effort by Indian peoples on the eastern Plains to highlight with mounds the location of burial grounds.

A specific example of a prairie mound built in the Historic Period is the burial of the Omaha chief Blackbird. He was buried on a high hill overlooking the Missouri River in eastern Nebraska about 1800. At the base of the hill is an outcrop of rock with various petroglyphs, and there are substantial springs issuing from the cliffs below the summit (Sheldon 1919:20-22). Lewis and Clark visited the mound with ten of their men in 1804. The mound was described as about twelve feet in diameter and six feet high (Mussulman 2011). In 1832 George Catlin described the mound as still present. Today, it is no longer visible. In many ways this describes many prairie mounds, including those in the Bend region. At the Okiedan Buttes, for instance, mounds are placed in prominent positions on the uplands over the Sheyenne Valley. Numerous springs may be found running from the base of the uplands, sometimes forming creeks that flow into the Sheyenne. Above the town of Fort Ransom several prominent mounds feature a series of petroglyphs in a field below, including the Fort Ransom Writing Rock.

In the Sheyenne Valley excavation of mound burials was occasionally done by archaeologists, commonly in the earlier part of the 1900s. Henry Montgomery (1906) performed a number of burial excavations in the late nineteenth century, mostly outside the Bend area in northeastern

North Dakota. In the early to middle twentieth century Edward Milligan excavated burial sites in the Sheyenne Bend region, including a mound group on the Okiedan Buttes. Gordon Hewes (1949) dug into two burial mound sites on the bluffs above the Sheyenne near Valley City (northwest of the Bend region) in 1948 to salvage them prior to construction of the Baldhill Dam. One of the latest burial excavations was performed by a University of Minnesota crew at the Anderson site, in the eastern Bend area in 1960.

One burial was found in a gravel pit with no evidence of a mound. This burial, near Lisbon, dates by the radiocarbon method to AD 700–1000 (Schneider 2005). It was the grave of an adult woman. Squash and gourd seeds found with the burial may be from wild species, but since squash was commonly used as a domesticate by Plains people during this period the most reasonable explanation for their presence in the burial is that they reflect the practice of gardening by the group this woman belonged to. The squash seeds also stand as a reflection of the role of women in Plains societies. Women were most often the ones responsible for tending gardens (men usually cleared and prepared the fields). Including some produce from the garden in a female burial is consistent with their role in society. Furthermore, the discovery of a bison metatarsal fleshing tool and a set of stone scraping tools are also a reflection of women's tasks in Plains cultures. While hunting was often the focus of males, women prepared hides for clothing and shelters. They used fleshers and scrapers to make the hides pliable and usable. In several ways the Lisbon burial provides a small commentary on women's culture on the prehistoric Plains.

There are numerous unexcavated mound sites in the Sheyenne Bend region, mostly on high ground overlooking the river lowlands. Perhaps the greatest concentration of mounds is on the bluffs at the southernmost extremity of the Bend, the area known as the Okiedan Buttes. Here there are not only numerous individual mounds, many now plowed down and difficult to identify, but groups of mounds disposed in complex arrangements that are presently undecipherable.

Based on ancillary data we maintain that many of the earthen mounds were constructed during the Late Prehistoric in the Bend Region. We have concrete data on material from one mound based on digging by Milligan. He is reported to have unearthed a pot with an Oneota (Late Prehistoric) design from the Ranes Mound Group. This pot likely dates from the fourteenth or early fifteenth century. Another pot from the Nelson Mound (Wood 1959), the so-called Sydna Vessel, is grit-tempered with a plain surface and bizarre composite shape. We regard it as

Late Prehistoric. Although it appears that many mounds in the region have been "potted," we have no data on what was recovered from this vandalism. At one site excavated by E. Johnson, the Anderson Mound, there is a radiocarbon date of between 1343–1563, directly indicating a Late Prehistoric age (Vehik and Vehik 1985). Besides this dated mound, there are occupations characterized by ditch enclosures and distinctive ceramics that have mounds situated close to the settlement. The occupation sites are well dated to 1400–1600, and it is pretty safe to assume that the nearby mounds are the same age.

On the other hand, mound building has been established as a cultural trait dating to the Woodland period in the adjacent James River Valley, as well as in other parts of the Sheyenne Valley itself (cf. Hewes 1949). Native Americans have been erecting earthen mounds since at least Middle Woodland (ca. AD 1-500) times in the Northern Plains (Kordecki and Gregg 1986; Neuman 1975; Schneider 1982) and occasionally in the Bend Region (Vehik 1979:69-71) and elsewhere on the Sheyenne River (Haury and Schneider 1986:131-132; Hewes 1949). Excavations at the Jamestown Mound in the James River Valley (Snortland 1994) showed an occupation associated with successive use of burial mounds beginning during the Middle Woodland (here, part of the Initial Woodland) Period (ca. AD 100), and continuing for over a thousand years! If we are correct about the relationship between nearby occupations and the timing of mound construction, we must think of the mounds as becoming more popular after about AD 1000. Analysis and synthetic treatment of this mound data by a number of researchers (Chomko and Wood 1973; Michlovic 1990b; Syms 1979; 1982; Wedel 1961) indicate that most of the burials derived from the Late Prehistoric period and that the ceremonialism reveals a blending of Eastern US and Plains traits.

Several authors construed the presence of burial mounds as the by-product of seasonal bison hunters (Neuman 1975; Syms 1979:294-295; Wedel 1961). In part this characterization was colored by historic chronicles, the favored notion being that no group lingered in eastern North Dakota, but rather passed through, some of whom went on to contribute to the cultural diversity of the Middle Missouri River in the eighteenth century (Henning and Toom 2003; Syms 1979; Toom 2004). This model has been challenged by survey and testing in the James, Sheyenne and Maple River (Michlovic 1990a, 2008a; Michlovic, Holley and Dalan 2019; Michlovic and Schneider 1993; Schneider 2002, 2008) and by Nicholson (1990) in southern Manitoba. This new interpretation holds that the Northeastern Plains generally, the Sheyenne Bend included, was occupied by bison-hunting cultivators represented by the Northeastern Plains Village Complex. Burial mound construction need not have been the result of nomadic bison hunters visiting the Northeastern Plains. Mounds are expressly about settling in. What is telling is that in some areas there is continuity—signs of usufruct based on long-term use, as at the Jamestown Mound. By placing the dead in visible "earth" models, that is, mounds, we believe the people in the Northeastern Plains were claiming the land. These mounds created, in essence, ancestral estates (Layton 1995), serving as lasting monuments with symbolic value that legitimated rights over use of an area.

Although there is evidence of Woodland Period occupation in the Sheyenne Bend region, it is not possible to reliably link burial mounds with specific Woodland settlements. We have found sherds that may date from the Woodland from the cultivated surface near the Ranes Mound Group, which would support the idea that the very large mound groups were the by-product of centuries of use. Not until the very end of the Woodland can we speculate that some settlements, such as the Lucas site complex in the Okiedan Buttes locality, have an evident relationship with mound construction (see Holley and Kalinowski 2008) (The Lucas site is discussed below in the chapter on the Late Prehistoric). We presume a date of AD 1000–1200 for the Lucas complex, and it may be that the incorporation of the linear embankments associated with the mounds is tied to widespread elaboration of mounds in the latest portion of the Woodland Period in the Midwest. This was a time of great change throughout the Eastern United States, and the Northeastern Plains was not immune from changes in other parts of North America. We strongly suspect that these changes are tied to the emergence of horticulture in the area.

The practice of excavating mounds was ended with protests by various groups, including the American Indian Movement (AIM), that began in the 1970s. Native Americans argued that excavating graves was offensive and demanded an end to the practice. These protests culminated in 1990 with passage of the Native American Graves Protection and Repatriation Act (NAGPRA). By the terms of this federal legislation American Indian groups were provided with a mechanism to re-bury previously excavated human remains affiliated with their tribes or nations, and to repatriate any object from federally funded institutions or state or local governments receiving federal funds. Since 1990, prehistoric burials, historic-era burials, and modern cemeteries have the same protections in North Dakota. Any burial discovered on federal or tribal lands follow the regulations set forth under NAGPRA, while those discovered on state or private land follow the protocols set by the North Dakota Century Code and administration rules. Occasionally when a modern cemetery is threatened with a disturbance by development of some sort, perhaps a new road, or urban expansion, or even natural erosion, an archaeological excavation will be performed to remove the burials carefully so that they may be documented and re-buried at another location. Most prehistoric burials threatened with disturbance, including mounds, that cannot be avoided are excavated according to protocols set down by the Native authorities. The contents are recorded and the human remains and accompanying grave goods are re-buried on land chosen by the group that claims jurisdiction over the burials in that region.

Early Excavations in the Sheyenne Bend

In 1938 W.D. Strong, an archaeologist associated with the Smithsonian Institution and Columbia University, excavated a major site on the eastern side of the Bend region. This site is known as Biesterfeldt. It is the "old village" noted on some early maps, and is universally assumed to be the village of the Cheyenne that David Thompson claims was destroyed by the Ojibwa. The excavation here was considered an important moment in Plains archaeology since Strong argued that at Biesterfeldt, he had documented the Cheyenne people in the eighteenth century during a period when they were in transition from river valley farmers to a new life-style in the nineteenth century as horse-riding nomads (Strong 1940).

During the 1940s the State Historical Society of North Dakota sponsored an excavation at the Schultz site, an archaeological station covering several acres on the Sheyenne River about eight miles east of the town of Anselm. This work was done by E.A. Milligan and T.C. Hecker in the early 1940s. There is not much information about the actual work at the site, since a formal report was not written and the field notes are not available. A surviving comment from Hecker indicates that pottery from the site was recovered from "... the lower levels of the ... village ash pits." (Wood 1963:231). Artifacts from the site, including pottery and stone tools, are housed at the State Historical Society in Bismarck. The stone tools include a few projectile points for arrows and are typical of the Late Prehistoric Period on the Northern Plains. Stone hide-scrapers and knives are among the dozen or so stone artifacts. The pottery collection from the site is substantial and includes a large sample of vessel rims with distinctive decorations. The pottery was originally described by W.R. Wood (1963), which he regarded as affiliated with an archaeological culture known as the Stutsman focus. The Stutsman focus is recognized in the Sheyenne and James valleys and dates to the Late Prehistoric or very early Historic Period. It is regarded as ancestral to the Hidatsa people (Wheeler 1963). Bowers (1965:213) agreed with this assessment of Schultz and the Hidatsa. From the Sheyenne Bend we now have three ethnic groups believed to have been present in early Historic times; the Cheyenne, Hidatsa, and the Yanktonai. The Hidatsa are not recorded in the area, but are placed there by Hidatsa oral traditions, and by some archaeologists like Wheeler who argue that ceramics from some of the sites in the region are Hidatsa. The Cheyenne and Yanktonai are mentioned in the written documents and may have been present in prehistoric times as well, although this at present is a matter of speculation.

In 1960 a University of Minnesota crew working under the direction of Elden Johnson initiated a project that extended from the Minnesota forests onto the prairies of the Red River Valley. Johnson was concerned to understand the nature of archaeological materials across the ecotone, or environmental transition zone, situated between the grasslands in North Dakota, and the forest and lake country in Minnesota. This evidently included forays into the Bend region. While his work is mostly unpublished, some of the collections he made are still available and were used in composing some of the later portions of this volume.

Waldo Wedel, a Smithsonian archaeologist who specialized in Plains archaeology wrote an overview of work on the Great Plains up to 1960. Wedel (1961) summarized the research that had been done in what he referred to as the Northeastern Periphery of the Plains. This included eastern North Dakota and the Sheyenne Bend region. Wedel stated that in early historic times the Dakota people used this region, and that there was no traditional evidence that they had displaced anyone as they left the lake and forest country of Minnesota and moved to the eastern Dakota prairies. Therefore, he speculated, the peoples who left the archaeological remains, including the many mounds and earthworks, must have left the region long before.

The greater part of Wedel's discussion of the Northeastern Periphery is focused on the mounds and earthworks, most of which had been recorded during the survey work of T.H. Lewis seventy years earlier. However, by the time Wedel wrote, many artifacts from the mounds and from some habitation sites had been described. For this reason, he had some basis to associate the builders of the mounds with specific prehistoric cultures of known affiliation and temporal placement. He felt the mounds had several purposes, of course including burial of the dead. Pottery from the mounds was distinctive and not entirely similar to that found in habitation sites. That there was no evidence in the mounds of European trade goods confirmed their prehistoric date. Pear-shaped marine shell gorgets were found in some burials and had masked faces carved on their convex surface. Vertical zigzag lines descending from the eyes suggested tears. These shell gorgets Wedel recognized as very similar to those found in burials from the Mississippi and Ohio valleys, and they are decidedly Late Prehistoric. He felt there must be some association between the eastern Dakota mounds and the cultures of the Mississippi Valley to the southeast. On the other hand, he thought that perhaps many of the mounds were built by the Assiniboine, particularly in the northern part of the Northeastern Periphery.

Searching for Sites in the Sheyenne Bend Region

Throughout the Sheyenne Bend there have been several systematic efforts to find archaeological sites, a procedure referred to as survey. Some of them were small scale projects completed in a day or two, and designed to discover whether any archaeological properties would be disturbed by land development, such as wastewater treatment ponds, road realignments, and bridge construction. These minor undertakings aside, there have also been major surveys covering the Bend region, mostly conducted between the late 1970s and early 1990s.

One of these surveys was a study of the Sheyenne Valley in Griggs, Ransom, and Cass counties and performed for the U.S. Army Corps of Engineers during planning for proposed dam construction. The survey was supervised by Rain Vehik (1979). In the Bend region of the Sheyenne, Vehik discovered 36 prehistoric sites, extending from approximately Timber Coulee south of Lisbon to about one mile west of the Richland County border. Eleven of these are burial mounds, one is a stone circle, popularly called a tipi ring, one is a possible earth lodge site with surface depressions indicating house locations, and one is an earthen ditch or embankment. All the others are artifact scatters on plowed field surfaces (Vehik 1979:53). The pottery includes some sherds that are probably Woodland in age, that is, dating prior to about AD 1100, while others are similar to Late Prehistoric Northeastern Plains styles and Missouri Valley Coalescent pottery from the early Historic Period. The projectile points, like the pottery, all appear to be from later Woodland assemblages or from the Late Prehistoric Period (after AD 1100).

In 1985 the University of North Dakota conducted additional survey in the Bend area (Haury and Schneider 1986). In keeping with then current research preferences, this survey was a stratified sampling procedure, with research "strata" consisting of different geomorphic and topographic positions in the Sheyenne Bend. In this instance, the strata consisted of floodplains, terraces adjacent to the floodplain, valley slopes, and uplands. The project was directed at assessing the chronology of sites in the region, identifying different types of sites, such as lithic scatters, earthworks, major settlements, and the like, and at documenting evidence of inter-regional relationships. In the Bend region the survey involved work from Little Yellowstone Park to a point midway between Fort Ransom and Lisbon. Survey was also completed on the eastern side of the Bend, and in the Maple River bend area.

Site density in the survey area estimated as a result of the survey was 0.9 sites/km^2 in the Sheyenne Bend area, and 0.3 sites/km^2 in the Maple River Bend area. Archaeological materials were found in the floodplain, terrace, and upland settings. The most common site type was the cultural material scatter, or artifacts found scattered in plowed fields. Burial mounds were the next most frequent site type. Of great interest was a finding made not in the field, but in a collection of artifacts found by an artifact collector in the vicinity of Alice. Here, the survey crew identified a number of Paleoindian projectile point types, mostly from the later portion of the Paleoindian period.

In 1992 a dam on the Maple River was planned to alleviate flooding along the Red River during the spring melt and heavy summer rain events. One of the best locations according to engineers was at the eastern edge of the bend in the Maple River at a location just upstream from its entry onto the flat Lake Agassiz Plain, that is, the Red River Valley. In the heavy clays of the Red River landscape the Maple is little more than a trench on the flat plain. A dam there would be useless. But to the west of the Lake Agassiz Plain the Maple River cuts through old deltaic sands and silts and in these relatively erodible sediments the Maple has carved out a generous basin-like valley ideal for damming water to maximum effect.

An archaeological study was required over an area of about 3000 acres (Michlovic 1993a). The survey included investigation of the river flood plain and the immediately adjacent uplands since in both areas cultural properties might be affected by the high water. Archaeological sites in the floodplain might be covered with mud in the ponded water or eroded away if the course of the Maple was modified in the flood pool. Sites on the valley rim might be damaged or destroyed if wave action from the pooled water began eroding the valley walls causing sites on the bluff tops to collapse downslope.

In all, 48 prehistoric sites were found, including sites on the floodplain, buried in alluvial deposits visible in the river cut banks, and on the edge of the bluff tops. The total number of sites present may be much higher. For instance, 10 sites were in pasture and wooded areas using the shovel test method. This procedure is believed to be effective at finding about 10% of the sites actually present. Even surface pedestrian survey, that is, walking over plowed fields, is believed to miss numerous sites where, for one or another reason, artifacts that are present may be obscured or covered with soil at the time of the survey. Furthermore, inspecting cut banks for buried archaeological material is haphazard, depending on access and vegetation cover at the time the survey was conducted. Undoubtedly, many more buried sites, under two or three feet of river sediment (alluvium) must be present.

Based on the style of artifacts found in the survey there were no Paleoindian or Early to Middle Archaic occupations discovered. If present, these sites may well be buried deep in the Maple River alluvium. A possible Late Archaic point was found at one site, and several upland sites with only lithic flaking debris, but no pottery, may indicate pre-ceramic (Archaic) occupations. On the other hand, these upland lithic finds could be from later peoples who used ceramics at other places, but simply did not leave any in these particular locations. Two of the sites in the survey area are of major significance. These are the Shea and Sprunk sites. Both are on the uplands of the valley rim, both are undisturbed, or un-plowed in pasture grass, and both are characterized by circular to oval ditches defining an area of roughly an acre or so. Also, both of these sites are now on the National Register of Historic Places. They will be discussed later.

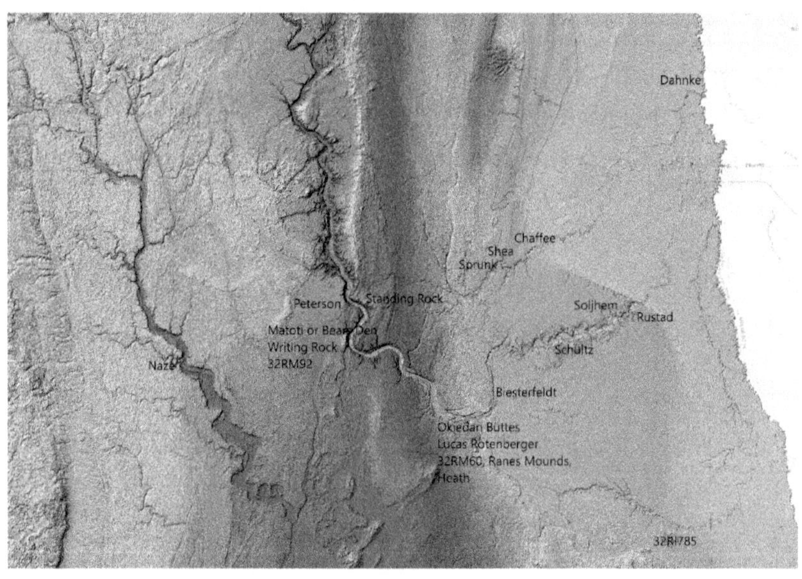

Figure 14. Major archaeological sites mentioned in the text and their approximate location within the Sheyenne Bend landscape.

Chapter 4
Early Cultures, Paleoindian and Archaic

The following review of regional culture–historical periods from earliest to latest comes with the caution that this system of dividing ancient time is largely for convenience (see the chronological table in chapter 1). It is actually unusual for any one area to provide equal amounts of information on each of these periods, and in fact, sometimes it is not clear that the period definitions are appropriate. Naturally, the earliest of periods are often under-represented in the archaeological record, while sites from later periods are present in greater numbers. There are several reasons for this. Earlier periods in time undoubtedly featured smaller populations than later ones, and thus fewer archaeological sites were created. Also, when population density is lower, people tend to live in smaller social groups, creating smaller settlements less visible to archaeologists. Another reason that earlier sites are rare in that they tend to be more deeply buried by sediments than more recent sites. A settlement buried under 5,000 years of deposits will be more difficult to find than one buried under 500 years of sediment. Finally, over time natural forces will often destroy archaeological sites. The chances of a site being completely distorted or eroded away over 5,000 years is much greater than of the same happening to a site that is only 500 years old, although we acknowledge that in more recent times land disturbance is more likely to damage shallow sites. Keeping all of this in mind is important when the reader assesses the relative paucity or abundance of archaeological information from different periods in time (Figure 14).

Paleoindian

The earliest of the archaeological periods in our region, and in North America generally, is known as the Paleoindian (13,500–8,500 years ago). The Paleoindians are regarded as the immediate descendants of the first peoples who came to the American continents from the Old World. Most archaeologists are of the opinion that the Paleoindians arrived after crossing into America over the Bering Land Bridge, a paleo-geographic feature called Beringia. This was the dry expanse of land between Siberia and Alaska during the Pleistocene. It was a result of lower sea levels when much of the earth's water was in glacial ice. Some archaeologists believe that early migrants came by a coastal route from northeast Asia to the west coast of America, perhaps by boat. Whatever the case, by at least 11,000–10,000 years ago Paleoindians would have been able to move into the Sheyenne Valley region, since by then the glaciers had receded from the area. The distinctive artifacts made by Paleoindian hunters have been found in the Sheyenne Bend, and at one site a buried Paleoindian-age deposit was uncovered.

Paleoindians may be thought of as the Upper Paleolithic peoples of the Americas, since it is from the Upper Paleolithic Period of the Old World that they derive. These peoples were formerly thought of as hunters who focused on late Pleistocene megafauna such as mammoth, mastodon, ice age bison, horse, caribou, and other large game. More recent study shows that the Paleoindians were also, and quite naturally, able gatherers of many types of plants, hunters of small game, and most likely accomplished at the utilization of many resources, as hunter gatherers known from ethnographic reports show us was typical of this adaptation throughout the world. The Paleoindians made a unique type of point for their spears. Archaeologists refer to them as projectile points, but they may have served a variety of functions, such as being hafted to bone or wood handles to serve as cutting tools or knives. Certainly, they must also have been used as projectile points. Much about the Paleoindian Period in this part of the Sheyenne Valley comes from artifacts found by private collectors. Some of these artifacts are now housed at the Minnesota Historical Society, and others at the State Historical Museum in Bismarck.

Archaeologists became aware of the Paleoindian as an archaeological phenomenon around 1930, and the term was introduced in 1940 (Hofman and Graham 1998:87). During the nineteenth century there was much speculation about the earliest Americans and some antiquarians believed that America had a prehistoric past similar to the Old World, with pre-human fossils and very crude stone technologies dating to hundreds of thousands of years ago. These ideas were rejected, and for a time, the reigning orthodoxy was that no humans were in America before the end of the Ice Age, around ten thousand years ago. However, during the 1920s several finds came to light in the Southwest US where Ice Age animals such as mammoth and giant bison were found with distinctive stone projectile points embedded in their bones; proof positive that humans were in America before the Ice Age ended. How long prior to the end of the Pleistocene would be a question not solved until the advent of radiometric dating methods around 1950.

The distinctive stone points found associated with Ice Age animals were elongated and parallel sided artifacts with concave base and unusual flake scars running longitudinally from the proximal end of the point toward the middle. These flake scars, often resulting from the removal of large flakes from both sides of the artifact, were called 'flutes,' and the points were thus known as fluted points. These fluted points come in an earlier, somewhat larger variety known as Clovis, and a more delicate-looking, later version known as Folsom. Sites with these types of artifacts have been excavated in various places with associated (calibrated) radiocarbon dates. Roughly speaking, archaeologists now date Clovis from around 13,500–12,900 years ago, while Folsom generally follows at about 12,900 and persists for another millennium or so. Together sites with these points are sometimes referred to as part of the Llano Tradition. After this time, we continue to find lanceolate points like Clovis and Folsom in outline shape, but without the distinctive flute scars. These latter artifacts are variable in some aspects of their generally lanceolate form and are often referred to collectively as representative of the Plano Tradition (Meyer, Beaudoin, and Amundson 2011). So, in simple terms, the Paleoindian Period consists of an earlier fluted point, and a terminal unfluted point expression. In the Northeastern Plains Clovis finds are rare. There are only a few reports of Folsom artifacts. Most of the Paleoindian diagnostic artifacts found in the region consist of Plano tradition forms (Figure 15).

There are many unanswered questions about the Paleoindians in North America. Most of what is known comes from archaeological sites outside the Northeastern Plains. For the Sheyenne Bend we know very little; however, a few generalizations are possible. The Paleoindians lived toward the end of the Pleistocene epoch and persisted into the early portion of the modern climatic period. In geological time this would be the Late Pleistocene–Early Holocene. They were hunters and gatherers and depended for their subsistence on wild plants and animals. Numerous Paleoindian archaeological sites feature the presence of large game animals, and especially in Clovis times, megafauna such as mammoth. By Folsom times the only Ice Age megafauna remaining seem to be *Bison antiquus*, an earlier and larger species of bison (Hofman and Graham 1998:118). Previous notions that the Paleoindians focused their hunting primarily on giant Pleistocene animals are now regarded as exaggerations. Pearsall (2012:82), for instance, notes that goosefoot, sedge, sunflower, and chokecherry have all been documented at Plains Paleoindian sites, indicating a substantial use of plant foods.

Figure 15. Clovis point (left), Folsom (center) and Plano point (right). Folsom point courtesy of the National Park Service; Clovis, and Plano points, MSUM Archaeology Lab.

Paleoindians are known largely from their lithic, or stone, technology. They made not only the well-known diagnostic Paleoindian projectile points, Clovis, Folsom, and Plano, but a range of other tools, including scrapers, knives, drills, engraving tools called burins, as well as artifacts made from bone, antler, and wood. Critics sometimes complain that archaeologists working with early sites have only stone tools to interpret past ways of life, and ancient cultures must surely have been richer than their stone implements might suggest. While there is truth in this, technology only makes sense within a particular adaptation (Bettinger 2001:154). Tools used for fishing are different from those used for hunting bison. So, while stone tools do not tell the entire story, they allow archaeologists to say something important about these prehistoric peoples. And part of the technology of the Paleoindians on the Plains was clearly designed, among other things, for hunting large animals.

Studies of Paleoindian site assemblages from across the Plains show that from Clovis to Plano there are several significant changes, besides the obvious loss of fluting in projectile points. For one, the megafauna, particularly mammoth, associated with Clovis sites are not present in the later phases of the Paleoindian. By Plano times, bison hunting became routinized and large-scale kills are evidenced in the archaeological record in the western Plains (Hofman and Graham 1998:103). Also, Plano assemblages are much more common on the Plains and extend into areas abandoned by the glaciers after about 11,000 years ago. Besides this, Plano sites tend to have more specialized tools than Clovis in the lithic assemblage (Irwin and Wormington 1970:33), suggesting perhaps some changes in the way people obtained and processed food. For example, there is an increase in Plano times in the frequency of end scrapers, drills, and burins (small stone chisels), indicating changing ways of preparing hides, and working bone, antler, leather, and wood.

The Paleoindian Period in the Sheyenne Bend region is poorly known. Many localities within the Bend region, and throughout the Northeastern Plains, experienced erosional episodes during droughty conditions in the middle portion of the Holocene (after around 8000 years ago), that is, immediately following the Paleoindian Period. Some sites dating to before the Middle Holocene may simply have vanished from the archaeological record (Artz 1995:81). Not only is direct evidence scanty, but this period is so distant in time that making comparisons with the Historic Period peoples of the Northeastern Plains is unwise. The Paleoindians were less populous, they had no domesticated plants, they lacked the bow and arrow, and there is no good evidence they lived in settled communities for any length of time. Drawing analogies from the life-ways of historic peoples such as the Yanktonai, the Cheyenne, or the Hidatsa, and applying them to the Paleoindians is not appropriate.

Nevertheless, there are a few things about a Paleoindian presence in the Sheyenne Valley that may be said. Elden Johnson reports finding Folsom points in a private collection from somewhere near Lisbon (Johnson 1962). Unfortunately, there is no information on the location of the sites where the Folsom points were found. There has always been some suspicion that they were in a local collection, but exactly whose collection is not known for certain. In any case, they are the only Folsom artifacts reported from this area. An avocational archaeological collector from Lisbon, Dr. Dick Herring, showed one of us (MGM) a collection from about ten or so miles east of Lisbon. There is reason to believe that this collection belonged to the same person who showed Elden Johnson the Folsom points. It is clear that the artifacts in this assemblage came from the Bend region, but precisely where is not documented. The collection also contains other identifiable point types, many belonging to the Archaic Period.

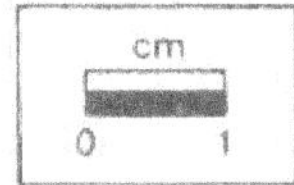

Figure 16. Late Paleoindian projectile point from the Bayley collection. State Historical Society of North Dakota, Bismarck.

Edgar Bayley, formerly of Alice, North Dakota, provided a substantial private artifact collection for a study undertaken by Ralph Thompson (1983). The collection consisted of artifacts from the central portion of the Bend region where the Sheyenne flows north along the western edge of the Sheyenne National Grasslands. This was probably in and around Shenford township, Ransom County (Figure 16). Mr. Bayley made the collection between 1925–1930. It includes artifacts from the Paleoindian Period through historic times. Thompson describes various projectile points from the collection that belong to several different Plano point styles. Four of the points are known as Agate Basin, and one each of varieties named Hell's Gap, Scottsbluff, and Eden (Thompson 1983: figure 3). All of these are unfluted lanceolate styles with slightly different shapes, which fit within the Plano Tradition. Projectile points similar to these have been found elsewhere on the Great Plains at excavated archaeological sites with associated radiocarbon dates. The presumed ages, based on dates from outside the Bend region, range from before 11,000 years to 8,000 years ago.

Figure 17. Late Paleoindian point fragments from near the Okiedan Buttes. Both are made of Swan River chert. The one on the left has a basal tang and an indented base. The point on the right has affinities to the Agate Basin type.

Other Paleoindian artifacts have been recovered from the surface of sites in the Bend region. This includes two sites on the floodplain below the Okiedan Buttes, both of which are unfluted specimens, and undoubtedly belonging to the Plano tradition. The artifacts are broken; however, the fragments that were recovered have the characteristic features of late Paleoindian implements. They are illustrated in Figure 17.

One Paleoindian component has been excavated in the Sheyenne Bend region. This is the most deeply buried of three occupations at the Rustad site. The site is on the Sheyenne River several miles southwest of Kindred. The site's several occupations are layered one on top of the other, each of which is referred to as a component. The major component of this site dates to the succeeding Archaic Period; however, radiocarbon dating and stratigraphy indicate a Paleoindian use of the site which dates to about 9,500 years ago. There are two radiocarbon dates for this level of the site. The earlier of the two dates on this level is about 10,000 years ago. This is in a downslope position of the site, while a 9,500-year date is a few feet upslope. The Paleoindian materials are found in a paleosol, or buried soil, that developed on the land surface exposed after the recession of Lake Agassiz. This soil was probably exposed and weathered for a thousand years or more, and the lower, or downslope date is the older one

Figure 18. Late Paleoindian remains at the Rustad site.

(10,000) and was assayed from organic material in the soil. We believe the date represents an early stage in the formation of this soil (Running 2005). The 9,500-year-old date was assayed on soil from higher in the profile and represents organic material in the soil closer in age to the time when people used the site, and to the time when this soil surface was buried. This date, of course, would place this component of the site within the time span of the Plano cultures of the Plains.

The Rustad Paleoindian layer is defined, then, on the basis of its stratigraphic position below an Archaic layer, and on the radiocarbon dates. Unfortunately, the diagnostic projectile points associated with Plains Paleoindian are not present. However, both large and small game animals were found. These include bison, fish and rabbit. No discrete living floor with features was discovered; only flaking debris and animal bones scattered vertically through about 10 or 15 cm of the deposit. A few square meters on the eastern side of the site contain these remains in their original location, but there is also a scatter of large bison bone that seems to have been washed down from upslope that is, oddly, above the in-place Paleo deposit (Figure 18). It is interpreted as a part of the Paleoindian component. Taken together, there is little to be said about this occupation. The radiocarbon dates tell us the age of these remains, and the animal bones suggest that the people here made their living from resources found in the grasslands (bison), the riverside woodlands (rabbit) and the river itself (fish). In other words, their way of life does not seem to have been that different from later peoples who lived by hunting various animals and gathering wild plants.

There is another element of the Rustad site Paleoindian component worth remarking on. Almost all the stone flaking debris from this level of the site is Knife River flint, an exotic stone material from west-central North Dakota. This brown, somewhat glassy stone is the best raw material for flint-knapping anywhere in the region. Knife River flint was used by people for thousands of years and was still being used for stone tools in the Historic Period. The people at the Rustad site, living about 200 miles east of the source area for Knife River flint, were either migratory, picking up flint in the area west of Bismarck and carrying it with them to the Rustad site, or they were involved in an exchange system with people to their west. At this point we do not have enough evidence to decide the issue one way or another.

If Paleoindians from the Folsom and Plano phases were present in the Bend region, they would have been living just to the west of glacial Lake Agassiz. Fortunately, some extensive work has been done on Paleoindian finds from the Assiniboine Delta region in southern Manitoba. The Assiniboine Delta is the largest deltaic deposit on the Lake Agassiz perimeter (the second largest is the Sheyenne Delta). The Manitoba Paleoindian data is better documented than the Paleoindian in the Sheyenne Bend, and the geographic setting is very similar. It seems appropriate to take the Manitoba materials as a comparable situation for the one that would have existed for Paleoindians in the Sheyenne Delta region.

A study of 28 Paleoindian sites in the Assiniboine Delta showed that there were few Paleoindian sites below the Campbell beach of Lake Agassiz. This means that when the Campbell beach formed about 10,000 years ago, Paleoindian groups were in the region. Most of the sites, however, were in locations some distance back from the beaches. This suggests that there may have been a resource-rich fringe area somewhat removed from the shoreline of Lake Agassiz. The glacial lake itself was probably not especially bountiful from a human perspective. After all, this was glacial meltwater, cold and not very accommodating to aquatic life. The dunes and hummocks back from the lake shore, on the other hand, may have featured ponds, wetlands, and diverse vegetation communities that would have supported waterfowl, fur bearing animals, and other game. These areas would have been attractive to the Paleoindian groups and explain the frequency of Paleoindian (mostly Plano) sites in this region (Boyd 2007). The Sheyenne Delta, smaller than the Assiniboine but similar in character, may have hosted Paleoindians in the same type of locations as the Assiniboine Delta in Manitoba. The presence of Plano points along the Sheyenne River on the western edge of the Sheyenne Delta does suggest that as Lake Agassiz receded ancient populations may have been exploiting the resources in the wetlands near the abandoned edges of the great glacial lake.

Additional study of the regional Paleoindian expression is badly needed. There are several areas that may contain very old sites dating to this period. These may be found along the perimeter of the Sheyenne Delta where there is a topographic drop into the lowlands of the Lake Agassiz Basin. Here, water running downslope off the uplands and into the Red River lowlands create local deposits known as alluvial fans. They are small deltas of sediment left as water moving downslope loses its energy and dumps its sediment load. These alluvial fans often accumulate in sporadic and repeated episodes of deposition. Layered archaeological sites, sometimes dating far back in time, may be found in such locations. The Rustad site is one such example. There are probably more if only they could be found.

Archaic

The Paleoindian Period lasted until about 8,500 years ago, the approximate date offered here for the beginning of the Archaic Period (8,500-2,200). Both of these terms, Paleoindian and Archaic, are used across all of the U.S. and Canada, and into Mexico. The standard chronology for North America posits the Archaic as the period following the Paleoindian, but this span of time is transgressive geographically. In some areas it begins and ends earlier than in others. In the Eastern US a standard date for the beginning of the Archaic is about 10,000 years ago and it continues to about 3,000 years ago. In the Great Basin, the dates are from 9,500 until, in some areas, the Historic Period (Fagan 2005:214, 370). We regard the Archaic Period in our study area as lasting from about 8,500 years ago until about 2,200 years ago, a span of about 6,000 years, the longest of all the prehistoric periods in the Bend region.

The Archaic was first defined in the 1930s. It was understood as a time after the disappearance of the fluted and lanceolate projectile point traditions of the Paleoindians, and the extinction of the Pleistocene megafauna. The Archaic was also recognized as flourishing prior to the introduction of agriculture and pottery making. Also, the construction of earthworks and mounds, common in later periods, was absent at most Archaic sites. Over time this definition has been modified, and we now know that some pottery was made toward the later portion of what we call Archaic, and in some places earthworks of various types were also built. Neither pottery nor earthworks are known for the Archaic period in the Northeastern Plains.

On the Plains the Archaic is often seen as beginning with a large-scale climatic warming trend known sometimes as the Altithermal. Some date this warming from 9,000-5,000 years ago, others from 8,500-4,000 years ago (Kay 1998:23-27). Often, terms with a slightly different meaning are used to refer to this climatic period, including Middle Holocene, Hypsithermal, Climatic Optimum, and Holocene Thermal Maximum. The climatic warming on the Plains during this period is known from pollen studies at various sites, including Elk Lake in Minnesota, where two dry pulses are recorded in pollen cores; one from 8,500-5,400 years ago, and another from 4,800-3,800 years ago (Kay 1998:26). During much of this period grassland vegetation extended east of its present boundary into north-central Minnesota toward the headwaters of the Mississippi River.

The Archaic was previously considered distinct from the Paleoindian in the use of a wider variety of resources. Today, that notion has been modified. The archaeological record suggests that Archaic peoples in some areas were less likely to depend on large game hunting than their predecessors, but this was not always true on the Great Plains. Here, large game, mostly bison, continued to be a major focus of subsistence for native groups. On this score the Plains Archaic people lived pretty much the same as the Paleoindians, perhaps with a growing use of plant resources. However, one aspect of the Archaic on the Plains is different from the Paleoindian; they made very different types of stone artifacts to serve as tips for their hunting weapons. These were mostly smaller in size than Paleoindian points, and often featured notches, either at the corners of the base or on the sides. Sometimes they had a shank extending down from the base of a triangular blade as a kind of stem. These notches and stems were designed to assist in hafting the point to a projectile shaft, a spear or a dart point (darts are a term used for a spear-like projectile cast with an atlatl or spear-thrower). In simple terms they are often referred to as notched and stemmed points. Exactly why ancient peoples changed their preference in making projectile tips from lanceolate and fluted forms to notched and stemmed is not really clear. Some think that it had to do with the invention of the spear-thrower, and that these lighter projectiles or darts required smaller points with a different hafting design. Others believe that the Paleoindians also used the atlatl, implying that the change in point forms was not related to how the projectile was launched.

Figure 19. Ground stone artifacts. Grooved mauls, above and lower left. Small celt lower right. MSUM Archaeology Lab.

Besides this, some archaeologists feel that the type of raw material used to make the points are an important factor that affected the change in point form from Paleoindian to Archaic times. Still others are convinced that so-called projectile points were used for other purposes as well, such as cutting tools, knives or saws (cf. McElrath et.al. 2009:7). Whatever the reason, archaeologists can easily distinguish Paleoindian from Archaic sites if projectile points are present, and on the Northeastern Plains and in the Sheyenne Bend, this is the easiest way to recognize these periods in archaeological collections.

There are some additional technological changes during the Archaic. Besides the new point or biface technology (a biface is simply any stone tool chipped on both sides, or faces, of the stone), the Archaic is also associated with ground stone tools. These include grooved mauls, axes, mortars, pestles, and other implements which were pecked and ground into shape using igneous rocks like granite and basalt, not chipped into shape from glassy rocks like flint. Pearsall (2012:83) points out that these begin to show up archaeologically in the Plano part of the Paleoindian Period, but they are certainly common in the following Archaic. Ground stone tools are very time consuming to make, involving many hours of effort to work into shape. They last a long time and may have been used over several generations, being very unlikely to break due to the toughness of the material they are made on. Ground stone tools were used for different purposes than chipped tools, including smashing bone to extract marrow, pounding posts into the ground, cutting down smaller trees for building, and grinding seeds, nuts, and berries. It is not a coincidence that along with the use of ground stone tools archaeologists sometimes find more evidence of plant foods at Archaic sites.

Ground stone tools became popular in the Archaic and continued in use throughout prehistoric times (Figure 19). Many farmers have examples of these tools in their sheds and barns. Being relatively large they are easy to spot in the field, even from the height of a tractor. Archaeologists are often asked by artifact collectors how old they are, but unfortunately, they are not diagnostic for time, and may reflect on any part of the prehistoric period, mostly after the Paleoindian.

Archaeo-botanists have documented the presence of many plants used by Archaic Plains peoples, including goosefoot, sedge, dock, smartweed, sunflower, wild bean, marshelder, chokecherry, buffaloberry, rose, wolfberry, grape, strawberry, and hackberry (Pearsall 2012:83). There may also be an increase in the use of small game, fish, clams, and waterfowl, as well as the continuing presence of large game resources. So, in addition to being a period in time, the Archaic seems also to represent a shift in the food-ways of the Plains peoples. This change may have involved not so much the use of resources never before exploited, but an increasing emphasis on resources that were less significant in earlier times.

Archaic Period sites in the Bend region are more common and better documented than the Paleoindian, both in private collections and in site survey results. For instance, in the Bayley collection from the central portion of the Bend region, there are over 50 Archaic-style projectile points. That compares with seven points from the Late Paleoindian Period that we counted in the same collection. Several recognizable Archaic point styles are found in the Bayley collection, and include types known as Oxbow, McKean, Hanna, Duncan, and Pelican Lake. Similar point styles were also observed in the collection shown one of us (MGM) by Dr. Herring of Lisbon. These Archaic point styles are dated at various sites across the Plains, although the dates from one site do not always correspond with those from another. Still, we have a rough idea that all belong to the Archaic Period, and to a certain extent, that the Oxbow appear earlier, and the Pelican Lake forms later. And at the very end of the Archaic, a side-notched point known as Besant is introduced (Frison 1998:144) (see figure 3b above).

Gregg (1985:100–116) reviewed the Archaic in North Dakota and laid out a chronology of diagnostic artifact (point) types from the earliest Archaic to the terminal part of the period. The earliest point styles for this period are small-sized side-to-corner-notched forms known as Logan Creek–Mummy Cave types. The name comes from two sites, Mummy Cave in Wyoming and Logan Creek in Nebraska, where similar points have been found in dated contexts extending to more than 7000 years ago. Following these types is the Oxbow style, a side-notched point form with an indented base and somewhat drooping "ears" on either side of the point base. This style is widely found throughout the Northern Plains. Oxbow is dated as early as 6,000 years ago (Dyck and Morlan 2001:119), although these types of points seem to persist in the archaeological record even after the end of the Archaic Period (Haug 1976). One way of understanding these projectile points styles is to think of them as becoming popular for a time and declining in popularity without completely disappearing. They may be less visible after the passage of so many centuries, but they do not necessarily disappear entirely.

Succeeding, and perhaps to some extent also contemporaneous with Oxbow is a complex of point styles known as McKean. The McKean style includes almost lanceolate shaped points known as McKean, and two other types named Duncan and Hanna. Duncan is a slightly stemmed point, while Hanna points have a broad side-notch. All three types typically have indented bases. The McKean complex is usually dated to the Middle Archaic on the Plains, from around 4,500-3,000 years ago, although Dyck and Morlan (2001:120) offer a beginning date of 5,700 in the Canadian Plains. They argue that the McKean Archaic hunter-gatherers were more opportunistic than their predecessors, making use of more plant and aquatic resources.

The final point types typical of the Northeastern Plains Archaic, referred to as the Late Archaic, are a well-made corner-notched form known as Pelican Lake, and the side-notched Besant points. During Pelican Lake through Besant times peoples on the Northern Plains were involved in highly efficient bison hunting with indications of mass hunts and even the construction of pounds or corrals to trap the animals (Frison 1971). By Besant times a network of long-distance trade in Knife River flint was apparently established, presumably along with other archaeologically less visible materials as well (Clark 1984). Also, during this time, around 2,000 years ago, moundbuilding and pottery making are introduced as well, which takes us into the succeeding Woodland Period.

Point types are useful when found on the surface or in private collections since they give us a rough idea of the age of a site. Unfortunately, they do not tell us much more than an educated guess about chronology of the site where they were found, and an indication that hunting tools were used or discarded there. Most of what we know about how people lived during the Archaic Period comes from the study of excavated archaeological sites, and from an understanding of the climate and environment of that time. We now turn to these special places to learn more about the Archaic in the Sheyenne Valley.

There are several well-excavated sites on the Northeastern Plains that help us understand the life-style of the peoples from this time. Most of these sites are from the earlier portion of the Archaic, and they include the Gowen site in southern Saskatchewan, Smilden–Rostberg in eastern North Dakota, the Itasca site in northwestern Minnesota, and the Cherokee site in northwestern Iowa. Several sites from the Sheyenne Bend may qualify as Archaic in age, and one site in particular is definitely part of the earliest Archaic on the Northeastern Plains. We deal here with three sites; two of which are undated, and the third a well-dated and extensively excavated site. Two of these are from eastern side of the Bend region, and the other is from a short distance south of the Bend area.

Site 32RI785

This site is unnamed so we refer to it with the Smithsonian Institution number (32 is the alphabetical place of North Dakota in the lower 48 states, RI stands for Richland County, and 785 is an arbitrary number given by the state). It was found and eventually excavated as part of the resource management plan for the Alliance Pipeline which passed through the site. It was dug in 1999 by a cultural resource management firm (Dobbs, ed. 2000). Located in southern Richland County, 32RI785 is on the Wild Rice River where it flows through the Campbell beach deposits of Lake Agassiz and onto the lacustrine plain. It is not within the Sheyenne Bend as we define it here, but is close enough that we are comfortable suggesting that the finds made there are relevant for the Bend area.

The site features two primary stratigraphic units. One of these, lower in the profile, consists of clayey sediments formed by Lake Agassiz. On the top of this unit is a gravelly lens that is found over much of the site and probably represents a lag deposit; that is, the remnants of a layer that was once present but was eroded away, probably by the wind, leaving only the larger sediment particles (gravel) as an indicator of its former presence. On top of this gravel-topped clay is a windblown deposit. In much of the site, it is difficult to separate artifacts into one or another of these natural deposits, but in at least one locality, the crew was able to isolate cultural materials in each of these two sediment bodies separated by a culturally sterile layer.

Unfortunately, no radiocarbon dates are available for the site; however, the Middle and Late Archaic are attested at the site based on the types of diagnostic artifacts present. One is Middle Archaic and indicated by Oxbow and McKean complex points. These are in the lower of two cultural strata at the site. The other is Late Archaic represented by the Pelican Lake and possible Besant-like styles. The Late Archaic is associated with the windblown deposits, while the Middle Archaic materials are situated in the lag deposit.

Besides documenting the two different time periods, the work at 32RI785 showed some significant differences between the Middle and Late Archaic occupations at the site. For example, in the lower, or Middle Archaic deposit, most of the stone material for tools is locally available, while the Late Archaic assemblage is primarily exotic stone, especially Knife River flint, and even including several pieces of obsidian from the Rocky Mountains. Besides this, the Middle Archaic deposit contains a very diverse tool assemblage with many expedient tools. These are more or less amorphous flakes with sharp edges used as they fall off the core and with little finishing into a final, formal, shape. Dobbs feels that this earlier component at the site represents an actual residential area for the people. In the Late Archaic, the tools are mostly formal, well-designed tools, suggestive of a field camp; that is, a place where people came with a well-designed tool kit for a particular purpose. Since spear points and knives are dominant tool types, the educated guess is that they were here for mostly hunting.

No plant remains of any significance were found at the site, but animal remains included dog or coyote, muskrat, rabbit, and some other small animals and birds. As with so many sites in the region, bison bones were ubiquitous. The way the bison bone was fractured indicate that bison were probably killed nearby and in small numbers, rather than in major drives where dozens of animals were killed in a single catastrophic kill event.

Dobbs believes that more mesic conditions after about 4000 years ago may have allowed more extensive use of the Northeastern Plains. The earlier Middle Archaic peoples may have lived a more stationary life, indicated by the diverse tool assemblage and by the quantity of expedient tools. By the Late Archaic improved environmental conditions allowed a life-style covering more expansive territories where hunters and gatherers were able to fan out from central settlements and exploit large areas with short-term resource-acquisition camps of the sort represented by the Late Archaic level at 32RI785. The high incidence of exotic tool-stone in this Late Archaic assemblage also reflects an adaptation that involved the capacity to travel or trade more widely for raw materials, including Knife River flint and obsidian.

Solhjem Site

A possible Archaic Period site in the Bend region is the Solhjem site (32RI718). This is on a terrace of the Sheyenne River as it winds a path through the sandhills on the eastern side of the Sheyenne Delta (Michlovic 1996a). The site was discovered by Garry Running in 1994 during geomorphic study of the Sheyenne Delta region. He found several flakes of Swan River chert in a plowed field on the south side of the river. The artifact scatter was interesting largely because of its position on the landscape. The cultivated field sloped toward the river from south to north. On the sloping ground a dark lens believed to be a buried soil horizon was exposed on the surface. Running surmised that the higher ground here was a terrace of the Sheyenne River formed when that stream emptied into Lake Agassiz sometime around 12,000–10,500 years ago. The dark lens visible on the slope of the field might well be an old land surface (soil) formed on the river terrace.

The site was excavated in 1996, when an area of about 3000m^2 was surveyed. Flaking debris and animal bone fragments were found on the surface, and a scatter of test excavations were placed over the field in order to search for a buried deposit. These units were dug to a depth of just over half a meter. Lithic items and animal bone fragments were found in the excavations, matching the finds from the field surface. Several of the bones are believed to be of bison, although they were badly broken. We do not know for certain whether the bones are from modern domesticated stock, or from prehistoric bison—cattle and bison being quite similar skeletally—but the fact of their burial suggests that they are bison bones. The lithic sample, including the material from the surface, consists of about 30% Knife River flint, the remainder being Swan River chert and some flaking debris of other types of material. No ceramics were found in either the surface or the excavated portions of the site.

The lack of ceramics and the position of the Solhjem site on a relict terrace of the river suggest the site may be quite old, very likely of Archaic age or even earlier. Since there are no radiocarbon dates from the site, nor any diagnostic artifacts, the age cannot be determined with any certainty. The robust representation of Knife River flint at about 30% of the total lithic sample indicates open access to the Knife River source area west of the Missouri. At the Rustad site (see below), Knife River flint is rare and its scarcity attributed to the periodically harsh climatic conditions on the Northern Plains during the Middle Holocene. If the lack of ceramics and the location of this site on an old terrace reflect a preceramic age, the abundance of Knife River flint might be taken as an indication that the site is not of Middle Holocene age. It probably is not from the Late Pleistocene/Early Holocene period since the buried soil exposed in the plowed field is formed in eolian sand, not river alluvium. The sands may have accumulated here during the Middle Holocene when sand dunes were forming, making a Paleoindian age unlikely. After the sandy sediments were deposited a topsoil formed on them. This soil may have lasted for over 1,000 years, indicated by the translocation of clay particles into the portion of the buried soil horizon below the topsoil. But the high incidence of Knife River flint tends to rule out a Middle Holocene date for the actual occupation. This leaves the earlier portion of the Late Holocene,

Figure 20. Rustad site during excavations.

after 5,000 years ago but before 2,500 years ago, as a likely age for the site. It is likely the people who lived here hunted bison. More than this is impossible to say about its age or function.

Rustad Site

The Rustad site (32RI775) is on the south bank of the Sheyenne River near the boundary between the Sheyenne Delta and the Lake Agassiz lowlands (Michlovic and Running 2005) (Figure 20). The Delta is south and west of the site, the Lake Agassiz Plain is north and east. The site is strategically located between the lush bluestem prairies of the clay-rich Lake Agassiz basin and the mosaic grasslands and wooded copses of the sandy Sheyenne Delta. It is in a soil pit or quarry, and it was discovered in the disturbed floor of that pit. Although the central portion of the site was destroyed by the removal of soil, a good portion was preserved in higher positions on the eastern side of the pit, in the eastern pit wall, and in a remnant bench of only lightly disturbed materials on the western side of the soil pit. The sediments are largely silt and sand dating to Early through Late Holocene times. Archaeological and geomorphological work was done at the site from 1993–1998.

At the base of the Rustad soil pit profile are lacustrine sediments laid down by Lake Agassiz. The topmost portion of these sediments have weathered into a robust soil, or paleosol, buried after perhaps 1,000 years of pedogenic development. The sediments that buried the paleosol eroded from the Sheyenne Delta upland on the southern perimeter of the site. This later deposit, dating to the Middle Holocene, was brought down by water shed from the higher ground, probably during the spring melt and summer storms. The deposit is known technically as an alluvial (stream deposited) fan. Finally, the fan deposits that buried the Early Holocene soil were buried by eolian (windblown) sand in the Late Holocene. These eolian deposits are the sediments that have presently weathered into the modern soil. Before the soil pit was exposed by heavy machinery, the archaeological site at the Rustad site was under almost two meters of sediment. The site was wooded before it was used as a soil pit.

There are three occupations, or archaeological components at the Rustad site. These range in age from about 9,500 to perhaps 1,500 years ago, giving the site an important place in North Dakota archaeology as a representation of human use of the Sheyenne Valley extending over about 8,000 years. Of course, the site was occupied intermittently rather than continuously, but the three components do provide us with snapshots of regional life at several points in the past. Beside this, each component is associated with sediment bodies representing different agencies of deposition. The earliest of the components is related to Lake Agassiz deposits, the middle component in the alluvial fan is associated with the down-washed sediments from the uplands, and the most recent component is in windblown deposits. These different deposits are themselves related to climatic conditions that were pervasive at the time of the various occupations.

Resting over the Early Holocene soil containing the Paleoindian component discussed earlier is the alluvial fan. There are actually two buried A-horizons in this fan deposit which tell us that erosion from the upland washed sediment down from the Delta and formed at least two surfaces that stabilized and weathered into topsoil. These A-horizons suggest periods of minimal upland erosion when vegetation would have covered the fan surface. The earlier soil was named the Ab3 horizon (A-horizon number 3, b is for buried). Additional upland erosion created another deposit of down-washed sediment that buried the previous A-horizon. This new deposit then weathered into another topsoil, Ab2 (A-horizon number 2, buried). In some areas of the site the two buried A-horizons are distinct, while in others they merge into a single dark layer (Figure 21). Apparently, the region was cycling through drier (erosion) and

Figure 21. Rustad site, Ab2 and Ab3 welded. Note the earlier, Paleo-age soil layer in the lower right of the photo.

wetter (soil building) periods. This seems to have characterized conditions during the Middle Holocene. The evidence from the Rustad site is that in eastern North Dakota the Middle Holocene, or Altithermal, was a period of relatively mesic, or modern, conditions, punctuated by severe droughts during which average annual temperature increased and precipitation decreased. It would have been during these dry periods when upland sediment was most likely to erode and wash downslope, creating the alluvial fan. After all, even during dry periods there is some snow cover, and occasional summer thunderstorms. During these events the dry, denuded, sandy Sheyenne delta would have easily eroded and provided the sediment for creating the alluvial fan at Rustad.

Several 14C dates provide age estimates for this landform (Figure 22). The Early Holocene date and Paleoindian materials discussed previously are about 9,500 years old. The soil developed on top of the Middle Holocene deposit, marking the end of that sub-period, is about 4,900 years old. The buried A-horizons within the Middle Holocene deposit date the Archaic. This Archaic component is about 8,000 years old in calibrated radiocarbon years, this date being based on six radiocarbon assays on charcoal and soil organic matter from the alluvial fan in the main area of the site, and from a seventh date on charcoal from a corresponding landform on the west side of the quarry. The calibrated dates range from 5990 B.C. to 6460 B.C., or about 8,000-8,400 years ago. These dates place the Rustad site very early within the Early Plains Archaic period.

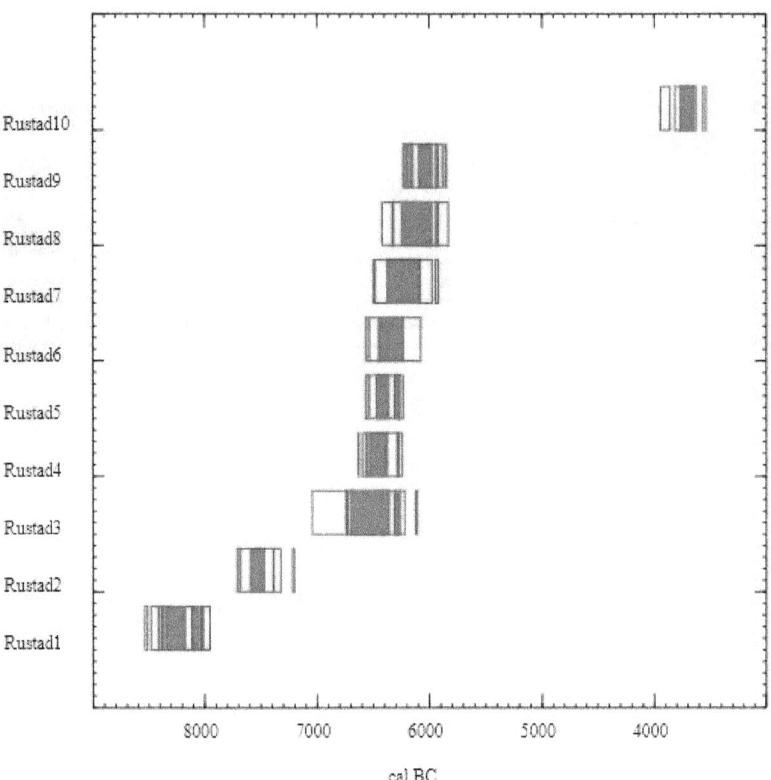

Figure 22. Radiocarbon dates from the Rustad site. Calibrated dates are from Calib 8.2. Dates in the 6000 BC range are from the Early Archaic component.

At this site there are some significant material differences between the Paleoindian and Archaic components, but it is also clear that there are similarities reflected here in the life-style of people during these two archaeological periods.

The greatest amount of cultural material was found in the Early Archaic fan sediments on the eastern side of the soil pit. A large quantity of animal bone, mostly bison, and a set of features comprising a living floor were present. One of these features is a fire stain situated in the center of a circular debris field possibly representing the outlines of a small structure (Figure 23). There are several other fire stains as well, and a continuation of the site on the western perimeter of the soil pit, which the artifacts, ecofacts, and a single radiocarbon date indicate was contemporaneous

Figure 23. Possible remnants of a circular structure at Rustad. Light colored area in the center of the debris field is a fire hearth.

with the main area. The small circular pattern of cultural materials with a central hearth, along with four other hearths absent any indication of a structure, suggest something of the nature of the community that lived at the Rustad site. The five features were positioned within about two to six meters from each other. They appear to be on the same level of the site and are within the merged or welded Ab2/Ab3 soil horizon. Excavations into the east wall of the soil pit show that most of the archaeological material actually seems to be in Ab3, the lower of the buried A-horizons, and in the main area, the cultural remains in the welded horizon (Ab 2/3) are in the middle of the deposit, also suggestive of Ab3 provenience. Our interpretation is that the main occupation is from Ab3, and that each fire hearth represents the living space of a small group, perhaps the size of a nuclear family of four or five people, or for a sub-family group, perhaps grandparents or older children. If each hearth represents an activity area for an average of a few people, there may have been 15 people in the excavated portion of the main area of the site. On the opposite side of the soil pit there is another hearth representing at least one other social group. We feel that both sides of the quarry were occupied at about the same time, based on the similarity in cultural material recovered, and the fact that a radiocarbon date from the western area matches those from the eastern area. Also, the activities represented by the cultural remains included hunting, cutting (butchery), wood and hide working (indicated by scraping tools), piercing, and, of course, various stages of tool making. All of this variety tells us that these were probably family groups.

The scattering of artifacts and bone in the disturbed/destroyed central part of the site indicate that the entire soil pit probably contained the occupation, and the excavated portion of the eastern area with its five hearths comprises only about 5% of the entire site area. So, there may have been many more than the few groups from the excavated area. The size of the Rustad occupation could have been as many as 100 people. This would constitute the equivalent of an ethnographic hunting and gathering macro-band, or a coalescence of smaller hunting groups, probably during the warm season. A warm season use of the site is inferred because on the Northern Plains large groups of people were likely to be found when resources were abundant and living conditions relatively benign. These conditions would not be expected during a North Dakota winter.

Alternatively, it may have been only two or three families visiting the site repeatedly over some indeterminate span of years, although we believe that the major occupation was in Ab3 and that either before or after the main use of the site, other visits were perhaps of a more limited nature. This is because the features and artifact scatter at the site seem to be patterned rather than randomly scattered. A random placement of features would be more likely if successive occupations were deposited independently.

Refuse pits, rock lined pits and post mold patterns are absent. There is very little cracked rock and no large piles of bone fragments. It is unlikely that bone grease preparation was occurring at the Rustad site (Bone grease was used in making pemmican, dried and pounded meat often mixed with berries). Most features are simple basin fire-stains, or in several cases, discard concentrations. None of the features are stratified, layered lenses that indicate they were re-dug or re-used time after time. A micro-morphological study of the soils containing the Early Archaic settlement did not yield discernible indication that the structure of the soil was altered by human use. There may have been several visits to this place; however, it is not possible to estimate how many, or even for how long people returned to this site. The radiocarbon dates span a period of 500 years, but they are statistically very close. The bison bone is of some help here. One of the partial tooth rows reflects a likely death during the winter, as opposed to the warm season indicators in the majority of the faunal assemblage. We might conclude the site was used on at least two occasions; possibly more than that. Even so, given the spacing of the fire-hearths mentioned already, we do believe that much of the site in Ab3 was created by a single, warm-season use.

The people who lived here were subsisting mostly on bison. Almost all of the animal bones in the Archaic level of the site were bison (Haury 2005). Not all elements of the bison skeleton are represented equally. Most of the bones are from the limbs and ribs. Some are also from the shoulder and pelvis. Not well represented in the bison bone collection are skull fragments, horns, or vertebrae. Based on this, we infer that the Rustad people were bison hunters who probably made their kills some distance from this site. Initial butchery would occur at the kill site, where the skull and vertebrae would have been discarded. The lower legs would have been used as convenient handles for carrying large meat packages adhering to the upper legs back to the settlement, including perhaps the shoulder and pelvic areas. Ribs with meat were apparently also returned to the site from the kill location. Rustad was clearly not a place where bison were killed, but one where bison carcass parts were finally processed and where people lived rather than where they captured or killed prey.

That part of the faunal collection that could be identified shows at least 14 bison are in the assemblage, including 9 cows, 2 bulls, and 3 juveniles. Most of the animals killed were mature, but not very old. They were probably killed in small-scale hunts. Since so many bison body parts were found, the kill was probably not very far from the Rustad site.

Bison bone from the site is on average larger than the bones from modern bison. This size difference is explained by the likelihood that these bison belonged to an earlier species of bison known as *Bison occidentalis*. This would make sense insofar as the Early Archaic occupation at Rustad is 8,000 years old and bison at this time may not yet have developed their modern size and form.

Rustad appears to have been strategically located to take advantage of the bison herds. Bison move throughout their range attracted by the grasses preferred as food. Grasses of different types mature at different times from spring through the fall. Bison prefer fresh, newly emerged plants to those that have matured and become tough or dry. The area around the Rustad site features a variety of habitats for grasses of different species and maturation schedules. The Lake Agassiz Plain supported the tall grass prairie which comprised an enormous amount of forage for the bison. The Sheyenne Delta was a more varied environment for grasses and would perhaps have featured greater diversity in grass species even though the total amount of forage per acre was less than the Lake Agassiz lowland. But the variability in the yearly growth patterns of different types of grasses would have given the bison good reason to remain in the vicinity of the Rustad site, possibly for much if not all of the year. We may add to these suppositions the findings from isotopic analysis of Northeastern Plains bison dentition. This shows that bison diets in this region consisted of local forage. The herds did not engage in long-distance migratory movements, but were more or less residential in their regional habitat (Widga 2006: 216).

Besides the availability of bison, the nearby Sheyenne River and its fringing gallery woodland qualifies the Rustad locality as a remarkably good place to live for a hunting and gathering population. Not only were there bison, but fish and mussels in the river, muskrat, beaver, raccoon, squirrel, berries, nuts, tubers, and greens. These would have supplied both food and pelts for clothing. There were also woodlands for fuel, for building material, and for making items such as wooden ladles, weapon shafts, and plant fiber for basketry and cordage.

There are some canid bones from the Early Archaic at the site. These are from large animals which may have been wolf. More likely, however, is that they are the bones of domestic dogs. The Plains Indians in the Historic Period were known to keep large dogs, often in considerable numbers. Historically, dogs were commonly used as pack animals by Plains peoples, and may certainly have been used this way at Rustad (Widga 2006: 214). Some of the bison bones also show gnaw marks, suggesting that they were being feasted on by dogs kept in the settlement, although faunal analysts caution that coyotes or wolves might have scavenged food remains after humans left the site.

The stone tool assemblage from this component includes many diagnostic artifacts. Numerous small notched projectile points were found, most of them are less than two inches long. Some of these would be classified as notched on the side of the point, others at the corner of the base. Almost all of the points were worked or flaked on both sides, although at least one is mostly unifacially flaked. We classify these notched points as part of a complex of Early Archaic point types collectively known as Logan Creek–Mummy Cave, named after similar points from Nebraska

Figure 24. Projectile points from the Rustad Early Archaic component.

and Wyoming. Some Rustad points were elongate and triangular in shape and are classified as a poorly known type called DeLong points. These are also known from the Northern Plains Early Archaic. There are about 20 points from the site that can be classified. Another dozen or so are badly broken and cannot be placed in any known category, although they are probably the blade tips from the same types of points that have been classified. The points from the Early Archaic deposit are similar to points from other sites on the Northern Plains, including Itasca in northwest Minnesota, Logan Creek in eastern Nebraska, the Cherokee site in northwest Iowa, and the Medicine Crow site in central South Dakota (Figure 24).

Small projectile points like those from Rustad are often believed to have been used to arm arrows rather than spears, since the aerodynamics of the arrow require restricted weight at the front of the projectile when using a bow of limited projective force. However, the bow and arrow are believed to have been introduced into North America or invented around 2,000–1,500 years ago, long after the Early Archaic. So why the small points at Rustad? Possibly small points were used with a new weapon system, perhaps with a modified shaft and fletching system that worked best with a small point. Possibly it was a weapon system that required a small point to penetrate large animal hides with perhaps a somewhat limited or reduced force of entry. For now, we archaeologists do not seem to have any adequate explanation for the reduction in point size at the beginning of the Plains Archaic.

The remainder of the stone tool collection from the site includes scraping tools for hide working and perhaps for fashioning wooden implements, bifacially flaked tools most likely used as knives or butchery tools, and a variety of miscellaneous worked flakes most likely used as expedient tools for immediate use and discard. The variety of tools at the site is an indication that the people who lived here did more than a single task and were involved in multiple activities that would be expected in a settlement of different genders and ages and one which sustained a relatively large number of inhabitants.

Many of the artifacts from the Archaic component at Rustad are waste flakes left over after a stone core was chipped into the shape of a tool; a projectile point, a bifacial cutting tool, a drill, or a scraper. Waste flakes are useful for archaeological interpretation in a couple ways. Sometimes the size and shape of the flakes may help us understand what stage in the tool-making process was happening at the site. For example, very large flakes are often produced in the early stages of core reduction and tool making. Much smaller flakes are made when a flint-knapper is finishing the edge of a tool to get it into final shape. In some cases, the shape of the flake even tells us what type of tool was being made, so even if the tool itself was removed from the site when people left it, the waste they left behind might leave a clue about the type of tool they made. Cores of stone from which large flakes had been removed were also found. These cores are the expended blocks of stone from which pieces were struck off to make tools. At Rustad, then, there were cores from the initial stages of reduction, and a variety of flake types suggestive of different, later phases of the manufacturing process. This reinforces the evidence from the features and from the sheer extent of the site that this site was a major Early Archaic occupation with evidence of multiple domestic activities.

Another bit of information comes from the waste flakes; they provide a picture of the kinds of stone raw material used at the site. At Rustad most of the raw materials are local cherts and similar flake-able stone like quartzite or siltstone. The incidence of Knife River flint is very limited—about 3–4% of the stone material is this exotic flint. Since KRF almost always comes from western North Dakota, we believe that the people who lived at Rustad had only limited access the KRF quarries. Either they had difficulty traveling to that area, or trade with intermediaries to the west was interrupted at this time. Since Knife River flint is present in much higher frequencies at regional Paleoindian sites, and also in later Archaic, Woodland and Late Prehistoric sites, we suggest that the climatic conditions of the Middle Holocene made contact across the Plains to the west difficult, and thus, limited the amount of KRF available to eastern North Dakota during this time.

Overall, the Rustad site provides a remarkable window on the early inhabitants of this region, and on the natural history of the last 10,000 years as well. Even though the site is mostly gone now, the opportunity afforded archaeological teams to work at this place has provided a major contribution to the history of the Northern Plains. Based on other sites from this period, such as Itasca (NW Minnesota) and Cherokee (NW Iowa), the eastern Plains in the Early Archaic was occupied by hunters who were largely dependent on bison. Excavated archaeological sites provide evidence of other subsistence routines, including small game hunting and fishing; however, in every case bison are the primary resource represented. The technology of these hunters included a small projectile point weapon system easily distinguished from the lanceolate projectile tip forms of the late Paleoindian period. The small un-notched DeLong points may be latter-day versions of Paleo-period lanceolate points, while the small notched Logan Creek forms represent the new, and eventually enduring point form. Larger points found at Early Archaic sites were probably used on thrusting weapons, or possibly as hafted knives, while the small projectile tips may have been used on shafts that were propelled either by hand, or with the assistance of the spear-thrower, or atlatl.

Figure 25. Late Archaic Pelican Lake point from a surface site in the Bend area.

Later Archaic in the Sheyenne Bend

Several archaeologists (e.g. Reeves 1990, Forbis 1992) identify a change in human adaptations on the Plains at the Middle–Late Holocene transition, sometime after 5,000 ago. This shift involved expansion of the McKean complex over the Northern Plains accompanying the climatic moderation in Late Holocene times. There may have been some improvements in the way ancient American Indian peoples used the Plains environment. Reeves (1990) feels that the appearance of stone filled pits and large quantities of smashed bison bone at Middle Plains Archaic sites reflect bone grease making and its use with pemmican. This practice would have given hunters an advantage surviving in the harsh and unpredictable Plains environment, although some believe there is evidence for bone grease making in the Early Archaic (Dyck and Morlan 2001:118).

Dobbs identified Middle and Late Archaic components for site 32RI785 on the Wild Rice River south of the Bend area. He argued from the evidence at this site that improved climatic conditions in the Late Archaic promoted a somewhat different life-style from the Middle Archaic. Considering the nature of the stone tools and lithic debris at the two components of 32RI785, he suggests that by Late Archaic times hunter-gatherers were able to fan out from central settlements to establish short-term resource extraction camps to more efficiently procure food for band members remaining in the base settlement. Is the evidence from this single site a reflection of real changes in the life-style of Archaic peoples, or is it rather simply the result of two different expressions of a single way of life being represented at a single locality? As more Archaic period sites are studied in the Northeastern Plains an answer to this question will eventually be reached. In the meantime, we offer possibility rather than probability.

From about 5,000 years ago until the beginning of the Woodland Period around 2,000 years ago, we feel that a more or less stable Archaic adaptation flourished on the Northeastern Plains. Throughout this period there was a focus on bison hunting, complemented with a variety of other resources, including tuberous plants, seeds, nuts, fish, and shellfish. The phases of the Middle and Late Plains Archaic in the Bend region may be subdivided based on changes in projectile point styles, specifically by the sequence from Oxbow through McKean–Duncan–Hanna to Pelican Lake (Figure 25) and finally Besant, the last of these representing a projectile point type that persists into the initial part of the Plains Woodland period.

Chapter 5
Plains Woodland

Woodland Culture and the Northeastern Plains

Following the Archaic is a time-period with the unfortunate name Woodland. The Woodland Period was originally defined as a time when people in the forests of eastern North America began making pottery, burying their dead in earthen mounds, and using domestic plants. All three of these cultural features are found on the Plains, and certainly on the Northeastern Plains, thus the term Woodland is normally used. It is disorienting, though, to refer to Woodland cultures on the Plains, since the two terms obviously bring to mind very different environments. Here we will follow the convention of referring to this period as the Plains Woodland.

The Plains Woodland in our study area probably begins about 2,200 years ago and persists until about 900 years ago. These dates are soft and involve some guess-work on both ends. The beginning of the Woodland coincides with the appearance of pottery in the Sheyenne Valley. Plains Woodland burial mounds are known from the James River valley, and from the Red River Valley, but are not attested in the Bend area. As for use of domestic plants, there is only very limited evidence for their use in the Sheyenne Bend Woodland.

Many archaeologists define the last part of the Woodland in the Northern Midwest and Northeastern Plains as persisting until the arrival of Europeans. In the Sheyenne Bend we place the ending date for the Woodland at around AD 1100, after which we envision a Plains Village adaptation arising, meaning the appearance of a more settled lifeway with good evidence for domestic-scale farming. On the Great Plains the appearance of substantial, more or less permanent communities known as Plains Villages, define a post-Woodland period and new life-way. The same is true for the Bend region.

The Woodland Period is normally divided into three parts; early, middle, and late. These terms are more pertinent east of the Mississippi than to the Northern Plains. In the Eastern United States, the Early Woodland is a time when burial mound construction proliferates, and thick, conoidal-shaped pottery, tempered with heavy fragments of grit or crushed rock, was first made. By this time also certain native plants such as Chenopodium, native squash, and marshelder were brought under domestication. This Early Woodland Period begins as early as 3,000 years ago in the east and lasts for 700–800 years (Fagan 2005: 422-427).

The following Middle Woodland is one of the better-known archaeological periods in the eastern half of North America. During this time, about 2,200–1,500 years ago, many conical earthen burial mounds and geometric earthworks were built. Some of the mounds were quite large, and earthen embankments in the shape of circles, squares, and even octagons were built, often with an impressive level of geometric sophistication. Also, at this time cultures in the eastern US participated in a trade network that featured the exchange of raw materials including obsidian from the Rocky Mountains, copper from the western Great Lakes, Knife River flint from western North Dakota, mica from the southeast US, and Gulf of Mexico seashell. Some of these materials were fashioned into ceremonial items executed in a variety of artistic motifs common to that era, including zoomorphs and stylized human figures. This complex of cultural activity is known archaeologically as the Hopewell Interaction Sphere.

The Hopewellian network of cultures dissolved after about 1,500 years ago when the Late Woodland began. Mound building continued for the burial of the dead, but the geometric earthworks were no longer constructed. The designs commonly used on pottery in the Middle Woodland also changed in the Late Woodland, and it is often with ceramic decorative designs that archaeologists distinguish between different divisions of the Woodland Period. And to the degree that differences in decorative preferences on pottery tell us about different communities, it seems that in the Late Woodland there may have been more diverse and localized populations, since the number of regional ceramic styles increases. Another, and an extremely important development occurred in North American during the Late Woodland. At this time the first good evidence for the widespread use of domesticates introduced from Mesoamerica is found at archaeological sites up and down the Mississippi drainage. The most important of these was maize. There is also evidence for domestic beans and tobacco. The addition of these plants to the pantry of the North American Indian peoples led to major changes in life. There seems to have been a population spike associated with the cultivation of these new plants. The population growth and the new domesticates are probably related to the diversification of ceramic styles and the increasing localization of Late Woodland cultures.

Figure 26. Ceramic vessels from Minnesota. In rear (left to right): St. Croix, Blackduck, Laurel, Sandy Lake. In front: three loop-handled Oneota vessels, and (second from right) Rainy River composite vessel.

On the Northeastern Plains we classify sites as belonging to one or the other of these sub-periods of the Woodland, but in reality, there is not much information for the Early Woodland as it is known in the Midwestern U.S. If anything, the Early Woodland of the Midwest corresponds chronologically with the Northeastern Plains Late Archaic. The Middle Woodland is more frequently referred to in the literature; however, Northern Plains sites with Middle Woodland designations mostly involve the presence of diagnostic projectile point types, such as Besant, known in some areas to be associated with burial mound ceremonialism or ceramics, even though these indicators of the Middle Woodland are not present at that particular site.

Since Early and Middle Woodland are so difficult to distinguish in our area, we prefer to use the terms Initial Plains Woodland for that time period in the Eastern US that would encompass the Early and Middle Woodland, and we use the term Terminal Plains Woodland for the more commonly encountered Woodland artifact assemblages found toward the latter portion of the Woodland Period. Initial Plains Woodland roughly corresponds to the time period from about 2,200 years ago to about 1,300 years ago, while the Terminal Plains Woodland persists from 1,300 to about 900 years ago.

In most of North America east of the Rockies the Woodland cultural period is characterized by the presence of pottery, although at many Plains Woodland archaeological sites, pottery is absent. Pottery is found at Plains Woodland sites in the Sheyenne Bend; however, it is more pervasive in the succeeding Late Prehistoric period. Woodland ceramics in the Sheyenne Valley are usually similar to ceramics found in adjacent parts of Minnesota (Figure 26).

Prior to firing ceramic vessels are wet clay and the procedures used to shape the pot left imprints on the soft, easily impressed surface. Also, the wet clay served as an inviting medium for decorative designs, often placed on the neck, shoulder and rim of the pot (that is, the upper portion of the vessel). For this reason, cultural chronologies constructed for time periods after the introduction of pottery usually depend on ceramic design features and decorative practices for arranging sites in sequences and into coherent cultural entities. Over time, ceramic manufacturing practices changed, so the temper used to prevent the fired or dried clay from cracking, and the marks left on the surface from the method of forming the vessel, changed over time, assisting the archaeologist in placing archaeological sites with pottery into rough time series. Even more useful are the decorative designs placed on the vessels, which were more sensitive to temporal and cultural variation than the manufacturing imprints.

Projectile points are another commonly used artifact to identify sites belonging to the Plains Woodland Period. Woodland points tend to diminish in size from the Initial to the Terminal Woodland, something most archaeologists attribute to the introduction of the bow and arrow. In the Initial Plains Woodland there are some larger point styles that may have been used on thrusting spears. Besides this, some large points found throughout the Plains Woodland period may have notches or stems that give the appearance of a projectile tip, but were hafted to handles and used as knives rather than on spears.

From earliest to latest these Plains Woodland point styles are commonly known as Besant, Avonlea, and Prairie Side-Notched. Pelican Lake points, the Late Archaic style, sometimes persist into the early portion of the Plains Woodland, sort of the opposite of Besant, a Woodland style that occurs in the later Archaic. These styles are very common on the High Plains west of the Missouri River, but they are also known from the eastern Dakotas and western Minnesota. They are found at sites that are radiocarbon dated to the Plains Woodland Period, and with other diagnostics of the Woodland such as pottery, and in some areas, burial ceremonialism involving mound construction.

Many archaeologists feel a cultural complex known as Besant most closely matches traditional Middle Woodland in the Eastern US, both in temporal and cultural features. Typically, this complex of archaeological

Figure 27. Besant (left) and Avonlea points, Bend area surface sites.

materials dates from 2000–1200 years ago (Wood 1998:12). As mentioned previously, Besant is the name of a side-notched projectile point. It is somewhat elongate, with a parallel-sided blade, and notches on the lower side of the point. Besant points are often found at sites with a high frequency of Knife River flint. Since Knife River flint is sometimes found in Hopewell sites in the Eastern US, some scholars believe that the contemporaneous Besant populations on the Plains were responsible for the eastward movement of this flint (Clark 1984). Besant artifacts are also found at sites on the Northern Plains with evidence of highly effective bison hunting, including the building of corrals that functioned as traps that bison were driven into. Besant sites also sometimes contain pottery, cord roughened on the surface and generally conoidal in shape. The burial mound associations, pottery, and dates of around 2,000–1,200 years ago combine to relate Besant to the Plains Woodland Period (Forbis 1998).

Another Woodland Period complex on the Northern Plains is known as Avonlea (Figure 27). It is a term applied to a style of projectile point; finely made, thin, with side-notches and often an indented base. They are smaller, and often thinner than Besant. Avonlea points are widely distributed over the Northern Plains and they are now commonly referred to as markers of an archaeological horizon. In archaeology, a horizon is a distinctive set of cultural traits that appear over a wide geographic area in a short span of time (Meyer and Walde 2009). The small size and thinness of the Avonlea points suggest that they were aerodynamically designed to arm arrows, and that their widespread and rapid diffusion across the Plains is evidence for the introduction of bow and arrow technology.

It is not uncommon to find pottery associated with Avonlea points at Northern Plains sites, and this is true for the Sheyenne Bend as well. The pottery is sometimes net or fabric impressed on the exterior, sometimes it is impressed with parallel grooves over the vessel surface, and sometimes it is simply cord-roughened. Much of this pottery is similar to ceramics from the forested regions of Minnesota. Yet there is considerable variability in the ceramic assemblage at Avonlea sites, and this suggests that it was the product of more than a single group of people (Meyer and Walde 2009).

Avonlea technology and point styles continue into the Terminal Plains Woodland Period, along with other types of points, including less finely made Prairie Side-Notched points. This simplifies the situation somewhat severely, and the variety of projectile points styles can confuse even veteran archaeologists. But overall, the trend over the entire span of the Plains Woodland is for the diagnostic points to diminish in size, almost universally accepted as an indication of the replacement of spear-casting technology with the bow and arrow, a weapon system widely used by the time of the European incursions.

Sometime during the Woodland Period on the Northeastern Plains domestic plant use began, possibly with some native species such as *Chenopodium* (goosefoot), and perhaps squash. By around 1000 years ago maize was introduced from the southeast US (originating in Mexico). Farming requires people to stay in one place for somewhat longer periods than hunting and gathering, so more stable communities such as small villages appeared in the Late Prehistoric Period. If Historic Period indigenous groups are a guide to the way their immediate ancestors lived, we may infer that most farming was done in the river bottoms where the soil was well-watered, and where the trees could be cut down and burned to form garden plots. The ash-enriched soil from tree burning was then mounded up with hoes, made from stone or from the shoulder blades of bison or elk, and planted. Upland prairies mostly could not be used for gardens because the root mass of prairie grasses was too thick to break without plows and draft animals. Furthermore, grasses grow back faster than trees and brush, so even burning off the grass would not prevent its immediate re-growth and competition with any planted crops.

The farms were household affairs and were not large by modern standards. For this reason, some archaeologists and anthropologists refer to this kind of agriculture as gardening, or horticulture, a term meant simply to indicate the relatively small scale of each planted unit. But very few Woodland sites on the Northern Plains show signs of domestic plants, so while we know that domestication was practiced during this period, there is not very much direct evidence for it on the Northern Plains in general, and in particular on the Northeastern Plains. A domestic squash seed was found in a pouch accompanying the accidentally exposed Lisbon burial, previously discussed. It is one of the few instances of direct evidence of domestic plants in a Sheyenne Bend Plains Woodland site.

Most of the evidence for Woodland period domestic plant use comes from Terminal Plains Woodland sites. In recent years, however, there have been developments indicating an earlier use of domestics on the Northeastern Plains, even though there is still some uncertainty about the reliability of the evidence. Doubts about the reliability of these claims are because the data consists of microscopic objects like phytoliths requiring high-powered magnification to observe. Usually, direct evidence for domestic plant use consists of plant macrofossils at archaeological sites—corn cob fragments, for instance. Seeds from domestic plants are sometimes larger, or shaped differently than their wild cousins. These kinds of remains are called macrofossils since they can be seen and studied without high magnification. Botanists usually make these routine determinations for archaeologists.

One of the earliest Woodland sites presently known for the Northeastern Plains is the Naze site on the James River about 30 miles west of the Bend region. Here, archaeologists from the University of North Dakota found a stratigraphically layered, multicomponent site with an Initial Woodland date for an occupation on the floodplain of the James River (Gregg 1987). There were thick, cordmarked potsherds with some incised or trailed lines claimed to be similar to an Early Woodland ceramic ware from elsewhere in the Midwest, such as Fox Lake ceramics from southwest Minnesota. There were also Besant and Pelican Lake projectile points, which would be expected in a Plains site of this age, perhaps around 2,000 years ago. Archaeologists also found a burnt set of eight posts arranged in a rough square several feet on a side. Michael Gregg, the excavator, felt this was a central, multi-post support for a conical shelter which would have leaners laid against it in a tipi-like fashion (Gregg 1987:98). In the area of the lodge structure excavators also recovered charred seeds of grape, *Chenopodium* (goosefoot) and Iva (marsh elder). Animal bones associated with this material consisted of mostly bison, but also some elk, dog, beaver, and possibly wolf and coyote (Gregg 1987:442-443). Naze fits well with our characterization of the Initial Woodland in the Sheyenne Bend.

There is another site near Naze that University of North Dakota archaeologists dug (Toom 2014). Known as the Akata site, work here was done to salvage some part of the site before it was destroyed by river bank stabilization. Like Naze, Akata is a stratified site with cultural materials superimposed one component on top of the other. At the bottom of the sequence in an alluvial soil is a Late Archaic deposit with Pelican Lake points. Radiocarbon dates range from about 3,000–2,500 years ago. Above this is an assemblage of Initial Plains Woodland materials dated to about 2,500–1,500 years ago. Some of the pottery in this level is similar to a type defined in Minnesota and named St. Croix ware. It is usually thought to date to the end of the Initial and beginning of the Terminal Woodland Period. Associated with this pottery are Besant and Prairie Side-Notched points, along with evidence that wild plum and chokecherry were eaten.

One other early site from eastern North Dakota, although somewhat removed from the Sheyenne Bend region, but nonetheless in the general Sheyenne River drainage, is the Bivouac site (32RY189) near Devils Lake. This site, also studied by University of North Dakota archaeologists, contains at least two Initial Plains Woodland components with pottery. The earlier of these features thick, cordmarked ceramics. There is no date for this occupation, nor are there any associated projectile points. A later component that Jackson and Toom (2004) define as Brainerd, is dated to between 1300-1250 years ago. Brainerd pottery is known best from the lake-forest country of Minnesota and characterized by ceramic vessels marked over their exterior by net and fabric impressions. This pottery type is sometimes associated with Besant points, and so we identify the site as Initial Plains Woodland. Avonlea and Prairie Side-Notched points are also present here, and although both fit comfortably into the later Initial Plains Woodland Period, the range of ceramics and point types at the site suggest that it was undoubtedly used over some considerable time span.

Even though the Bivouac site is on the shores of Devils Lake there is no evidence of aquatic resources being used at the site. Instead, bison is the most prominent food, making up to about 60% of the animal bone found at the site. Elk, deer or pronghorn, dog, and some waterfowl were also found in the deposit. Knife River flint makes up about 80% of the lithic material, suggesting a very close connection at this time period with the Knife River quarries west of the Missouri River.

It is fair to say that the Plains Woodland Period is most difficult to characterize, and any full understanding has still to be achieved. We have identified only traces of this thousand-year-plus period for the Bend region. This is attributable in part to the alluvial valley where these and earlier occupations are likely buried. Buried components have been identified in the Sheyenne River Valley, but the temporal association of most of these is not possible to ascertain. At the mouth of the Sheyenne, about ten miles north of Fargo, excavations at the Dahnke–Reinke site revealed buried Initial Woodland and Archaic under a Late Prehistoric occupation. Although this site is on the Sheyenne River, it is about 50 miles northeast of the Bend region. But it is one of the very few useful Initial Woodland sites in the Sheyenne Valley proper. At the Dahnke–Reinke site, R.G. Thompson (1990) found a thick, grit tempered ceramic ware represented well below a near-surface deposit containing Late Prehistoric Sandy Lake pottery. These early ceramics were dated to roughly 2,000 years ago and may be described as relatively thick, often with textile impressions on the exterior surface, and tempered with a grit or crushed rock. It is obvious from the deep deposits these ceramics were found in, and the radiocarbon assays in association, that they date from the earlier portion of the Plains Woodland Period. Comparable deposits have not yet been found for the Bend region itself.

The Initial Plains Woodland Period in the Bend region proper is first recognized in a few sherds similar to types known as Brainerd and Fox Lake in Minnesota. A rough time span of 2,100–1,700 years ago is likely for these ceramics. This pottery seems similar to the earliest found in nearby James River sites, such as Naze. The ceramics are thick-walled with horizontal cordmarking and incised lines laid over the cordmarked vessel surfaces. Fabric impressed and net impressed sherds may also date from this period or slightly later. Sherds of this latter type have been found on the Okiedan Buttes, southeast of Lisbon, and at the Rotenberger site, on the floodplain below the Buttes.

Several sites in the Sheyenne Bend area have other types of Woodland pottery. A.E. Jenks, of the University of Minnesota, collected some pottery from a site in the Sheyenne Bend in the earlier part of the twentieth century. These cord-impressed sherds have unusual elongate tool impressions as decoration, but there are too few to characterize the collection or compare it to others. Elden Johnson made a collection of ceramics from the Heath site, in the southernmost portion of the Bend, that also have the characteristic features of a Plains Woodland ceramic ware. Vehik (1979) described several surface sites west of Kindred that he regarded as Plains Woodland. While these collections are useful in documenting the presence of Woodland materials in the region, they do not provide any contextual information about the nature of the lifestyle of the people who made this pottery. Cordmarked surfaces, grit temper, and relatively thick sherds indicate they are not part of the more recent ceramic traditions from the Late Prehistoric Period and must therefore be Woodland in affiliation. To get a somewhat more rounded picture of the Plains Woodland occupation in the Bend area, however, we turn to several excavated sites from this time period.

Site 32CS13

One Woodland period site in the Bend region is 32CS13, the Chaffee (or Sprunk) site (Michlovic and McMaster 1982). Work at this Maple River site arose from the discovery of human bones while a landowner was digging for gravel. Unfortunately, this site was severely disturbed by machinery and the excavations were limited to undisturbed areas around the perimeter of what must have been the main area of the site, which probably included a mound. The location of the site is of some importance in assessing its cultural affiliation. The presumed mound was situated on a beach deposit of Lake Agassiz. Many prehistoric burial sites, particularly mound burials, are associated with the Lake Agassiz shoreline deposits. We believe that this is mostly because these deposits are elevated over the nearby terrain and make the burial structures visible from lower positions.

Most artifacts were found on the plowed surface of the site, or in the upper 20 cm of the soil. A few grit-tempered potsherds were found, almost all of which are cordmarked on the body and typical of Woodland wares. One was a decorated fragment with oblique corded impressions bounded above and below by horizontal twisted cord impressions. Below the decorations were parallel cord impressions running more or less obliquely from the decorative field. This decorated sherd is similar to pottery found associated with burial mounds in other parts of central and eastern Dakotas belonging to the Besant complex. These mounds are probably from the Initial portion of the Plains Woodland and it is reasonable to assume that the Chaffee site might be of the same age.

Figure 28. Blackduck vessel rim.

Several projectile points and scraping tools were recovered, along with several amorphous, modified flakes used as tools. Two of the points are classified as Pelican Lake, the Late Archaic artifact style which often extends into the Plains Woodland Period. The third point was a Prairie-Side Notched point, another style often associated with the Plains Woodland. Aside from the tools there were hundreds of flakes recovered, including three cores from which flakes had been struck. Nearly half of the flaking debris found here consisted of Knife River flint. The remaining lithic material was from various local cherts found in glacial till. The high incidence of Knife River flint is common for the earlier part of the Woodland on the Northern Plains.

Thousands of small animal bone fragments were found. Ninety percent of this was burned. The only species of animal identified was bison. What is most unusual about the bone is the small size of the fragments, and the fact that so much of it is burned. Normally, unburned bone is preponderant in regional archaeological sites. Some bone may have been tossed into fires as fuel, or simply as a way of disposing of waste.

The human remains from the disturbed mound included six individuals. We refrain here from a description of these burials except to say there were three juveniles and three adults, all found in the disturbed area. Some of the remains from the burial were stained with red ochre. All were reburied by Indian authorities on reservation land at the request of the landowner.

Site 32CS4899

Several probable Woodland sites were found in the flood pool area of the Maple River dam (see Stubbs, et al. 2001:123-133). These sites are characterized as belonging to this period because of the pottery found in them, normally cord roughened on the surface and tempered with grit. The pottery from these Plains Woodland sites on the Maple is relatively thin and this suggests to us that the sites belong to the Plains Terminal Woodland, since in general, earlier pottery in this region tends to be thicker than later pottery. The fact of their being buried, in some cases in plowed fields but below the level of disturbance by the plow, tells us that these sites, dating to prior to about AD 1000, are old enough to have been heavily covered by river-flood deposits. It also suggests to archaeologists that if sites that are only 1,000–1,500 years old are up to a meter or so below the surface, how much more deeply buried must be the older Archaic, or even Paleoindian sites?

One of the Plains Woodland sites discovered by the Maple River dam excavations was 32CS4899. The site extends from the levees of the Maple River eastward into a fallow field. Over 1,000 artifacts and ecofacts were found in shovel probes and excavations. The most significant find was Terminal Woodland pottery belonging to a ceramic ware well-known in Minnesota and named after the lakes-country town of Blackduck (Figure 28). This Blackduck pottery is widely distributed in Minnesota north of the Twin Cities and extending into Manitoba and Ontario. Blackduck ceramics are heavily decorated on the lip and rim of the vessel, and feature closely spaced impressions made diagonal to the lip with a rod or stick wrapped with cordage. Punctations on the exterior of the vessel neck are also common.

Blackduck pottery is radiocarbon dated at numerous sites and may be placed between about 1200-1000 years ago. At 32CS4899 the Blackduck pottery was found at a depth of about 40–50 cm below the surface. Above it the excavators found pottery belonging to the Late Prehistoric Period similar to the ceramics of the Northeastern Plains Village culture. Unfortunately, of the several hundred bone fragments found, only one possible identifiable element is reported, and this belonging probably to bison.

Rustad Site (Woodland component)

There is also a Woodland component at the Rustad site. On the west side of the soil pit in sediments above the Archaic level there was a light concentration of cultural material including burned bone, some lithic debris,

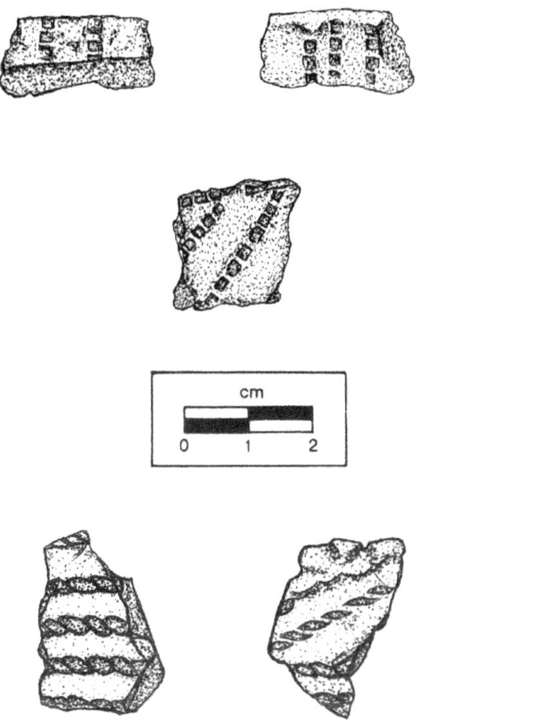

Figure 29. Dentate stamped (St. Croix) and cord-impressed sherds from Irwin Johnson.

and a small side-notched point common in Plains Terminal Woodland sites. A few cordmarked pottery sherds were also found. We do not know the age of this material, except that it is above the buried soil dating the end of the Middle Holocene (about 4,900 years ago), and the presence of pottery suggests an age later than about 2,000 years ago. The style of the small point and the cordmarking on the relatively thin sherds would indicate a Terminal Woodland assignment for this component. Unfortunately, the bone was so badly fragmented that no identification of skeletal elements was possible, nor was any evidence of plant material found that could be used to shed light on the precise nature of resource use. Even so, there is this tantalizing bit of material from Rustad showing the use of this site intermittently for a period of some 7,500 years!

Figure 30. Projectile points from the Irwin Johnson site. Upper points classified as Avonlea. Small triangular points below classified as Late Prehistoric.

Irwin Johnson Site

One of the better studied Woodland sites is Irwin Johnson (32RM172). It is located in the southern and central portion of the Sheyenne Bend, and is owned by *The Archaeological Conservancy*, a national non-profit organization devoted to the preservation of archaeological sites throughout the United States. The site came under *Conservancy* control when it purchased the immediately adjacent Biesterfeldt site, a Protohistoric farming village (discussed below). However, no evidence for occupations relating to the nearby Biesterfeldt site occupation was identified at Irwin Johnson.

Prehistoric ceramics, stone artifacts, and animal bone fragments were concentrated along the elevated margins of the terrace immediately above the Sheyenne River floodplain (Holley and Michlovic 2013). Most artifacts and ecofacts were found 20–40 cm below the surface. In the wall profile of five contiguous units there was a distinct layer of scattered bone fragments visible at a depth of about 20–35 cm. This we believe to be the occupation level at the site.

The artifact sample spans the Terminal Woodland into the early portions of the Northeastern Plains Village Complex of the Late Prehistoric

Period. The sherds, however, were consistently small and difficult to precisely identify. No stratigraphic patterns were observed in the distribution of ceramic attributes, such as decorative designs, the thickness of the sherds, or the fashion in which the exterior of the vessel was treated.

Most of the artifacts were pottery that featured cordmarked surfaces. These sherds are thin-walled. Also recovered were sherds from small, fine paste miniature vessels and plain surface jars with tooth-like impressions (dentate stamping) used to form geometric designs. Dentate stamping, a form of decoration that looks like a broad-toothed comb was pressed into the vessel surface prior to firing, is associated with St. Croix Stamped pottery known mostly from Minnesota and likely dates to the Terminal Woodland Period. Cord-wrapped stick or rod and cord impressed decoration is also present on several sherds (Figure 29). This pottery probably extends from the Plains Terminal Woodland into a poorly known initial expression of the Northeastern Plains Village Complex. This would coincide with the early farming villages in South Dakota.

The additional presence of simple stamping and a single Sandy Lake shell-tempered and cordmarked sherd also attest to later occupations at Irwin Johnson. Based on the ceramic remains we have identified, we posit recurrent occupations beginning sometime late in the Terminal Plains Woodland Period and continuing on an intermittent, short-term basis into the Northeastern Plains Village complex (after AD 1100).

While the pottery sherds are small and difficult to identify, stone tools include several small triangular, probably Late Prehistoric points and two Avonlea points (Figure 30). The Avonlea points date to the Plains Woodland Period. Over 50% of the lithic debris is Knife River flint. Most of the remainder is locally available chert and other silicate rocks found in glacial till. Oddly, no scraping tools were found, but only points, biface fragments and a few used and worked flakes. This suggests to us that the site may have involved only a limited range of activities.

A single radiocarbon date was obtained on a quantity of small bone fragments found associated with a relatively dense scatter of bone in the main excavation trench at Irwin Johnson. The date of the bone fragments is 970 ± 30, giving a calibrated radiocarbon age of about AD 1075. The date is interesting in that it could fit with the very end of the Terminal Woodland, a period we believe is well represented at the site, or with the very beginning of the Late Prehistoric, more poorly reflected in the artifact assemblage. Since the earlier and later components are mixed it is impossible to separate out the cultural material associated with one or the other of these.

The nearby Lucas site (about a mile west of Irwin Johnson) features an enclosure and mound complex and yielded a set of wrapped rod and cord impressed ceramics similar to some of the pottery from Irwin Johnson. Perhaps the late materials from Irwin Johnson are contemporaneous with the Lucas enclosure. So, based on the ceramic remains and diagnostic stone tools there were recurrent occupations at the Irwin Johnson site beginning sometime late in the Terminal Woodland Period and continuing on an intermittent, short-term basis into the Northeastern Plains Village complex.

The collection of ecofacts from this site was mostly animal bone. Close to 4,000 bone fragments were found although only about three dozen were identifiable. Two elk and at least one bison are represented in terms of the minimum number of animals that would have been needed to form the bone collection. There were also bones of at least two muskrats and one beaver. Hundreds of shell fragments from river mussels were also recovered.

Elk are not very common in the archaeological record of the Plains, although a few elk were found in excavations at Devils Lake and in the James Valley. Historic accounts show that elk were abundant in the region. Alexander Henry, on his journey up the Red River in 1800–1801 described hunting elk and bison, particularly in September. Elk were rutting at the time and Henry says their bellowing could be heard in every direction (Coues 1897:84, 90, 94). Elk are often successfully hunted, even today, in the early fall, and this fact offers the slight possibility that the elk at Irwin Johnson might represent an occupation during that season.

About 50 liters of soil was taken for flotation, a method for using water to float off organic remains in soil samples. The samples from artifact rich areas provided only identifiable fragments of oak and ash tree charcoal. No plant food remains were found.

Discussion

Characterizing the Plains Woodland in the Bend region is difficult due to the small number of excavated sites, and to the lack of a well-defined Woodland culture in the Northeastern Plains within which we might fit the scattered and scarce collections from the Bend. One of the challenges we face is that the collections are mostly small, and each ceramic collection features decorative traits distinguishing it from others. They are all assigned to the Plains Woodland, in some cases due to their similarity to well-known Woodland wares from Minnesota, and in others, their Woodland status is based on the thickness of the sherds, the presence of cord marked or roughened surfaces, and their differences with the pottery of the succeeding Late Prehistoric Period. We believe that some of the thicker, cord marked pottery in the collections may be classified as Initial Woodland, dating to before 1500 years ago. This material is not common and until more buried contexts from this period are excavated it is impossible to characterize it for the Bend region in detail.

There are Terminal Plains Woodland ceramics present at Irwin Johnson, which we feel are associated with the Avonlea points recovered from the site. These ceramics are broadly similar to the St. Croix stamped pottery defined in Minnesota. Blackduck, another well attested ceramic ware from the Northern Midwest, is present in an excavated site reported in the Maple River Bend.

Even though the data is spotty for the Woodland Period, we tentatively offer two phase names for the Woodland materials in the Bend region. The Initial Woodland we name the Dahnke phase, after the dated and stratigraphically early finds made at Dahnke–Reinke site. This is cordmarked, thick, grit tempered pottery which we presume would match chronologically to the Initial Plains Woodland point types such as late Pelican Lake and Besant. A diagnostic of this pottery is the presence of nodes or bosses on the exterior that are punched from the interior. The later phase we call Sand Hills. Characteristic of this phase are the type of materials we find at Irwin Johnson, including thinner, grit tempered ceramics with occasional decorations including dentate stamping similar to St. Croix pottery from central Minnesota. This phase corresponds to the projectile point types called Prairie Side-Notched and Avonlea.

Woodland in the Sheyenne Bend represents some changes in the way the Native peoples of the region lived. Even though big game continues to be a mainstay of life, as with the Archaic, there are some important differences from the Archaic. The evidence for domestic plant use is sparse, but the squash seed from the Lisbon burial indicates that some domestic plants were probably being used. Pottery was also introduced during the Woodland. The use of pottery is regarded as a major innovation by archaeologists since clay pots are useful for storing food, and perhaps more importantly, it makes boiling water an easy task. Prior to the use of ceramic vessels, boiling water for cooking could be done by dropping hot stones into hide-lined pits, or by using a skin bag of some sort, perhaps the stomach of a bison or elk, to hold the water into which the stones were dropped. Either way is cumbersome. Ceramic vessels may be placed directly over a fire and used repeatedly for boiling. Boiling is a most effective way to remove toxins from certain nuts or seeds, such as acorns.

Boiling also reduces tough cellulose to a digestible state, thus making many plants previously unusable, not only edible, but even desirable. The advent of pottery undoubtedly led to significant changes in the range and types of foods, particularly plant foods, on the menu of Plains Woodland peoples of the region. The other important Woodland feature found in the Bend are mounds for disposition of the dead. At least some of the mounds in the Sheyenne Bend may have been built during the Plains Woodland, possibly during the latter portion of that time span. Mound building is generally believed to have represented not only a change in the treatment of the dead. When societies change the manner in which they bury their dead it represents a re-orientation of their cosmology; their beliefs in the afterlife and possibly their relationship with the deceased. Aside from changes in the system of belief, mounds are visible monuments clearly meant to represent a place of ancestral significance. There must have been some reason that people began placing heightened importance on signifying places where their predecessors were laid to rest.

The similarity of some of the ceramics to those of the lake and forest country in Minnesota is significant. Clearly some of the impetus for the Plains Woodland Period developments in the Bend region had an eastern source. The presence of Blackduck pottery at one of the sites along the Maple River also illustrates an important Woodland practice, one that may have earlier roots in the Archaic, but which is clearly indicated in the Woodland. This is the routine practice of lake-forest populations moving into the prairies to hunt bison, and undoubtedly forage for other resources as well. There is evidence for this Woodland adaptation in the nearby Red River Valley at several locations (cf. Anfinson et al. 1978; Michlovic 2005), and it seems to extend into the Sheyenne Valley as well.

Chapter 6
Late Prehistoric and Village Culture

Late Prehistoric and Village Culture

Major changes in the life-way of people in the Sheyenne Bend, and throughout the Northeastern Plains begin to appear around 900-800 years ago (AD 1100–1200) (cf. Toom 2004). In the estimation of most archaeologists these changes were due to the introduction of routine farming based on maize, squash, beans, and some domesticated native species like sunflower, the establishment of semi-permanent settlements with visible surface architectural features, and ongoing cultural influences from the south and east. Sites from this period are the best known in the entire region, partly because they come at the end of the prehistoric period and they are most likely to be exposed on the surface or the near-surface. Besides this, people practicing farming are likely to live in larger communities that are more visible archaeologically than those of more mobile hunters and gatherers. Finally, the Late Prehistoric period endures for about 500 years, a time span long enough to allow for the accumulation of a significant amount of archaeological material and a substantial number of sites.

Major changes were occurring throughout much of North America prior to AD 1000. Mesoamerican crops such as maize, squash, and beans were replacing the less productive native North American domesticates, such as *Chenopodium* (goosefoot) and *Iva* (marsh elder). This led to a dramatic increase in productivity and undoubtedly in population as well. Throughout much of the Mississippi Valley large population centers appeared. The largest of these is Cahokia, located near St. Louis. This site featured monumental earthen mounds that served as sub-structures for temples, somewhat after the fashion of Mesoamerican cities. Similar, albeit smaller sites are found in the Southeast and Midwest US, many in the Mississippi drainage basin. These major centers, known collectively to archaeologists as Mississippian culture, had profound impacts on the regions surrounding their core areas. The eastern Great Plains experienced a number of cultural influences emanating from the Mississippi Valley after AD 1000, and these may be seen in southeastern Minnesota in both the Cambria culture and in the complex of archaeological sites in the Red Wing, Minnesota area on the Wisconsin border.

Mississippian life-ways centered around major towns and villages. The dynamic that led to the development of villages and towns in the Southeast may have been due to population increases, no doubt related to the on-going impact of farming on North American populations, and even cultural impulses from Mexico where civilizations developed in preceding centuries. In any case a similar adaptation spread into the Great Plains, west and north up the Missouri, and northward along the Mississippi, as well as along the major tributary streams. Village adaptations are well-known from the Historic Period in the Missouri River Valley in Nebraska, Iowa, North and South Dakota. Village culture included life in settled communities, sometimes of over a thousand people, use of agriculture, substantial semi-subterranean lodges, food storage in carefully prepared pits, and a varied set of industries in ceramic, stone, and bone. Wild food sources continued in use, especially bison hunting. For this reason, the adaptation of these Plains farmers is sometimes referred to as a dual economy, featuring a dependence on both wild and domestic food sources. These Plains village farmers were probably the ancestors of ethnic groups such as the Wichita, Kansa, Omaha, Pawnee, Iowa, Oto, Arikara, Mandan, and Hidatsa.

In the Northeastern Plains there are several archaeological complexes associated with these developments; Cambria on the lower Minnesota River, Oneota in Iowa, southern Minnesota and eastern South Dakota, and the Northeastern Plains Village culture in the eastern Dakotas, western Minnesota, and southern Manitoba. To the west of these developments on the Northeastern Plains were the village cultures on the Missouri River in the central Dakotas. To the east and north were lake and forest country hunter-gatherers who focused their subsistence efforts not on farming or gardening, but on the intensive collection of wild rice. Some of these hunter-gatherer groups were almost certainly the ancestors of the Eastern Dakota (Gibbon 2012:189ff).

In the Late Prehistoric Period these Plains peoples farmed along the river lowlands, raising maize, squash, sunflower, beans, tobacco, and a few other domesticates, and they did so more or less in the same way their successors in the same area did in the early Historic Period. While these Plains villages did not develop directly out of the Mississippian culture, they were part of the same cultural intensification involving farming and larger populations living in more permanent settlements.

Coinciding with these developments were two material culture indicators archaeologists found during the development of these village adaptations. These indicators are the widespread use of small, simple

Figure 31. Oneota vessel fragment, showing trailed line or broad incising with shallow punctations.

triangular and side-notched projectile points known as Eastern Triangular and Plains Side-Notched, and the frequent use among some groups of crushed shell to temper clay for making pottery.

One of the earlier of these archaeological cultures is known as Cambria, found most commonly in the Minnesota River Valley. Cambria dates to the late eleventh through the early thirteenth centuries, and the best known and largest Cambria sites are near the confluence of the Blue Earth and Minnesota rivers near Mankato. Cambria peoples were farmers and hunters, and their settlements were substantial, often covering several acres. Aside from their well-known life-style employing the dual economy of the Plains Villagers, Cambria people made use of a distinctive set of ceramics that included grit tempered, smooth surfaced vessels with several types of decorations. Some of those decorative designs include closely spaced parallel incisions within bordered panels. Other ceramics were largely undecorated and entirely utilitarian. Perhaps the

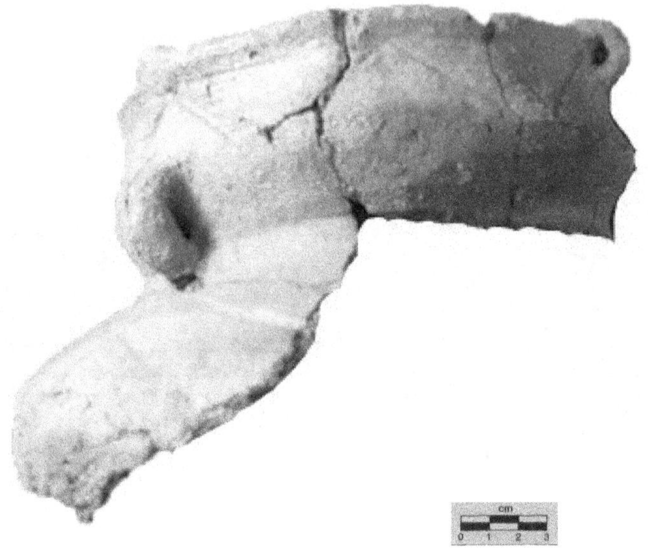

Figure 32. Initial Middle Missouri vessel fragment from the Bayley collection, State Historical Society, Bismarck.

most interesting of the decorative motifs were curvilinear, broad incised lines very similar to the designs on the ceramics from Mississippian sites to the southeast. These latter ceramics have led to a great deal of speculation about the relationship of the Cambria peoples to those Mississippian peoples of Cahokia, the center of the Late Prehistoric Missisppian culture. The modern descendants of the Cambria people are not known, although Toom (2004:294) has suggested an affiliation with the modern Hidatsa.

Perhaps the most widespread of these Late Prehistoric archaeological village cultures is Oneota. This prairie culture is also closely related to Mississippian. Oneota, like other Plains Village peoples farmed maize and squash, hunted bison, elk, deer, and other game, and continued the use of wild edible plants. Oneota is distinguished from other Plains Villagers in the use of shell-tempered, smoothed surface ceramics with incised linear and geometric designs (Figure 31). The use of shell to temper ceramics is relatively unusual in North America and has its origins in the Southeast and Midwest US. It is significant that shell tempered pottery with broad incised or trailed line decoration is typical in Mississippian sites, and the widespread presence of these traits in Oneota pottery reflects the intrusion of eastern influence into the prairie region of the Great Plains, where

Oneota is well represented. Oneota groups of the Minnesota–Iowa–Wisconsin region are believed to have been ancestral to Chiwere speaking Siouan groups such as the Iowa, Oto, and Winnebago.

A complex of archaeological cultures also developed in the eleventh century and later along the Missouri Valley in the Dakotas, and in portions of northwestern Iowa and adjacent areas. We refer to these groups here as Middle Missouri Villagers. Like Oneota and Cambria these people lived in farming villages and devoted a good deal of effort to bison hunting. Their distinctive ceramics come in a bewildering array of types, but are almost entirely grit tempered, and often simple or check-stamped on the vessel surface (Figure 32). This type of treatment was probably executed on the vessel with a carved paddle leaving block-like or crisscrossed impressions in the clay. Broadly speaking, the Middle Missouri Villagers were ancestral to the Three Affiliated Tribes of today; the Mandan, Hidatsa, and Arikara (MHA Nation).

In central and northern Minnesota, on the eastern border of the Northeastern Plains, shell tempered pottery, without the Oneota shapes or decorative designs, is found at numerous archaeological sites from the Late Prehistoric. It is known as Sandy Lake pottery, has simple globular forms, and is shell-tempered in roughly half the known samples. Otherwise, Sandy Lake ceramics appear much like earlier pottery from the Woodland, with cordmarked surfaces and sometimes the cord-wrapped stick or object impressions found earlier in ceramic wares such as Terminal Woodland Blackduck. Occasionally Sandy Lake vessels are even found with trailed-line designs, but for the most part, Sandy Lake pottery seldom has much in the way of decorative elements. Sandy Lake pottery, and Oneota, eventually show up in the Sheyenne Bend region.

Probably the most archaeologically noticeable cultural expression in the Sheyenne Bend region during the Late Prehistoric Period is the Northeastern Plains Village Culture. Village adaptations in areas surrounding the Bend are well-known in the Missouri River Valley in Nebraska, North and South Dakota. Until thirty or forty years ago, the village adaptations were not much discussed for the Northeastern Plains. However, during the 1980s excavations in the Sheyenne Bend, specifically on the Maple River, along the James River south of Jamestown, and in the Devils Lake area, made it clear that the village adaptation had developed in these areas as well.

Northeastern Plains Village Culture, as it is now called, is characterized by archaeological sites dating mostly to after the year AD 1200. It persists perhaps to around 1800 (Toom 2004:283, Gregg et al. 2016). The most characteristic sites are small, semi-permanent settlements found on the uplands in the Sheyenne and James valleys, and extending into the Red River Valley of Minnesota and Manitoba from south of Lake Winnipeg to Lake Traverse and Big Stone Lake at the headwaters of the Red River. The best known of these sites are found in undisturbed contexts and feature what are presumed to be defensive ditches surrounding relatively small areas, often no more than an acre or so. Lodge depressions, usually found in the village sites along the Missouri River, are not present at these sites and lodges are presumed to have been placed on the ground surface without any significant sub-surface excavation of a floor space. Storage pits are common, along with stratified refuse deposits, particularly in the abandoned ditches, which seem to signify episodic deposition as might be expected if the settlements were repeatedly used, as on a warm season occupation/cold season abandonment cycle.

These small villages—perhaps they are better called hamlets—are known from the Sheyenne Bend where Fred Schneider of the University of North Dakota first described them in the late 1970s. They include the Shea and Sprunk sites on the Maple River Bend, and Lucas, Peterson, and Nelson in the Sheyenne Bend proper. Other sites in similar upland settings and characterized by circumvallated ditches are found in the Lake Traverse–Big Stone area, and along the James River south of Jamestown. At the Shea site, one of the best known of these villages, the occupation extends considerably beyond the ditched portion of the site, where artifacts and features, while not as abundant as inside the ditched area, are nevertheless substantial in their frequency. Haug and Fosha (2008) describe a similar disposition of cultural material extending beyond the ditched occupation at the Hartford Beach site, located above Big Stone Lake in eastern South Dakota.

Some of these sites, such as Shea, Sprunk, Nelson, and Peterson are situated near burial mounds. These mounds are more or less conical in shape and roughly 15–25 meters in diameter. While we assume that the mounds are cemetery sites related to the settlements, excavations have not been performed in any of these mound sites and their actual affiliation to the village sites is likely, but still somewhat speculative.

The artifact assemblages from these sites include scapula hoes made from bison bone, although other bone tools are common as well. The lithic assemblage includes substantial percentages of Knife River flint, small notched and triangular projectile points, scraping tools, mostly end scrapers, often made on Knife River flint, as well as an assortment of bifacial cutting tools, drills, awls, and expedient amorphous flake tools. Ceramics consist of a combination of styles that seem to mix influences from east, west, and south. Much of the pottery is characterized as Northeastern Plains Village pottery. These are mostly globular jars, often smoothed on the upper surface and tempered with grit. Decorations include incised lines and tool or finger impressions, some of it similar to the decorative practices of Oneota peoples to the south and east. Some pottery mimics the ceramic traditions of the Missouri Valley, such as the occasional presence of a vessel with a wavy profile near the top of the vessel, known as an S-shaped rim. One of the most unusual aspects of the Northeastern Plains Village sites in the Sheyenne Bend, particularly within the Maple River Bend area of this region, is the heavy presence of Sandy Lake ware, the often shell tempered pottery commonly found in central to northern Minnesota lake-forest country.

Dennis Toom (2004), an archaeologist who contributed heavily to our understanding of the Northeastern Plains Village Culture defined it as an archaeological tradition. In archaeology, a tradition is a set of cultures that share similar ways of life, are generally contiguous with each other, and which persist in a geographic region over time. The Northeastern Plains Village Culture Tradition (NEPV) would thus comprise a set of cultures in eastern North Dakota and surrounding regions, which in Toom's (2004:283) estimation persisted from about AD 1200–1800. It was related in some way with the slightly earlier Cambria cultural complex to the southeast in the southern Minnesota Valley. This NEPV tradition, after flourishing for several centuries in the James, Sheyenne, and Red River valleys, and in the Devils Lake basin, shifted its focus to the west in its later phase, only to rebound to its old eastern territory after AD 1600. In this later phase, the NEPV ceramics begin to take on more and more features of the ceramic styles of the Middle Missouri Villagers (Toom 2004:289).

The Okiedan Buttes: Lucas, Rotenberger, and Site 32RM60

The Okiedan Buttes are steep slopes rising above the southernmost extent of the Sheyenne River on the dramatic 'elbow' in the river's course. These bluff tops were referred to in the journal of Joseph Nicollet, a geographer who mapped the upper Mississippi River basin in the 1830s (Bray and Bray 1976). Many sites are found here, and more are undoubtedly to be discovered. One of the most intriguing of these is the Lucas site (32RM225), a small upland ditch-enclosed site. Some believed that the site was a prehistoric settlement of native peoples in this area, while others argued that it was an American military installation, Camp Hayes, built by the expedition of Colonel Sibley into Dakota territory during the

Figure 33: Aerial view of the Lucas enclosure on the Okiedan Buttes. View to the west. Note three conical mounds just east of the enclosure, one with ridges radiating to the south into the plowed field. Another mound is visible to the west in the cultivated field, and the Ranes Mound group is visible just beyond the shelter belt to the west of Lucas.

aftermath of the 1862 Dakota War in Minnesota. Camp Hayes was only briefly used in 1863, but the small, circular enclosure at Lucas seemed unusual for a nineteenth century American military installation. Holley and Kalinowski (2008) show conclusively that Camp Hayes is actually on the other side of the Sheyenne, and is not the same as the Lucas site. Archaeological finds from excavations in 1989 consisted entirely of prehistoric artifacts and ecofacts; lithics, ceramics, and animal bone fragments (Michlovic 1990a). The complete lack of historic material such as metal fragments, glass, buttons, or the like made it clear that the site had nothing to do with the 1863 occupation of Camp Hayes.

The Lucas site consists of an almost fully circular ditch that runs just over 120 meters in circumference (Figure 33). The ditch is almost a meter deep in places and encircles an area about 40x40 meters. Earth is piled outside the ditch forming an embankment. There is an opening where the site faces the bluff edge, seemingly giving access from the interior of the enclosure to the lowland below. The steep bluff slope on the north side of the site is heavily wooded today, and below the site the floodplain of the Sheyenne is cultivated.

The artifact collection from the site is rather small. Just under 2000 items were found in the excavations; the thick pasture grass in the area made finding any surface materials impossible. The lithic assemblage consisted mostly of flaking debris from tool making, along with hundreds of potsherds. Animal bone and shell fragments were also recovered. Most of the bone was not identifiable, although at least two bones were from a large mammal, and two were from a small mammal. The shell fragments were river mussel shells. Some of the bones were burned. The nature of the artifact and bone collection indicates that there was obviously domestic activity at the site: flaking debris from tool making, broken pottery from daily household work, and burned bone from cooking and hearth cleaning.

Even so, the evidence for domestic undertakings at the site is not as substantial as might be expected at a site where considerable effort was expended in the construction of an encircling ditch. There is no surface evidence, nor any excavated indication of a house structure. Fire hearths, storage pits, or post molds indicating house walls were not encountered in the admittedly limited excavations. Furthermore, one excavation unit placed in the ditch did not yield any evidence of a trash deposit or midden.

The artifact assemblage from Lucas gives the impression of a Terminal Woodland use of the site. There is a single projectile point from the excavations, a Prairie Side Notched point, normally related to the

Terminal Plains Woodland, perhaps around 700–1300 years ago (Peck and Ives 2001:163). There were few lithic items that could be classified as core fragments, and not very many flakes with a weathered exterior cortex. These are characteristics of early phases in stone tool making, and since both are absent in the lithic sample at Lucas, and since there is only a small lithic debris sample, it would seem that tool maintenance rather than manufacturing is indicated. The percentage of exotic Knife River flint at the site, 21%, is not uncommon for eastern North Dakota. Locally available Swan River chert accounts for 40% of the sample. Other materials, mostly found in regional till deposits, constitute the rest of the lithic collection. As at many other sites, even though Knife River flint accounts for only about a fifth of the lithic sample, about half of the tools and utilized flakes (that is, showing use wear) are Knife River flint.

The pottery at Lucas is difficult to characterize mostly because of the small size of the potsherds. The collection is entirely grit tempered, and the surface treatment includes both cordmarked and smoothed surfaces, with cordmarking being somewhat more common. The small vessel rim fragments and occasional decorated sherds which archaeologists use to classify and date the pottery suggest an age in the very latest portion of the Woodland or the early Late Prehistoric Period. Some of the decoration consists of object impressed stamps, resembling somewhat the impressions of a broad-toothed comb, while other sherds have cross-hatched decoration on the rim or polished surfaces or linear incisions. These decorative features recall both Eastern US Woodland and Missouri Valley Villager affiliations. There is, however, a complete lack of shell tempering typical of the Late Prehistoric Sandy Lake and Oneota pottery.

The ceramics from the Lucas site provide us with the best way of understanding rstanding the cultural affiliations of the site. The combination of eastern and Plains ceramic traits are reminiscent of the Initial Middle Missouri Tradition, which developed along the Missouri River in South Dakota during the period after about AD 1000. The grit-tempered and cordmarked sherds, along with the cross-hatched decoration on some of the vessels are especially indicative of this affiliation. It is best, however, not to characterize the Lucas collection as Initial Middle Missouri, but it makes sense to assume that the date for the site matches the dates for that more southerly cultural manifestation. For this reason, we identify a regional archaeological phase called the Lucas phase, which we believe is transitional from the end of the Woodland to the earliest expression of the Northeastern Plains Village Tradition.

The ditch at Lucas is almost entirely circular, unlike other ditched settlements in the Bend region, which have more irregular outlines. Also, the artifact assemblage is relatively impoverished, so in some ways this does not look like a normal settlement. Based on these factors Holley argues that the Lucas site may have its origin in some less mundane function. In the eastern United States, there are many enclosures dating from Middle Woodland times and later that were clearly ceremonial in nature with little indication of heavy occupation. Perhaps the Lucas site represents a late manifestation of this eastern ceremonialism on the Northeastern Plains. Circular enclosures have been noted on the perimeter of the Northeastern Plains and are commonly interpreted to be associated with ceremonial activities. Skinner (1915:177) notes that among the Menomini a circular enclosure comprised of an embankment about a foot high was built for special feasts. In the middle was a drum set on four decorated supports. Spector (1993) also mentions that the nineteenth century Dakota village at Little Rapids had an enclosure for ceremonial dances, also consisting of an area cleaned of debris and surrounded by a circular ridge of mounded earth. Perhaps the Lucas enclosure had a similar function, even though the enclosure was defined by a ditch and embankment rather than an embankment only.

Adjacent to the Lucas site, about 80 meters to the east is an arrangement of three conical mounds. They are about 20–25 meters in diameter and 1.5–2.0 meters in height. The mounds are only a few meters apart from each other, and from the largest, and most easterly mound, linear earthen embankments radiate to the south and southeast. These linear embankments are today somewhat difficult to see, and in the plowed fields south of the fence line they are invisible on the ground; however, aerial photographs show these embankments once extended hundreds of meters to the south. Neither the conical mounds nor the embankments have been archaeologically tested, although each of the mounds has a small depression on its top. It is likely that soldiers from Camp Hayes, or later pothunters looted the mounds in the late nineteenth or early twentieth century.

The meaning of the mounds and embankments is not something archaeologists understand, although there are hypotheses that have not been fully investigated. Embankments and associated mounds are known in other parts of the Upper Midwest and Northeastern Plains. Numerous examples may be found in southern and southeastern Minnesota, and there is a complex of mounds and connecting embankments in the James River Valley not far to the west of the Lucas complex. Some archaeologists have suggested, informally, that they may have had some celestial significance, for example, marking an important solar or lunar position relating to seasonal changes. Others suggest that perhaps the embankments represent physical representations of spiritual pathways or tracks. Here, we can only describe these monuments and await further study to answer questions about their meaning. In any case, they add to the notion that the Lucas enclosure itself may have had a ceremonial significance, rather than serving simply as an enclosed settlement.

Aerial photographs show several additional conical mounds on the bluff edge and even in plowed fields to the south of the bluffs. About a half mile west of the Lucas site is another set of mounds known as the Ranes Mound group. Here is a complex arrangement of about 19 conical and linear mounds overlooking the Sheyenne Valley, and extending back into the upland. This mound group was originally mapped in the late nineteenth century, but intensive study or excavations were never conducted. Clearly the Okiedan Buttes was an important and ritually significant area for ancient Native American peoples.

About 200 meters to the immediate west of Lucas are a pair of sites resting at different elevations from the bluff top to the floodplain below. The largest of the sites is on the floodplain and adjacent terrace of the Sheyenne. It is the Rotenberger site (32RM226), which extends over about 30 acres of cultivated field and onto a terrace to the south of the floodplain. The terrace portion of the site is undisturbed and partly wooded, but mostly in pasture grass. A second site is on the bluff top directly west of Lucas. This site is also in pasture and is characterized by several modest surface depressions that may be house pits, and a small mound-like eminence around which the depressions are arranged.

The cultural material from Rotenberger was assessed as dating primarily from the Late Prehistoric period with stray examples of materials from other periods. Bison bone accounted for most of the faunal remains. One stone artifact has the characteristic features of a Late Paleoindian spear point, being well-thinned on both faces, with grinding on both edges of one end. The paucity of formal lithic tools is attributed to the heavy local collecting of the site (regional collectors favor lithic over ceramic finds). Test excavations revealed that this expansive floodplain occupation reflects recurrent use of the landform probably stretching back at least to the Plains Woodland period and through the Late Prehistoric, mostly from 800–600 years ago.

The later ceramics at Rotenberger are plain or smoothed surface vessels with far less cordmarking than is common in the Lucas phase. These are assigned to a post-Lucas phase named Matoti, about which more is presented below. Incising on the vessel surface, and the use of punctates is often observed. Some design elements are similar to those found on Oneota vessels. Based on these features the Matoti ceramic assemblage would best be dated to AD 1200–1400, and may overlap with the succeeding Shea phase, which is expressed most fully on the Maple River. A majority of the several hundred pottery sherds were smoothed or polished on the surface, while about a fourth were cordmarked. Other minor surface treatments included stamped, net and fabric impressions on vessel surfaces. The collection probably represents a minimum of about 16 different vessels. One is an Initial Plains Woodland Fox Lake vessel, while another is a Terminal Plains Woodland pot. There is one other vessel representing a type of pottery found in the Missouri trench. The rest of the pottery vessels are classified here as Northeastern Plains Village types.

The Rotenberger site extends upslope to a terrace immediately above the floodplain, revealed by shovel probes and several excavation units. Large mammal bone belonging to bison or elk was found. Artifacts included a Cambria-like rimsherd, a cord-impressed rim, projectile points, and quite a lot of small sherds and flakes. The projectile points include a well-made Knife River flint unnotched triangular point, and a small, jasper side-notched point that is classified as Prairie Side-Notched. Both of these forms would fit within the rough date of 800–600 years ago proposed for the Matoti phase. Not much may be said about this portion of the Rotenberger site, although the limited testing reported here may have been on the perimeter of the site, and more material might be found if testing were expanded.

A single radiocarbon date on bone recovered from one of the excavation units at Rotenberger gives a calibrated age of about AD 1000. This dates one of the occupations at the site, not all of the cultural materials present. The pottery suggests at least two ceramic occupations at different times. The size of the site and the variety of cultural material found indicates that floodplain sites like this one were the living places for people who used the upland Okiedan Buttes for more ceremonial purposes.

At least two springs usher from the bluff tops and drain into the Sheyenne River adjacent to the Rotenberger site. Springs are important sources of water and spiritually significant to Native Americans as the water comes directly from the earth. It is possible that this is one factor in the location of so many mounds on the Okiedan Buttes.

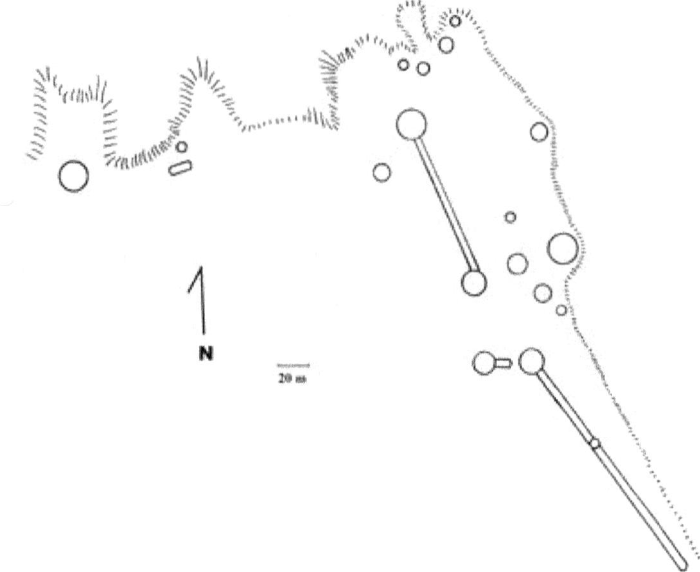

Figure 34. The Ranes Mound Group. Map modified from Haury (1990).

One additional site was tested on the top of the Okiedan Buttes west of the Lucas enclosure. This site, 32RM60, was first mapped by T. H. Lewis in 1890 as consisting of five circular depressions surrounding a small elongate mound. Small is a misnomer; it is a tiny mound not like any reported mound in the region. Haury (1990) returned to the site 100 years after Lewis as part of an assessment program directed at relocating the mounds mapped by Lewis. She noted that not all of the mapped depressions were present, particularly the westernmost depression.

The site lies in minimally disturbed prairie sod near a bluff edge of the Sheyenne. The soil in this area is thin and rests over a blanket of gravel not far below the surface. Little was found in the shallow topsoil above the gravel. The ceramics were all grit tempered with few diagnostics. The greater part of the ceramic collection consisted of sherds with simple stamped surfaces. This type of pottery is consistent with a radiocarbon date (about AD 1213) from a charred post which was presumably part of a structure. The ceramic sample is meager totaling only a few dozen items. Large sherds, decorated sherds, rims, and contoured sherds, useful in understanding the shape and size of vessels, are lacking. Nonetheless, when seen in the light of other collections from the area, a comparative perspective and possible phase association is arguably attainable.

The absence of shell temper places the collection either prior to AD 1300 or after 1600, as shell tempering appears to enter the region sometime immediately prior to the Shea phase and is absent in the mid-eighteenth century Biesterfeldt collections, a few miles to the east. Space plays a role in this as well. Collections from higher up on the Sheyenne River, for example Griggs County (Haury and Schneider 1986), have little or no shell temper, and, as a rule, shell temper is uncommon in the Bend Region. However, shell temper incidence increases on Sheyenne Valley sites as we move east towards the Red River. The mix of surface treatments is telling and points to an age range of late Terminal Woodland to early Northeastern Plains Village. We believe the ceramic sample from 32RM60 reflects the Lucas phase in part, and by the presence of simple stamping, the Matoti Phase. However, two diagnostics of the Matoti phase, broad incising and polishing, are absent from the collection. The radiocarbon date of about AD 1200 fits into this Lucas–Matoti time span. Ceramic wall thickness (average 4.39 mm) also is typical of ceramics belonging to these two phases. From much further afield we have a similar date from a small collection in the Browns Valley area, the Browns Valley "fort" (21TR9) at Lake Traverse. The collection from this site is consistent with 32RM60. The ceramics are also grit tempered; however instead of simple stamping the pottery displays a mix of plain, cordmarked, and cord-impressed decorated ceramic vessels, with some surface polishing present as well.

Southwest of the Lucas–Rotenberger–RM60 complex of sites is the Ranes mound group and adjacent occupation sites (Figure 34). This large archaeological complex has hardly been studied; in fact, the actual recording of the site is in question and we have trouble matching the location of sites indicated on official state site forms with the actual location of the sites in the field. This difficulty may be no one person's fault, but the result of several factors. Some of these locales were identified in the nineteenth century by T.H. Lewis, and some of his maps are now inaccurate due to changes and corrections in the old land surveys. Another problem is that some of the parcels that contain sites are owned by the same family. Thus, more than one site may be given the same common name. In this location, a site situated on a river terrace has the same name given to another site located on the blufftop. In any case, we cannot be certain without field-truthing where the boundaries of all the sites are, and whether some of the sites listed should perhaps be combined with other, adjacent sites.

Figure 35. Schultz site, view to the west.

This site complex on the western end of the Okiedan Buttes includes a number of mounds, some in a single related set (the Ranes group), and others standing alone. Two of the constituent sites are both known as Heath. One of these is on an intermediate landform partway down from the bluff top to the alluvial plain. Another Heath site is above and slightly to the east of this location. It is a cultivated field adjacent to the Ranes Mounds. Portions of the artifact collections from these sites are available, including material recovered by Elden Johnson during his brief project in the Bend region. Unfortunately, many of the artifacts were taken by private collectors and their present disposition is not known. The ceramics represent both Plains Woodland and Northeastern Plains Village styles. These sites, like those to the east near Lucas, illustrate the complexity of occupation in this area where the Sheyenne reaches its southernmost position. The heavy domestic use of the rich Sheyenne Valley is obvious from the many sites here, which is true of other portions of the Bend. However, at the Okiedan Buttes there is an overwhelming presence of ceremonial features, in the form of mounds, mound groups, linear earthworks, and perhaps as well the Lucas enclosure itself, which may have had more of a ceremonial than mundane function. The work done so far on these Buttes has only provided a preliminary understanding of the area; major projects in the future may allow us a fuller understanding of the significance of this important locale.

Schultz Site

About 13 miles or so east of Lucas and the Okiedan Buttes is the Schultz site (32RM210). Schultz was previously excavated by Hecker and Milligan, but unfortunately, they did not write a descriptive report on the site, and we have not been able to locate notes from their excavations. Our information about the previous excavation at the site comes from comments made by W.R. Wood (1963) in his discussion of affiliations the site has to the Stutsman focus, a Late Prehistoric to Protohistoric culture of the James Valley. Even though there is no report on the site, the artifact collection is available at the State Historical Museum in Bismarck. Our interpretation of the Schultz site includes consideration of this previously excavated material (Michlovic, Holley, and Dalan 2012). In the description that follows, it is important to keep in mind that the finds made earlier by Hecker and Milligan are distinct from most of what was found in our excavations. While our work at Schultz recovered evidence of Northeastern Plains Village and Sandy Lake ceramics, Hecker and Milligan found ceramics much more like pottery found at the villages on the Missouri River. This is the reason that the Schultz site has been affiliated with the ancestral Hidatsa. The differences between earlier finds and the ones we made in 2009–2010 is most likely due to the fact that the site as recorded includes a relatively large parcel of land extending over dozens of acres. Our work and the work of Hecker and Milligan may not have been in the same location within this expansive parcel.

Knowing the significance of the artifact collection from previous work we returned to the site during the summer of 2009, although we were not certain our work was at or near the location of the earlier excavations. The site area is bounded on the south by the Sheyenne River, and a part of it is split off from the remainder by an old meander scar of the river that is often filled with overflow from the Sheyenne. Even though we had re-established the location of the site, there was some disappointment as well. Hecker and Milligan had earlier described ash stains and pit features and found large pieces of pottery similar to ceramic types common to the Missouri River Valley. Our surface collection was impoverished by comparison and included only a few hundred items. Among these were about 60 very small potsherds, most of which were tempered with shell, and very dissimilar to Missouri Valley pottery. A few stone flakes

Figure 36. Storage pit at Schultz. Note the dark stain in the profile on either side of the chalkboard.

from stone tool making, and about 150 animal bone fragments were also found, along with miscellaneous shell, charcoal, wood, and daub fragments (burnt mud from house walls).

In 2010 we conducted excavations at the site. We chose a small pasture surrounded by woods to the south of the slough where shovel probes the previous year produced the most promising quantity of cultural material (Figure 35). A remote sensing survey was also done to discover whether there were remnants of any subsurface structures that might show up when the soils were probed by electrical induction. Altogether, this work yielded a modest artifact sample, one major feature, a variety of animal bones and a single radiocarbon date. Most of the cultural material from the site was found between 20–50 cm below the surface.

The radiocarbon date for Schultz is 400 ± 40 years before present. When calibrated the date is calculated in calendar years as AD 1480. This age is consistent with the type of artefacts found at the site and places it in the same temporal span as many of the other sites known from this part of the Sheyenne Valley.

A modest number of daub fragments were recovered from the excavations, just as they were from the shovel probes. They were found in all portions of the site both north and south of the slough. Daub is burnt clay

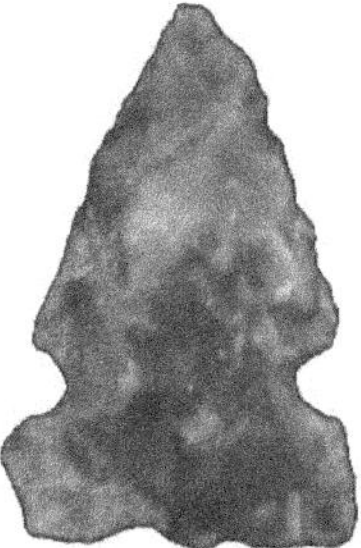

Figure 37. Plains Side-Notched point, Schultz site. Point length about 3 cm.

with the impressions of fiber or plant material. Daub was probably from lodge structures made with wooden frames and a wicker-work of small branches to fill in between the framing posts. This was then plastered over with mud. The daub results if the structure is burned, thereby preserving the fire-hardened pieces of the mud walls. The daub tells us something about the kind of structures that people here lived in. Unfortunately, we did not find other evidence of structures at the site, for example, in the form house outlines or sub-surface house pits. We may, however, infer that the site featured pole and thatch structures plastered over with mud.

There was one feature found at the Schultz site. This was a bell-shaped pit, a feature similar to those known to have been used by the village peoples who lived along the Missouri River. These pits, up to two meters in diameter and sometimes just as deep, are usually narrow at the top and widening below the neck of the pit. They were used to store food. Storage was important as populations grew larger and communities needed food to tide them over the winter months. Sometimes, after a pit was no longer in use for storage, the empty hole would be used for garbage disposal.

The pit at the Schultz site was discovered at the base of the topsoil, about 35 cm from the ground surface (**Figure 36**). We probably dug through part of it before we could detect its outline in the lighter colored subsoil. It was about a meter deep, contained bison bone, including an upside-down bison skull at the base of the pit, along with a few artifacts. It was apparently not used on purpose for refuse, which suggests to us that after the food stored there was removed the site was soon thereafter abandoned. The bone and occasional artifact found in the pit, except for the skull at the base, were probably washed in naturally as the pit filled in. Since bison skulls have been found at the bottoms of other bell-shaped pits on the Plains, we believe that this skull was purposely placed at the base of the pit, possibly when it was originally dug.

Figure 38. Rims and decorated sherds from Schultz

An electromagnetic sensor (EM38MK2) was used to measure the conductivity of subsurface deposits and to detect any variations in subsurface magnetic susceptibility, something regarded as advisable considering the finding of daub fragments and a bell-shaped pit, both of which are suggestive of structures being present. Variations in soil electromagnetic properties might be related to disturbances in the normal soil profile not visible from the surface. On either side of the area where the bell-shaped pit was found there were soil anomalies detected that might reflect the presence of structural remains. Since our own work was purely exploratory and minimally funded, we were not in a position to undertake a major open-area excavation to document entire structures. Any further archaeology undertaken at Schultz should, of course, focus some effort on the further investigation of these anomalies.

The lithic collection from the excavations and shovel probes is quite small and amounted to fewer than 100 items. Most of the debris is Knife River flint, followed by locally available Swan River chert. The collection of flaking debris seems to represent two different phases in the stone working process; core reduction, the early stage in stone toolmaking, and the actual fashioning of finished tools. All core fragments are of local raw materials, not Knife River flint. This is worth our attention, since Knife River flint was apparently not available in large chunks or cores, but only in already reduced cores that were finished into tools. The lithic collection shows that the people who lived at the Schultz site were performing many different tasks with flaked stone, and this was probably the product of an extended stay by the people who used this site.

Since few actual stone tools were recovered, the stone implements in the collections of the State Historical Society from work by Hecker and Milligan allow for some more fully informed conclusions about the site. The diagnostic points are late prehistoric in style and include small triangular and Plains Side-Notched types (Figure 37). Most of the actual tools from the site, including points, scrapers, and bifaces, are Knife River flint. We feel that this indicates Knife River flint was mostly brought to here as already made tools. Swan River chert was being made into tools at the site and the finished products were removed and continued in use elsewhere.

The pottery from Schultz is Late Prehistoric in style, a conclusion that fits well with the radiocarbon date. Based on the ceramic collection, the Schultz site fits between Late Prehistoric and Post-Contact times. The Schultz site was occupied around the same time period as other regional Northeastern Plains Villages such as Shea and Sprunk, which are part of the Shea phase (Michlovic 2008a; see below), dating to around AD 1400–1500. Schultz does have some features of Shea phase sites, but when the collection from the earlier work of Hecker and Milligan is considered, the site seems to be only marginally related to those of the Shea phase.

Grit temper predominates the ceramic collection, but shell temper is also represented, unlike some other Northeastern Plains village sites farther to the west in the Bend area. The presence of shell tempering is interesting since it was a popular part of ceramic production in central Minnesota and in areas southeast of there during the period after AD 1200. Less common traits include braced rims and channeled lips. Schultz features Plains-derived treatments such as cord-impressed braced-rim jars, a preponderance of straight-neck jars, horizontal incising, and check stamping. Incisions on cordmarked surfaces are also found at Schultz (Figure 38).

The ecofact assemblage from the site included both plant and animal remains. Some wood charcoal fragments were identified on the basis of cell structure as ash, hophornbeam, poplar, elm, and birch. There were also fragments of plum pits and one or two fragments of maize. The animal bone included mostly bison elements, but also a few bones from fish, beaver, frog, and rabbit.

Schultz fits in with local cultural traditions in the types of ceramics and lithic artifacts found. The people who lived here relied on the local flora and fauna, with some amount of horticulture as well. Even though only one or two fragments of maize were recovered, maize does not grow wild, and the people at Schultz either grew it themselves or traded for it. The presence of a bell-shaped pit and daub fragments are indicators of a stable residential community, which is likely when people are farmers. Daub found in shovel probes and in the excavations shows that relatively substantial structures were built at the site, reflecting a semi-sedentary adaptation, that is, one involving living at the site for entire seasons or more.

Site 32RM92

While the Schultz site is toward the eastern side of the Bend region, another excavated site, 32RM92, is on the western edge of the Bend. This site, which lacks a colloquial name, is located on the floodplain of the Sheyenne River a short distance north of the town of Fort Ransom. It was test excavated in 1993 prior to proposed construction that would disturb the site (Michlovic 1993b). Both shovel probes and excavation units were dug at the site. Samples of soil from the excavation units were also water-screened with a fine mesh to recover small cultural items. Excavations extended to between 50–70 cm below the surface. Most of the cultural material was recovered from between 10–40 cm. Cracked and fire cracked rock at the site was mostly in the upper 30 cm, leading us to believe that the occupation rests at around a depth of 20–30 cm, which seems to be the occupation level of many regional sites.

In both dry and water screened samples, hundreds of bone fragments and some shells were found. These included identifiable elements from bison, dog, and a few river mussels. About one-fourth of the lithic items were Knife River flint. The other lithic material is local chert, although two pieces of broken catlinite from the Minnesota Pipestone Quarry were recovered as well. Two projectile points, one side-notched and one a simple triangular form, both suggest a date of Late Prehistoric. The ceramic assemblage consists of about 100 potsherds, mostly small. All the pottery is grit tempered, and all but two cordmarked sherds have plain or smoothed surfaces. Several of the sherds have paired parallel broad incised lines impressed into the surface, and another has a narrow-incised line. Other ceramic decorations include two rims with tabs, and two rims with lip notches.

The ceramic and lithic assemblage from 32RM92 clearly places this site within the Northeastern Plains Village Tradition. The two projectile points fit comfortably in the Late Prehistoric period, and the ceramics are quite homogeneous and clearly like assemblages from the Northeastern Plains Village sites in the James Valley, and from the Maple River sites such as Shea and Sprunk. What is different about RM92 in relation to these latter two sites is the paucity, or the complete absence of Sandy Lake ceramics, which are well represented along the Maple River (about 25

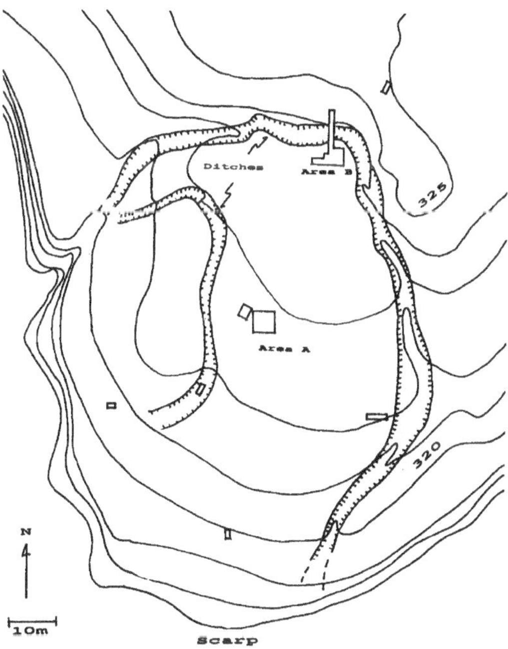

Figure 39. Aerial view and map of the Shea site.

miles northeast). We do note that Sandy Lake pottery generally appears more common in the northern and eastern part of the Bend at sites like Schultz, or those in the Maple Valley and in locations closer to the Red River Valley.

Shea Site

Shea (32CS101) is located on an upland about 16 meters (~50 ft.) above the Maple River in southwestern Cass County (Michlovic and Schneider 1993). It sits on a point of land that projects toward the river on three sides, while the north side of the site extends into the upland prairie. The site is on ground that drops abruptly toward the lowlands to the south and west. The eastern slope is not as dramatic, but still steep. There were erosional features on the west side of the site at the time of excavations, and artifacts, cracked rock, and animal bone could be found exposed on this side of the site. Even so, the south and most of the west slope were covered with a heavy blanket of vegetation, much of it being leafy spurge, and for the most part, these slopes were quite stable at the time of excavation.

The Shea site is one of the most significant sites in the Sheyenne Bend region. Its importance derives from the site's excellent state of preservation, the nature of the artifact assemblage found, the number and types of features documented, the suite of radiocarbon dates obtained for the deposit, and from the fact that it formed a significant part of the definition of the Northeastern Plains Village culture, and even more directly, the archaeological entity now known as the Shea phase. The main portion of the site is defined by a ditch about three meters wide and up to a meter deep. The ditch encloses an area against the bluff edge of about an acre, so while the steep scarp into the valley below defines the south and west side of the site, the north and east sides are enclosed by the ditch. There is a second, almost invisible ditch interior to the outer one. This feature is best seen in aerial views. We believe that the interior ditch defined the perimeter of an earlier phase in the settlement of the site, which was expanded over time to the dimensions of the outer ditch. There is an undisturbed circular mound (32CS45) approximately 200 meters north of Shea. We assume this is a burial ground for the people who lived at this site.

The Shea site was not really discovered at any particular date. Roger Shea, who owned and farmed the site for many years, said that his father always knew about the site and that it was a settlement of the Indians long ago. Roger and his father both refrained from cultivating the site and only allowed their cattle to graze the pasture grasses there. Shea was a vocal advocate for the protection of the site, and always took pains to make our work there as pleasant as possible.

The site was recorded in 1966, and Fred Schneider made a topographic map (Figure 39). Schneider later reported on Shea and other similar sites known from the Sheyenne Bend region, bringing an entire set of previously unknown sites to the attention of the archaeological community. Intensive archaeological work at the site began in 1985. A much larger effort followed in 1987. Additional, but more limited work was completed in 1989–1990 (Michlovic and Schneider 1993). We estimate less than 5% of the site was affected by excavations.

The entire upland formation on which Shea rests is part of the Maple River delta and the natural sediments are loams and very fine sands. A soil profile just outside the site (where the soil was not disturbed by human activity) shows a haploborall with an A-B-C (topsoil, subsoil, parent material) sequence. This is the type of soil that forms under grasslands in cool climates. Within the perimeter of the ditch, the natural soil profile is almost unrecognizable, a result of the intensive domestic activity by the people who lived there.

Today the Shea site is less than a kilometer from the Maple River dam, which became operational in 2006. During the construction phase for the dam, the river below Shea was re-channeled, and the south and west slopes were re-graded. Engineers thought that grading the bluff edge on the south and west of the site to a more gradual slope would stabilize the site and prevent erosion. The concern of both archaeologists and engineers was that wave action from ponded water when the dam was full would cause slippage on the slopes and collapse of the southern side of the site into the Maple. Unfortunately, the reduction in the grade of the slope involved heavy machinery in stripping the deep-rooted spurge and exposing the highly erodible fine sands in the sub-soil. Even though a protective netting and planted grass were installed on the newly sloped land, erosion began almost immediately. The status of the site may be judged precarious.

The excavations at the Shea site probed the interior ditch to its base, a depth of about 150cm. The exterior ditch was cross-sectioned as well. The depth of the cultural deposit on both sides of the ditch was relatively shallow, being between about 8–25 cm below the surface. In the ditch deposits (both inner and outer ditches) cultural material was found to extend

Figure 40. Profile of the Shea site interior ditch.

to over a meter below the present surface. There were about 40 features identified at the Shea site consisting of fire stains, large pits, post molds, rock concentrations, and of course, the ditches.

The features tell us some interesting facts about the occupation of the Shea site. The arrangement of post molds, especially interior to the outer ditch, suggest that there may have been a wooden palisade built on the interior side of the ditch, undoubtedly for defensive purposes. Interior to the ditch, two of the several fire hearths overlap each other, suggesting a repeated, or ongoing use of the site. Some of the features were clusters of rock and other debris, probably from cleaning out fire hearths. These discard features indicate the process of cleaning or maintenance, something that happens at sites where occupation is for the long term rather than temporary.

Some of the features are relatively large pits that were used as storage facilities, but when emptied, were re-used for refuse disposal. There were seven of these found at Shea. A couple of the pits expand below the orifice and take on the classic bell-shape of storage pits known from the villagers of the Missouri River Valley. Furthermore, many of the pit features have an internal stratigraphy with distinguishable layers of sediment, indicating that they were infilled over some time period. In other words, there was a duration to their formation. And this re-use occurred only after these pits, originally created to store food, were emptied of their storage.

The excavations across the exterior or main ditch also told a story about the site. While the exterior ditch today is about three meters wide and a meter deep, excavation across the ditch showed that it was originally about 1.5 meters deep (~5′). If there was a wooden palisade interior to this, the combination of ditch and palisade would have formed a considerable defensive barrier to any external threat, especially in the days before horses and firearms. Also, on the immediate interior of the external ditch is a layer of very light-colored sand, obviously from deeper layers in the natural deposit. This light-colored sand is present above the darker colored topsoil. This must have been created by the digging of the defensive ditch, which brought up light-yellow sands from several feet below the surface that were tossed up to the interior and over the top of the darker colored near-surface soils, creating a ridge interior to the ditch.

One of the most informative features at the Shea site was the second, interior ditch (Figure 40). This ditch must have been used as a dump for some time during the occupation since it was completely filled with refuse. In fact, about half of all the cultural material from the site came from a two-square meter unit dug into this ditch! Perhaps the most significant aspect of the deposit that filled in the interior ditch is that there were many layers, perhaps as many as 14, although these were often interrupted with dumps of debris, presumably by the site occupants. The more or less uniform horizontal layers we feel were possibly washed in naturally as snow melted, or perhaps by heavy rains. Some of these layers contained no artifacts. Other layers, including some of the irregularly shaped layers, were rich in cultural materials, containing stone artifacts, ceramic fragments and animal bone. We feel the most reasonable interpretation of the deposit is that after the interior ditch was abandoned for the more extensive exterior ditch that encompassed it, the interior ditch became a dump. Over time people at the site discarded debris into it, while at other times sterile or non-cultural sediment ran into it. This might suggest that at times the Shea site was abandoned. Those periods are represented by the sterile deposits. At other times the site was occupied and people tossed kitchen debris into the ditch. This makes sense in terms of our understanding of how some Native people lived on the Plains. During winter their camps were often in lower elevations—wooded or protected areas—while during the warm season upland villages, like the Shea site, were preferred for settlements. And based on the number of lenses in the ditch, it would seem that at least six or seven cycles of occupation and abandonment occurred, maybe as many as twelve. The site may have been used for a decade or more, being abandoned in the winter and re-occupied during spring–summer–fall.

The question of when the Shea site was occupied is a somewhat simpler issue. Six radiocarbon dates, all from secure contexts in the occupation layer, provide a good estimate of the time that people lived at the site. The average radiocarbon age for the site is 421.8 ± 25.6 years ago. When these dates are calibrated, they indicate an occupation around AD 1450 (Michlovic and Schneider 1993:124). This is about 300 years before European explorers passed through North Dakota. This age would place Shea at the time of the western expansion of Oneota (Henning 2005:172-174), and during the Northeastern Plains Village middle period (1300-1600) as defined by Toom (2004:287).

We get a glimpse of the life-ways of the Shea site people from the foods they ate, and evidence for this comes from plant and animal remains found at the site. Plant fragments were found in several features using simple flotation. Most of the features at the Shea site produced a sample of mostly burned seeds and other durable plant fragments. Over a dozen different species of plants were identified. Ash and aspen charcoal were present. Also found were remains of various usable plants; some possibly medicinal, others used as foods. These include swamp honeysuckle, burdock, wood sorrel, dock, cinquefoil, nettle, marsh elder, goosefoot, vetch, pulse, wild cherry, and most importantly, maize. It seems clear that the people at the Shea site made use of a large variety of plants, and the ones actually found at Shea probably represent only a fraction of the actual variety of plants regularly in use. Most of these species are wild, although both goosefoot (Chenopodium) and marsh elder (Iva) were sometimes domesticated by ancient American Indians.

The people here certainly domesticated maize. By the fifteenth century maize and other domesticates, such as squash and beans, were being used by North American peoples. The Shea site was one of the earliest discoveries of maize being used in eastern North Dakota, although today evidence of maize use extends into Manitoba north of Winnipeg. In any case, the Shea people were at least part-time farmers. We know this because maize was found in different parts of the site, indicating it was not a rarity. Also important is that both kernel and cob fragments were found. Normally, we expect that shelled corn was traded, since cobs would have been awkward to transport. If the Shea farmers were anything like the Historic Period village farmers of the Missouri Valley, they would undoubtedly have had the gardens and fields in the floodplain of the Maple

River below the site. As we mentioned previously, the prairie sod was difficult to break up without machinery. The wooded lowlands, on the other hand, had moist soils and trees, which could be cut down and burned after they dried. The ash-fertilized topsoil could then be mounded up and planted with the corn and any other plants they wished to grow.

The most common animal remains found at this site were bison. Over 150 identifiable bones from bison were recovered, although many more that were probably bison could not be positively classified. While some of these may have been elk, no clearly identifiable elk were found at the site. If the bison bone that could be identified were matched to different portions of a bison body, it would have taken at least 13 animals to create the sample that was found. Other animal bones that we may be certain were present include dog, beaver, skunk, rabbit, weasel, a few bird and fish bones, and various river mussels.

Clearly bison were a very important food for the Shea people. This corresponds well with the historical records that suggest Plains cultures were focused on bison hunting. Most of the bison bones are from mature animals, with few bones from juveniles or very old animals. The Shea hunters seem to have been targeting healthy adults. Mass drives where large numbers of animals are stampeded was probably not the preferred hunting method here. If that were the case a better cross-section of the herd would be represented in our sample of bison bone. Hunters may have scouted out local bison herds and stalked the animals individually or in small groups, with the hunters taking what they needed.

We should be careful not to underestimate the importance of other animal foods as well. Bison bones are large with thick cortex and they preserve well in archaeological deposits. Smaller animal bones are more likely to be totally destroyed by scavengers, including dogs, which were present at Shea. In any case, the Shea faunal collection indicates the hunting and trapping of a variety of animals from the local environment.

The artifacts from the site consist of bone tools, stone tools, flaking debris from tool making, and pottery fragments. The bone tool collection includes several worked bison scapulae probably used as hoes for gardening. There were also bone awls, bone fleshers (for removing flesh from the interior of hides), and a few bone tools for flaking. One fragment of a bone bracelet and a single bone bead were also recovered.

About 80 projectile points or point fragments were found, the vast majority being simple triangular shapes small enough to have been used as points for arrows. More than two dozen scraping tools were present in the excavated sample. These were used for hide preparation. There were

Figure 41. Large fragment of a Sandy Lake pot from the Shea site.

Figure 42. Northeastern Plains Village decorated potsherds from Shea.

also stone tools with a roughly ovate shape most likely used as cutting tools, perhaps functioning mostly as knives. Some of the stone artifacts were polyhedral cores. Pieces struck from these cores would have been fashioned into tools. Finally, there were numerous expedient tools, that is, amorphous flakes with no patterned shape. These were mostly lightly worked on one edge, possibly to blunt it so the opposite, sharp edge of the flake could be used for cutting.

A few thousand pieces of flaking debris left over from making stone tools were recovered. Different types of raw material were found, including a couple flakes of obsidian, or volcanic glass, from a source somewhere in the Rocky Mountains. A few fragments of catlinite, or red pipestone, from the Pipestone Quarry in southwest Minnesota were also found. One of the pieces may have been a broken fragment of a large bead. Another bead was made of rolled copper, most likely from the Lake Superior region. Knife River flint represents over thirty percent of the lithic debris at the Shea site. A type of quartzite, Tongue River silica, may have been imported from South Dakota, although there are small amounts of this raw material found in the local glacial till deposits of eastern North Dakota. It comprises about a quarter of the lithic debris sample. The most common of the local raw stone materials is Swan River chert. This is fairly common in local till deposits and may have been the most easily obtainable stone-working rock. Ease of acquisition was, unfortunately, offset by the fact that Swan River chert is very difficult to work into tools. Archaeologists who have experimented with knapping Swan River chert say that it is easier to work when heated in a fire, although heating it too much wrecks the potential for tool making.

Possibly the most significant artifact type is pottery. Approximately 5,200 pottery sherds represent about 80 vessels. Some of the pottery was tempered with grit (sand or crushed rock), while the rest was tempered with crushed clam shell or both shell and grit. Many of the sherds were relatively large and could be matched to other sherds to give us a good idea of the size and shape of the vessels. For the most part they were not very large and would have held less than a gallon of liquid, although at least a couple were larger than that. Black residues on some of the vessel interiors indicate they were certainly used for cooking. At least one of the pots had small loop handles on the sides.

The pottery has been assigned to two major types or groupings of pottery recognized by archaeologists (Figures 41 and Figure 42). One type is Sandy Lake. There are just over 40 vessels identified as belonging to this type. The other major pottery type is Northeastern Plains Village

Figure 43. View of the Maple River from the Sprunk site.

pottery. About 33 of the vessels belong to the Northeastern Plains Village type. There is a third type of pottery at Shea, a minor type represented by only four vessels. These are classified as Oneota. Obviously, the people at the Shea site had communication with the Oneota peoples, perhaps involving trade, intermarriage, or some less-intensive contacts of a more irregular nature.

The Shea site is a very important archaeological property on the Northeastern Plains. It is well-dated, provides important insights into the life-way of regional populations in the fifteenth century, and illustrates the variety of cultural influences present in this part of the Plains in later prehistoric times. For these reasons, and because of the intact nature of the archaeological deposit, the Shea site was placed on the National Register of Historic Places in 1996.

Sprunk Site

Sprunk (32CS4478) is a companion to the Shea site. The site is about three miles southwest of Shea and, like its sister site, is located on a bluff top overlooking the Maple River (Michlovic, Holley, and Dalan 2019). Two mounds are visible from the field below on the crest of the valley upland. These burial structures are about 75 meters apart and were part of a pasture that had not been plowed. About 10 meters beyond one of the

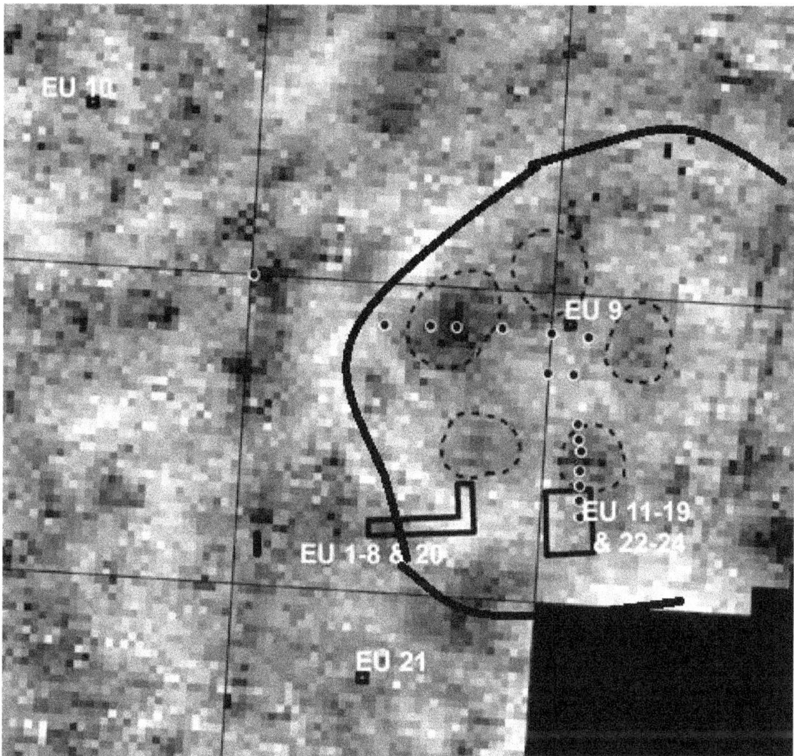

Figure 44. Geophysical depiction of house-sized anomalies detected by electrical resistance survey at the Sprunk site. The dark circular line indicates the center of the ditch; dotted circles are presumed structures.

mounds is the Sprunk site ditch. The interior area of the ditch is 40 meters in diameter, defining a hamlet-sized settlement similar, but somewhat smaller than Shea.

The Sprunk site is important for several reasons. Like other ditched settlements in the Sheyenne Bend region, Sprunk is in an upland setting with a panoramic view overlooking a wooded floodplain below (Figure 43). It is relatively undisturbed, and two seasons of excavations impacted less than 3% of the site. Unfortunately, the small area of less than 30m^2 excavated does not count the destructive activity of rodents like ground squirrels and gophers, nor does it account for the potential erosion from the flood pool of the Maple Dam, which periodically floods the valley floor below. Nevertheless, the Sprunk site's intact archaeological deposit, its similarity in location, content, features, and chronology to the Shea site, gives archaeologists a much more rounded picture of fifteenth

Figure 45. Projectile points from Sprunk.

century life in this portion of the Northeastern Plains. Finally, like the Shea site, Sprunk was placed on the National Register of Historic Places in 2007 because of its cultural and historical significance.

The excavations recovered stone tools and flaking debris from flint knapping, numerous pottery fragments, animal bone, shell, and plant fragments. Two radiocarbon dates on charcoal provide an approximate age of 1400–1500. We suggest an average calibrated date of AD 1470 here. This date matches the known age of the ceramic styles from the site, and is close to the set of dates from the Shea site.

All of the artifacts, ecofacts and features from Sprunk were found either in shallow soil levels, mostly in the lower A- and upper B-horizons, or from the ditch that surrounds the site. The site matrix interior to the ditch contained cultural materials in shallow levels (15-30 cm below surface); however, the ditch deposit contained artifacts to a meter below the present surface.

The obvious construction activity identified at the Sprunk site is the encircling ditch. There is also a single post remnant from one of the excavation units. This post was found in the vicinity of a geophysical anomaly. It was a wood (charcoal) post base placed in a roughly square hole, which was refilled after the post was put in place. This may be a support for a structure, unfortunately no other structural features were found associated with this post. There are other indicators of structures at Sprunk, and these were identified using geophysical methods, in particular electrical resistivity and magnetometry. This work, by R.A. Dalan, resulted in the discovery of five circular anomalies within the ditched area of the site. Each of these had a diameter of about five meters. We interpret these as signatures of small, circular structures. If each of these housed a small extended family, they may represent domiciles for a total of 30 or 40 people (Figure 44).

Figure 46. Sandy Lake vessel rim from Sprunk.

Figure 47. Northeastern Plains Village pottery from the Sprunk site. Fragmentary vessel above shows Oneota decorative motifs.

The artifacts from Sprunk consist of lithic, bone, and ceramic items. The lithic debris amounted to over 600 pieces. Based on the actual implements and the debris from tool making it seems that some core reduction was completed, but probably not intensive core reduction. Possibly early and middle stages of tool making are represented by the sample, although Sprunk was not any sort of special purpose stone reduction station. There were 40 actual implements found including scrapers, general purpose bifaces, and projectile points. As mentioned previously, scrapers were needed for hide preparation so they could be used for clothing or for tipi covers. About two dozen projectile points are variable and may represent more than projectile tips. One with an asymmetrical blade is probably a hafted knife. Some are notched at the base for hafting, and others are simple, very thin triangular forms (Figure 45). The point assemblage is typical of the Late Prehistoric Period on the Northern Plains. The point styles include mostly Eastern triangular forms, along with one Plains Side-Notched point, two Prairie Side-Notched, and several anomalous, heavily re-worked notched points.

The varied tool assemblage reflects on a range of activities conducted at the site. Many of the implements are broken, which is predictable at a settlement of any type, since the tools archaeologists find are normally the broken or dulled implements that were discarded when a living site was abandoned. The lithic debris sample is somewhat unusual for a regional site insofar as Knife River flint is preponderant, representing over 60% of the lithic debris sample. Locally available Swan River chert is only about 15% of the total sample. Compared to Shea, Knife River flint is better represented and Swan River chert is less common.

About 1,500 pottery sherds were found in the Sprunk cultural material sample. The collection of potsherds represents at least 26 vessels, all of which are identified as jars (globular, wide-mouth container). The ceramic collection was divided between shell and grit tempered sherds, although shell is slightly more common in frequency and weights. Most of the sherds were cordmarked on the exterior, a few were stamped and others, smoothed. The shell tempered pottery with cordmarked surfaces is Sandy Lake. The grit tempered sherds with smooth surfaces are Northeastern Plains Village ceramics. Decoration on the latter pottery includes parallel linear incising or trailing, with a few examples of chevrons, hachure, crisscrossing, and zoomorphs (fragmentary thunderbird/hawk). A few sherds contain small punctates. Of the total vessel count, 11 are identified as Sandy Lake, 14 as Northeastern Plains Village ware, and one as Oneota (Figures 46 and Figure 47).

These are pretty much the very same ceramic types found at the Shea site. The two major ceramic wares might be taken as a reflection of two occupations at the site; however, in one level of the ditch deposit a large Sandy Lake vessel fragment was found next to a Northeastern Plains Village vessel. There is no stratigraphic evidence from any part of the site to counter the evidence from the ditch that the ceramic wares at the site were in simultaneous use. The vessels are mostly small. Orifice diameters range from 11-24 cm. The lack of larger vessels here may reflect the limited nature of the activities that occurred at this site. Along with the lithic data indicating only some of the stages of stone reduction, this ceramic data may reflect seasonal use interspersed with periods of abandonment.

Plant remains were naturally more limited, although dozens of maize kernel and cob fragments were found in flotation samples. Also, evidence for tobacco use in eastern North Dakota was present. Amaranth and *Chenopodium* in the samples may reflect some of the wild foods used by the people, and the single morning glory seed, perhaps intrusive, may also reflect the use of this hallucinogen. Some wood charcoal was identified as birch. This tree is native to the Minnesota woodlands and is not expected on the Maple River. It may have been transported from an eastern source. Overall, the evidence in flotation samples make it clear that maize was consistently used at the Sprunk site.

Animal bones were common in the deposit, and consist largely of bison. At Sprunk, most bison body parts are present, including vertebrae and skull fragments. This suggests a nearby kill or kills, since these types of bones are not commonly carried far from the kill site. Other identified animal remains are only a fraction of the number of bison, but indicate the use of white-tailed deer, badger, beaver, otter, and canids. Although the canid bones may be wolf/coyote or domestic dogs, the common use of domestic dogs in the Historic Period suggests these remains at Sprunk are dogs. Some fish were present, and river mussels were unusually common. Somewhat unusual for regional sites, there were a large number of waterfowl present, including Common Mallard, Northern Shoveler, and Wood Duck.

The people at the Sprunk site were hunting, fowling, using river resources, gathering wild plants, and evidently practicing routine gardening. It was a life-way that made use of the wide range of resources present on the prairie, in the river below the site, and in the pothole lakes and ponds nearby to the west of the settlement.

Figure 48. View of the Sheyenne Valley below the Peterson site.

One of the important implications of the finds made at the Shea and Sprunk sites is the relationship of Sandy Lake ceramics to populations that lived contemporaneously in the central Minnesota lake and forest country from the Late Prehistoric Period and into the early part of the Historic Period. Sandy Lake ceramics were first described by Cooper and Johnson (1964) as a Late Woodland pottery style of that region, and later, it was reported as present in archaeological deposits with French trade items in the Mille Lacs area of central Minnesota. When early French explorers penetrated into this part of Minnesota, they described the area as the territory of various Dakota groups, including the Mdewakanton. The association of French trade goods with Sandy Lake pottery at archaeological sites in the homeland of Dakota peoples made an association of Sandy Lake pottery with the Dakota people an easy inference, and many archaeologists concluded that Sandy Lake was the ceramic production of the Dakota.

At the Shea, Sprunk, and other sites in the Maple and Sheyenne Bend region, the Sandy Lake pottery most likely also represents the ceramic tradition of the same or closely related people. Our inference is that in the Late Prehistoric Period the Dakota or Lakota were active in the Sheyenne Bend, and that they were practicing the dual economic pursuits of bison hunting and river-bottom gardening, and living seasonally in small, fortified settlements, not as nomadic hunters, but as semi-sedentary farmers, hunters and gatherers. This stands in contrast to the traditional historical reconstructions of Dakota and Lakota movements in the very early Historic Period. This standard historical view sees the Dakota and

Figure 49. Aerial view of the Peterson site, Google Earth.

their western relatives, the Teton (Lakota) as recent migrants from Minnesota onto the Great Plains, where they lived as nomadic bison hunters. A revision to this view has been argued for several decades (Michlovic 1985); however, historians continue to neglect the archaeological record, neither reporting these finds, or finding them inadequate. In any case, from our point of view, the presence of some groups of Dakota on the Northeastern Plains in the Late Prehistoric Period is highly likely, probably extending back at least to the thirteenth century, a time when Sandy Lake pottery is abundantly attested just east of the Sheyenne Bend on the Red River.

Other Sites in the Maple River Valley

We have already reviewed one Terminal Woodland site found on the floodplain of the Maple. However, most of the sites in the Maple Valley have Late Prehistoric material. From the finds made in test excavations it is safe to conclude that the ones in near-surface deposits may be characterized as Northeastern Plains Village sites, and they include ceramics that resemble the collections from Sprunk and Shea, such as smooth and cordmarked, grit tempered, thin-walled pottery (Stubbs et.al. 2001). One of the more productive of the sites that was tested is situated in the floodplain field directly below (east) of the Sprunk site. The deposits are relatively deep and extend to a depth of over 60 cm below the surface. The artifact assemblage from the site is similar to the Sprunk collection in the presence of diagnostic Northeastern Plains Village ceramics, and generally comparable lithic materials as well. It is very possible that the two sites are related, and that the floodplain site is the lowland location that the Sprunk people occupied during the winter months when weather conditions on a high, exposed blufftop would be most uncomfortable. The surprisingly deep burial of these Late Prehistoric materials is no doubt a product of heavy sediment dumping during river floods and subsequent soil disturbances moving artifacts through the soil profile.

Peterson Site

During the summer of 1974 two University of North Dakota archaeologists, Fred Schnieder and Rain Vehik, were looking for archaeological sites in the Sheyenne Valley. After camping one night at Little Yellowstone Park on the far northwest side of the Sheyenne Bend region, the two decided in the morning to climb the steep slopes above the river to get a look at the valley from the top of the rim (Figure 48). The very steep climb up the west side of the valley wall paid off. On the valley rim they found two small ditched settlements from the prehistoric period. One, the Peterson site (32RM401) and the other the Nelson site (32RM402). In 1977 Schneider presented a lecture on these and other similar sites at the Plains Conference, an annual meeting of anthropologists and archaeologists. It seemed then that Peterson must be part of some previously undefined culture. Schneider called for more study of these sites. By 2010 we had already worked at several other sites that were regarded as part of the same culture as Peterson: Shea and Sprunk. If the Lucas site is included as a small village, Peterson would be the fourth excavated site in the catalog of such sites in the Sheyenne Bend region. The archaeological testing that was eventually carried out at the Peterson site (Michlovic 2008b) was limited in extent and purpose. The primary goal was to affiliate the site with others of a similar surface configuration in the Sheyenne Bend region and to determine as far as possible the extent of the cultural deposits.

The Peterson site is a small fortified domestic settlement with a typical range of debris making up the archaeological deposit. The area enclosed by the ditch is about the same as the Sprunk site (Figure 49). There were small ceramic sherds, stone tool making debris, used and broken stone tools, shattered animal bone and a few fragments of fire cracked rock. Several small, triangular projectile points were found. These are similar to the same type of artifacts found at the Shea and Sprunk sites. In the lithic collection there are many flake fragments and pieces of shatter-like debris. These have neither striking platforms nor ventral/dorsal differentiation. This means that these flakes were not carefully planned removals from the original core, which happens as stone-knappers are in the middle and late stages of stone tool making. This type of flake assemblage is typically created in early phases of stone tool making. Also, there are many cores and thick, chunky fragments for a collection of this size which may indicate cobble testing or other early phase stone reduction activities. Reinforcing the positive indicators of early phase stone tool preparation, pressure flakes were not found in the collection. This negative finding suggests that edge finishing and other late phase lithic production activities were not conducted at the Peterson site, although we offer this with the caveat that only limited testing was done here.

The ceramic collection may represent as many as 14 different vessels, but this estimate is based on a few sherds of very small size. The size of the sherds may indicate heavy traffic and trampling of the broken vessels. The field has not been plowed so it is unlikely that any recent human activity is responsible for the small sherd size. No ceramic rims or decorated pottery fragments were recovered from the site. This is especially unfortunate because decorated pottery fragments and the rim sections of vessels often display culturally sensitive features or decorations that allow archaeologists to place them in a particular time frame, and to affiliate the makers of the pottery with similarly decorated ceramics in the same general region.

Peterson is one of the sites in the Sheyenne Bend classified as belonging to the Shea phase. The characteristics of this archaeological phase will be reviewed below. We believe that this small, ditched hamlet size community on the uplands above the Sheyenne River is another example of the settlements of this phase. As with other Shea phase sites, the artifact assemblage contains Sandy Lake (shell tempered, cord roughened) and Northeastern Plains (grit tempered, and primarily stamped or plain surfaced) ceramic wares, the settlement is encircled by a defensive ditch, and there are no obvious pit features visible on the surface. Peterson does not display all of the features of Shea phase sites, but the setting, the ditch, lack of other surface features, and the technology of the people who lived here do match that of Sprunk and Shea.

Associated with the Peterson settlement are an eagle trapping pit to the east of the ditch (32RM164), and a low, circular mound, undoubtedly a cemetery, to the southeast of the site (32RM165). The eagle trapping pit is situated on a point of the bluff top from which there is a very steep decline into the Sheyenne trench. Elgin Crows Breast (Mandan–Hidatsa–Arikara Nation), consulted with archaeologists prior to excavation and suggested that the pit was clearly made for this purpose, and that its location would take advantage of the updrafts rising against the steep valley sides that eagles would use when they circled over the prairie. At his request, no work was done in or near the eagle trapping pit. The proximity of the pit to the Peterson occupation may indicate that it was not used at the same time the site was occupied, since eagle trapping might be compromised by a nearby settlement. While it is typical of fortified sites in the region to have burial mounds nearby, Peterson is the only known site of this phase to be associated with an eagle trapping pit.

The mound near the Peterson site is almost certainly a cemetery, but we cannot be sure whether or not this was used for the people who lived at Peterson or others who buried their dead here prior to or after the settlement was used. The mound is about 25 meters in diameter and not more than a meter in height. We assume that as with other mounds on the Northeastern Plains this one dates to the later portion of the prehistoric period. The proximity of the mound to the Peterson site, and the nearby Nelson site, make it very likely that the mound was in fact used by the people who lived in these settlements.

There is little that can be said about the nearby ditched settlement, the Nelson site. It is located about ¼ mile to the south of Peterson. Access to this site was denied by the owner and no direct links between the two sites could be established. The Nelson site is about the same size as Peterson and is surrounded by an irregular fortification ditch, although the ditch at Nelson is somewhat deeper. In common with other Shea-like sites, this one also overlooks the river valley below, and some short distance west of the site is a low, circular mound. It is very similar to the one near the Peterson site. Exactly why two such settlements and possibly associated mounds are located so close together is not known, and the question will probably only be answered when additional excavations can be carried out at both sites.

The End of the Prehistoric Period

There are a number of Historic Period archaeological sites in the Sheyenne Bend region, and most of these are from the Euro-American settlement and from the earlier portion of the twentieth century. For instance, in the Maple River portion of the Bend area, there are several older farms with remaining buildings that are regarded as historic in age. In terms of the National Register of Historic Places, "older" means a site that is more than fifty years old. Our concern here is not with these relatively recent sites and structures, nor is it with other, and older Euro-American sites, even though some of these have attracted a great deal of attention. One example is Camp Hayes, mentioned earlier. Another example, near the modern town of Fort Ransom, are the remains of old Fort Ransom, the military installation built in the aftermath of the US–Dakota war of 1862. It was constructed in 1867 to protect travelers on their way west,

Figure 50. The Biesterfeldt site, aerial view. The lower part of the picture shows the abandoned river meander. Dark circles are lodge depressions. The remnants of the fortification ditch are on the left and right of lodges. Note how plowing has obliterated the southern half of the site.

but was shortly thereafter abandoned and taken down in 1872. It is now a protected North Dakota heritage site and may be visited and toured, with on-site interpretation to aid the visitor. Many other sites from the Historic Period may be found in the Sheyenne Bend; however, our focus is on the Native American past in the region, and for this reason we now attend to one of the most important archaeological sites in eastern North Dakota.

Biesterfeldt Site

Of all the archaeological sites in the Bend region, none is more imposing, both in its physical appearance and its place in the archaeological literature, than the Biesterfeldt site. It has been studied and remarked upon for over 100 years. The site is mentioned in multiple early histories by explorers who heard about it, but never visited it. We believe that the site represents the continuation of cultural processes that developed in the prehistoric period and that, ultimately, were instrumental in the archaeological expression we find at this site.

Biesterfeldt (32RM1) is on the east side of the southern extremity of the Bend and it sits about 100 meters east of the present course of the Sheyenne River (Figure 50). It was named after a farmer and landowner,

Louis Biesterfeld (a T was later added to the end of this name). It is sometimes referred to as the Cheyenne–Sheyenne site. This is because it is almost universally believed to have been an occupation of the Cheyenne people when they lived in eastern North Dakota. The Sheyenne River takes its name from these same people. The site is mentioned in the accounts of David Thompson in 1799 and Alexander Henry in 1801 as a village of the Cheyenne that was destroyed by the Ojibwa sometime in the eighteenth century. A rough dating of the Biesterfeldt would be from sometime between about 1720–1780 (Wood 1971).

Biesterfeldt sits on an elevated prominence above an abandoned Sheyenne River meander that abuts the site to the north. To the south is level land while gentle slopes descend from the site to the east and west. Today, farm fields border the site to the east and south, while gallery woodlands along the Sheyenne River are west of the site. The meander scar on the north describes a rough semi-circle, and during wet years the meander trench itself may be filled with water. The area within the meander is filled with trees, brush and lush grass.

The site is about 100 x 170 meters in extent, covering around four acres. Part of it has been heavily disturbed, mostly the southern half where plowing has obliterated surface features. The northern half of the site is mostly undisturbed and features a fortification ditch and numerous lodge depressions. These depressions are similar to those found in the earth-lodge villages of the Mandan, Hidatsa, and Arikara along the Missouri River in the Dakotas. Although lodge depressions and the encircling ditch are not visible today in the southern portion of the site, there are multiple reports from earlier in the twentieth and nineteenth century of the site in essentially undisturbed condition. Before being disturbed by farming, there were over 60 lodge depressions at the site. At an estimated 10 or more occupants per lodge, the population of Biesterfeldt may have been 600 or more.

There are maps of the site dating to the late nineteenth century, and an 1814 map of the Lewis and Clark expedition even illustrates an "old village" on the eastern side of the Sheyenne River bend, where Biesterfeldt sits today (Figure 51). When T.H. Lewis was conducting the Northwestern Archaeological Survey in 1890, he visited Biesterfeldt and noted 65 earth-lodge depressions within the perimeter of the defensive ditch, and many more houses outside the ditch. O.G. Libby and A.B. Stout prepared a good map of the site for the State Historical Society of North Dakota in 1908, showing the outlines of all earth lodges prior to plowing (Wood 1971).

Figure 51. The "Old Village" recorded on the 1814 map of the Lewis and Clark expedition. Note the name of the river is spelled "Cayenne." Available at http://hdl.loc.gov/loc.gmd/g4126s.ct000028, Library of Congress.

Figure 52. Pottery vessel rims from Biesterfeldt, above. Late Woodland Blackduck and Sandy Lake pottery similar to Minnesota ceramic wares are below. Biesterfeldt vessels are unlike the Minnesota ones, making it unlikely the people at Biesterfeldt left Minnesota only shortly before settling in the Sheyenne Bend.

In 1938, W.D. Strong, then of Columbia University, came to study Biesterfeldt. Strong had a few years prior worked in Nebraska where he pioneered an archaeological methodology known as the "Direct Historical Approach." For Strong, the best way of understanding the prehistory of a region was to work backward through time from the known, Historic Period, to the most recent portion of prehistoric times, then to continue back in time from the better known to the less well known. In this way a sequence of connected cultures and their development could be traced with confidence to the distant past from the well-known recent period.

By the time Strong excavated Biesterfeldt it was generally understood that the Cheyenne people had migrated to the Great Plains from the Minnesota lake-forest country. The popular reconstruction of this migration was featured in the authoritative work of Cheyenne culture and history by George Grinnell (1918). This was based on historical accounts of the Cheyenne having once lived in Minnesota, where they were farmers, eventually moving up the Minnesota River to the vicinity of Lake Traverse, and from there to the northwest where they established their village on the Sheyenne River. This notion of a Minnesota origin for the Cheyenne was reinforced by the fact that their language is Algonquian, related to other Great Lakes region peoples such as the Ojibwa and Cree, and different from the Siouan speaking Dakota and Assiniboine. Biesterfeldt, then, was regarded by Strong and most other scholars as a Cheyenne farming village of the middle part of the eighteenth century, settled just after these people left their Minnesota homeland for the Plains where they would eventually become bison hunting nomads.

Since Biesterfeldt had been known as a settlement of the Cheyenne from the eighteenth century, just after the end of the prehistoric period, Strong felt it would be a perfect case study for his "Direct Historical Approach." He excavated all or parts of ten structures visible as surface depressions. These lodges were round in shape and were dug into the ground to a depth of two or three feet. Lodges had a central hearth, and the floors of some were littered with the charred logs and beams that had formed the walls and roofing. Numerous large cache pits were also found between houses. Broken pieces of pottery were found throughout the deposit, along with stone tools and some metal artifacts as well (Strong 1940). Strong never published a full report on the work he did at the site, but W.R. Wood (1971) analyzed Strong's collection and notes from the site and published a full monograph on Biesterfeldt through the Smithsonian Institution.

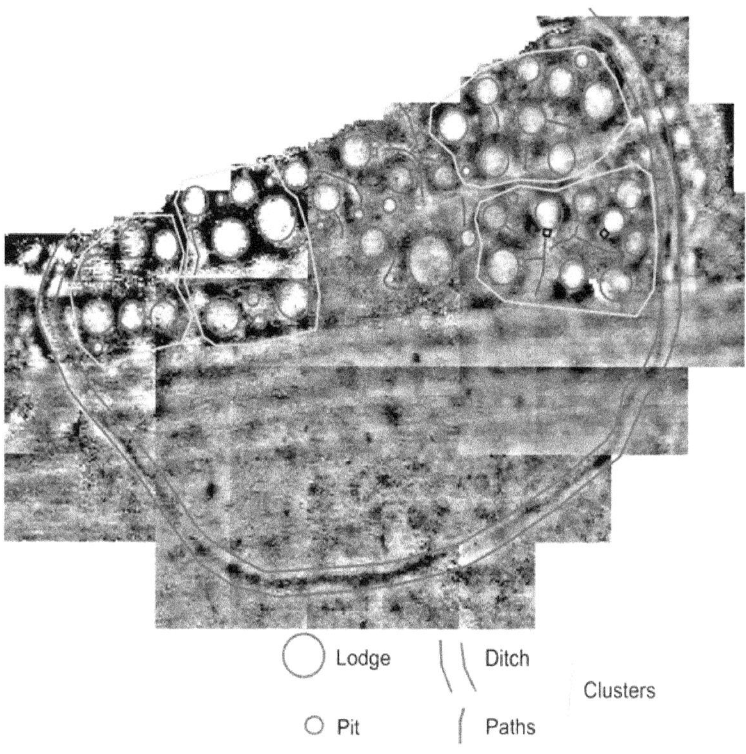

Figure 53. Resistivity map of Biesterfeldt with hypothesized house clusters outlined. Map by R.A. Dalan, neighborhood outlines by C. Harris.

There are serious problems with the interpretation of Biesterfeldt as a settlement of the Cheyenne as they moved out of the Minnesota forests. First, the site does not look at all like a settlement of people who lived in the early Protohistoric Period in Minnesota. In fact, the lodge depressions, the encircling ditch, and the layout of the site all look exactly like the type of settlements found along the Missouri River in North and South Dakota. Second, the pottery from the site was unlike the types of pottery used in Late Prehistoric and Historic Periods in Minnesota. Instead, the ceramics are somewhat similar to those found at Arikara sites in South Dakota (Figure 52). These issues were touched on in Wood's monograph. Wood, after careful examination of the artifact collection, concluded that archaeologically, the Biesterfeldt site was most closely affiliated with the cultures of the Missouri Valley, and he classified it as a part of the Coalescent Tradition of the central Dakotas. This placed the site in the same category as the Mandan, Hidatsa and Arikara sites. This was a rather troubling move from the point of view that saw Biesterfeldt as the settlement of a people who had only recently left Minnesota.

In 2005 the Biesterfeldt property was purchased by the *Archaeological Conservancy*. Shortly after this the National Park Service Midwest Archaeological Center in Lincoln made the decision to pursue National Landmark status for Biesterfeldt. The site had previously been placed on the National Register of Historic Places as a location important in the history of the Cheyenne people. Its significance was judged to be worthy of even greater recognition that would be bestowed by National Landmark status, in part because of Wood's re-analysis of the site which highlighted its place in northern Plains culture and history. In 2007 the Midwest Archaeological Center's Vergil Noble requested additional study of the site in order to provide the up-to-date descriptive material that would be needed for a National Landmark nomination. This led to two additional seasons of work at Biesterfeldt in 2007–2008. This work involved standard archaeological excavations and remote sensing as part of a National Park Service Workshop (Holley, Michlovic, and Dalan 2011).

The Park Service's remote sensing, or geophysical study at the site included a varied set of procedures including magnetometry, electrical resistance, downhole magnetic susceptibility, electromagnetic induction, along with several other methods of subsurface detection. An updated topographic map of the site was created which involved geo-referencing current findings with previously compiled maps. Minor errors in previous maps of lodge locations were reconciled with their actual position as determined by a total station survey. Following the remote sensing procedures archaeological excavations were completed in targeted areas to answer certain questions about the site that were deemed worth pursuing in light of the findings of the remote sensing surveys.

The findings of remote sensing were dramatic. The entire circuit of the fortification ditch was recorded including that portion of the ditch that had been obliterated by plowing. In the southern, plowed portion of the site magnetometry and down-hole magnetic susceptibility showed the location of features under the ground and invisible on the surface today. Two of these were later excavated and shown to be vitally important to understanding the remaining potential of the site as well as helping in the interpretation of the occupation. The resistance survey was also useful for revealing pathways within the village, that is, the actual routes taken by people walking through and between the lodges. The same survey also showed the orientation of the lodges in terms of their entryways. When

Figure 54. Storage pit at Biesterfeldt. The subtle layers in the fill mark the passage of time as the pit filled in.

these results were mapped, it seemed clear that the houses at Biesterfeldt were arranged into something like neighborhoods, with five or six lodges clustered together, sometimes with doorways facing each other in a somewhat circular arrangement. In the unplowed northern portion of the site there may have been five of these clusters. The southern, plowed portion may have contained several more (Figure 53).

This new information about the site, along with what was known previously about the site layout, helps us to understand something more regarding what the organization of the site might have been. We know from Strong's excavations and from early maps of the site that there was a large structure in the north central portion of the site. This was known as house 16. The circular depression from this house is still visible at the site today. Using our knowledge of the village layouts at the Historic Period Missouri River settlements we assume that house 16 was home to an important family at Biesterfeldt. Near this structure was a cache pit so large it was sometimes mapped as another house. House 16 faces a rather large open area or plaza. In many Plains Village sites such a plaza would have been used for major ceremonies and group activities or community meetings.

Excavations served to ground-truth the findings of the remote sensing and also answered one or two questions raised by Strong's previous work. Two areas of digging were placed in the disturbed, or plowed, southern portion of the site. Here magnetometry and downhole magnetic susceptibility had indicated two potential cultural signatures preserved below the zone of soil disturbed by plowing. Upon excavation, one of these areas yielded a large hearth, circular in shape, and probably in the center of a lodge no longer visible from the ground surface. In the second of these areas a jet-black floor was found at a depth of 30 cm with charred log fragments later identified as elm. There was also a cluster of substantial cobbles adjacent to a pit that extended about 15 cm deeper into the ground. The log fragments were very likely the rafters of the lodge given their modest diameter of about two inches. The black soil was undoubtedly the organically enriched floor of a house that had been in use for some time period, perhaps several years.

On the northern rim of the site overlooking the now-abandoned meander scar of the river another excavation was completed, this one to a depth of about 1.3 meters, or four feet. The feature was just off the top rim of the Biesterfeldt landform on slightly sloping ground. This was a large cone-shaped pit with a diameter of one meter at the top (Figure 54). This was undoubtedly dug originally as a storage pit by the people who lived here, and then re-used as a refuse pit after it was emptied of its contents. There were not many finds in this pit, although some artifacts were found throughout the deposit. Bones from fish, bird, dog, turtle, and bison were recovered. Only a few ceramic sherds and pieces of lithic debris were found, but there was a substantial quantity of cracked rock. The pit profile showed about ten layers suggesting that the infilling occurred over some period of time. Some of this was likely intentional disposal by the people who lived at the site, some from natural sedimentation, perhaps during spring snow melts and summer rain storms. It would seem clear from the stratigraphy of the pit that disposal took place into this pit over a period of at least several seasons. Adding to this the time that the pit was used for storage, and we might conclude that a number of years passed in the life-history of this single feature at Biesterfeldt.

Outside of the fortification ditch the remote sensing had indicated some sub-surface anomalies in the soil. Since some early visitors to the site mentioned houses outside of the ditched areas it was thought that maybe these sub-surface anomalies represented lodge structures. Excavations were therefore opened on the east side of the site adjacent to the ditch. No house structures were found, but, instead, there was an inversion of

Figure 55. Stratigraphy on the edge of the ditch, showing original topsoil at bottom, light-colored subsoil from ditch digging above that, and mixed topsoil-subsoil above that from cleaning the ditch. Entire sequence is topped by modern sod.

Figure 56. Portion of the bone pit at Biesterfeldt.

the normal soil profile. Apparently, after the ditch was dug it had partially infilled with surface sediment. The ditch was then re-dug or cleaned out and the infilling surface sediment shoveled out on top of the lighter colored sediment from the bottom of the original ditch that had previously been deposited on the ground-surface. We know from this that the site was used long enough for the ditch to partially infill and require cleaning out (Figure 55). Along with the evidence from the pit feature already described it is apparent that the Biesterfeldt site was occupied probably for a number of years. In this regard it is worth noting also that on the basis of Strong's excavation, W.R. Wood concluded that the houses at Biesterfeldt showed no indication of having been re-built. Since earth lodge houses of this type among the Missouri villagers were normally re-built after about 15 years, we estimate the Biesterfeldt site to have been used for fewer than 15 years, but for perhaps up to about 10.

Excavations were also placed near House 16 in the vicinity of the cache pit exterior to that lodge. An old photograph from the Strong excavation showed a large pile of bone in this location. We re-excavated in the same place and located the bone pile. Only a portion of the bone was recovered, but even from this partial collection we documented the presence of 11 bison, including bulls, cows, one juvenile, and three calves. Such a collection suggests a catastrophic kill in which a large number of animals were killed in a single episode and included animals of both sexes and all ages. Perhaps this bone pile represents a major feast with community-wide significance. This suggestion is reinforced by virtue of the fact that the bone pile was adjacent to the largest structure at the site (Figure 56). This is, incidentally, the only instance of a possible mass kill in the archaeological record of the Sheyenne Bend.

Other excavations outside the ditch produced little in the way of important finds, although in one excavation unit artifacts clearly unrelated to the main occupation were found. These were cordmarked potsherds belonging to a culture pre-dating the Biesterfeldt occupation by a century or more.

In all of the excavations at Biesterfeldt there were small artifacts such as potsherds, stone tools, and even implements made of metal. The pottery that was found consists of earthenware ceramics, some with smoothed exterior surfaces and many others with stamped surfaces resulting from the use of a carved paddle in shaping the jar. These finds, along with those from the Strong excavation show that vessels were globular in shape with incurving shoulders and constricted necks. Pots were decorated with a variety of impressions, sometimes made with trade beads that were occasionally left in the body of the vessel. Sometimes fine lines were incised in the wet clay prior to firing. These decorations are of great importance in calculating the cultural relationship of Biesterfeldt to other sites. The decorations and the shape of the vessels look unlike the pottery from Minnesota and more like the ceramics of the Missouri Valley villages in South Dakota, particularly those of the Arikara (Johnson 2007). There are also some similarities to pottery from earlier periods in the Sheyenne Bend. Stone tools include arrow points, either triangular or notched, hide scrapers, stone knives, hammer stones and mauls, manos and metates for grinding seeds, shaft abraders and even a catlinite elbow pipe found at the site by a local collector. There are bone tools including fleshers and bison scapula hoes. Several iron and brass arrow heads and knife blades were recovered. Microscopic examination of the metal revealed that some of the artifacts were re-worked items probably made by native craftsmen rather than imported as finished tools.

The Biesterfeldt site is unique in eastern North Dakota and is certainly the only site of its kind in the Sheyenne Valley. It is one of the few archaeological sites in the region that can be associated with a known people, in this case the Cheyenne. It is also the only known earth lodge village in eastern North Dakota. Biesterfeldt obviously dates to the eighteenth century. The technology at the site consists of stone, bone and earthenware implements, but there are also artifacts made from iron and brass introduced by Europeans. An Ojibwa elder who David Thompson spoke with in the 1790s claimed that as a younger man he was involved in a raid that destroyed the village of the Cheyenne and drove them to the west. Besides this, a large oak post taken from the site in the early twentieth century was the focus of a dendrochronological study, or a tree ring count. The result of this study dates the tree used for a structure at the site to the early eighteenth century. An occupation of a decade or so between 1720–1780 would seem to best suit evidence for the site's age.

As already mentioned, the site has been regarded as a settlement of the Cheyenne people immediately after their move from the Minnesota lake-forest country. While everyone seems to agree that the site is Cheyenne in cultural affiliation, the nature of the architecture at the site along with the clear evidence of Missouri Valley ceramic types is far more suggestive of a movement of people from the west than from the east. The pottery is similar in many regards to Arikara pottery, and since the Cheyenne in the nineteenth century had a somewhat close relationship with the Arikara we might assume that the site represents a substantial group of Cheyenne who moved east from the Missouri River region to the Sheyenne Bend for reasons we may only guess at. One possibility is that the Cheyenne at this time were eager to expand their trading options with Europeans. Another suggestion that has been made is that the Cheyenne moved here to escape the epidemics diseases that were spreading among the villages of the Missouri Valley during the eighteenth century. Whatever the reason the occupation did not last very long. Biesterfeldt was probably used for only a generation or less.

Chapter 7
Concluding Discussion

The archaeological record of the distant past in the Sheyenne Bend is incomplete and leaves open many questions about what happened over the span of prehistoric time. The admittedly spotty record we have assembled here does allow for a few conclusions. These touch on some important issues for archaeologists, and for anyone else who wants to know about North Dakota's past in particular, or the deep history of the North American Plains generally. We hope some of the inferences we conclude with will give readers a sense of why we think that the prehistory of the Sheyenne Bend is worth knowing and understanding. The native peoples of this region and their ancestors of remote times persisted and adapted to conditions that changed dramatically over hundreds of generations, from the Ice Age through the Altithermal, to the variable conditions of more recent times. It is a story worth knowing—certainly as presented here, an imperfect story with holes, but a foundation for the future.

The Northeastern Plains and the Sheyenne Bend

The Sheyenne Bend region is part of the Northeastern Plains, or the prairie grasslands. Here, annual precipitation is higher than on the Western Plains, and lush, tall grass communities are extensive. While these grasslands were susceptible to fire, they also recovered quickly from the repeated conflagrations and their regeneration was integral to the process of re-invigorating the grassland communities themselves. This environment has been home to innumerable bison, and to a surprising variety of smaller game, as well as a natural pantry of many edible and otherwise useful wild plants. A short distance to the east of these prairies are the forests of Minnesota, and, indeed, the boundary between the woodlands to the east and the grasslands was and still is today a dramatic divide. For much of the prehistoric period the peoples of the forest lands moved into the prairies to hunt bison, and these movements had a clear impact on the archaeological record of the Sheyenne Bend.

The prairie itself, however, was not the focus of human settlement in spite of the resources found there. Most archaeological sites in the Bend are in the forest-fringe along both the Sheyenne and Maple rivers.

Communities of any size, from a small village or hamlet to a temporary camp, were mainly located there. The gallery woodlands along the rivers had wood for fuel, construction, and for manufactured items. Here was water along with the resources in the water; mussels, fish, beaver, and muskrat, for instance. In the woods along these rivers were deer, bear, elk, and occasional bison seeking escape from winter storms. There would also be small game such as rabbit, squirrel, and raccoon; and nuts, fruits, berries, tubers, and greens. Away from the rivers there were occasional camps, smaller occupations of more limited duration. These we believe represent forays into the upland prairie for game, plants like prairie turnips, or simply stops on journeys from one more enduring settlement to another. Also, often on uplands bounding the rivers were the ceremonial sites: mounds, petroglyphs, and other locations of ritual importance. Standing Rock and Bear's Den Hillock are examples recognized in the region to this day.

This prairie has been the focus of archaeological attention since the time of T.H. Lewis' survey in the late nineteenth century. Until recently, however, it has been seen as peripheral to the more dramatic cultural developments along the Missouri River in the central Dakotas, and those of the eastern United States woodlands, where the well-known mound building cultures flourished: Adena, Hopewell, and Mississippian. Waldo Wedel, the Smithsonian archaeologist, saw the Northeastern Plains as an area peripheral to both the high Plains cultures to the west, and the woodland cultures in the east. The anthropologist A.L. Kroeber, based on his understanding of historic Plains peoples as well as on the archaeological record at the time, saw the prairie portion of the Plains as largely a reflection of eastern cultural developments (Kroeber 1939).

The archaeological record for the Northeastern Plains, and certainly of the Bend area itself, has seriously eroded the forcefulness of Wedel and Kroeber's claims. Kroeber's belief, eighty years ago, that farming could only be practiced along the Missouri River in the Dakotas, or up to Big Stone Lake in Minnesota (Kroeber 1939:212), or that, without the horse, the Plains peoples would have had but a "meager stock of culture" (Kroeber 1939:77) is challenged by the archaeological work in the Bend region, where small agricultural hamlets have been documented on both the Maple and the Sheyenne, and where a lengthy sequence of cultures has been uncovered. Besides this the Bend region illustrates the rich ceremonial and ritual life of prehistoric peoples. Kroeber's and Wedel's argument that the people who lived on the prairie were outliers of the eastern woodland cultures has real merit. But we now know that the peoples of this region in the prehistoric period had a long and complicated history, certainly reflecting eastern influences from as early as the beginning of the Archaic, and that they were equally tied to the Plains toward the west, where raw materials and cultural influences penetrated in an easterly direction.

The First People

The earliest peoples of the Bend region seem to have moved into the area from the west, since the diagnostic Paleoindian projectile tips we find throughout the region are similar to those found farther west on the Great Plains. These include the occasional Folsom fluted points reported for the Bend area, and the more common Plano points found in regional private collections and in the State Historical Museum.

To the modern observer, Paleoindian life in the Bend region would have been unrecognizable in some ways. The late glacial environment made the Sheyenne Valley a different landscape than it is today. The ice sheets were still present in southern Canada, and there was an enormous lake to the immediate east; Lake Agassiz. This expanse of water covered the land from just west of Kindred to the vicinity of Barnesville, Minnesota, about 33 miles to the east. The climate would have been cooler than today, and woodlands were probably more common. There was still ice-age megafauna, like mammoth and giant bison.

The single excavated component from the Paleoindian period in the Sheyenne Bend is the oldest cultural level at the Rustad site on the far eastern perimeter of the Bend southwest of Kindred. Here, we estimate from radiocarbon dates an occupation of Plano peoples around 9400 years ago. They were using bison, probably an extinct species of bison called *Bison occidentalis*, and small game as well. This is an important matter, since the later peoples of the Archaic period seem to have continued this type of life, but with a very different style of making their hunting implements. A Plano point style known as Agate Basin is the most common diagnostic from the local Paleoindian Period, although this conclusion is based on meager evidence from surface collections.

Archaic Period

During the subsequent Archaic Period, it is not clear that there is any major change in the adaptation of the people of the Bend region, or indeed, the Great Plains generally. Large game hunting focused on bison continues, and it is documented at several archaeological sites. Bison hunting was the fundamental subsistence adaptation of the people of the Northeastern Plains from the time of the Paleoindian. This is apparent at sites such as Cherokee in northwest Iowa, Granite Falls, in the Minnesota River Valley, at Itasca in northern Minnesota, and of course, at the Rustad site on the Sheyenne River.

The major difference between the earliest portion of the regional Archaic and the Paleoindian seems to be an interruption in the movement of Knife River flint for tool-making from its western North Dakota source area to the east. We feel that the most economical explanation for this are the environmental conditions on the Plains resulting from the episodic aridity of the Middle Holocene climatic maximum, or Altithermal. Knife River flint across the Northeastern Plains seems to often show a pattern of distance frequency decay; meaning that the amount of this high-quality flaking material diminishes in a more or less constant fashion in sites more distant from the source area. This is interpreted by archaeologists to mean that the material is being traded from one group to the next, and at each transfer, less of the material is traded than previously. This down-the-line trade is typical at most regional Sheyenne Bend sites after the Middle Holocene. The very low incidence of Knife River flint at the Rustad site Archaic component almost certainly has to do with an interruption in the transmission of this flint, which would suggest that there were portions of North Dakota east of the Missouri River where human groups were absent during this often warm, and periodically arid Middle Holocene climatic episode.

Another major difference between the Archaic and the Paleoindian in the Bend region is the dramatic change in the styles of projectile points. The reduction in size and the change in the shape of points has been a puzzle to archaeologists. While some have suggested that the appearance of the small, notched Mummy Cave and Logan Creek points, similar to those found at Rustad's Archaic layer, were made to arm atlatl darts, recent finds have shown the atlatl to have been used in the Paleoindian, so atlatl use is probably not the explanation for the appearance of notched and stemmed points in the Archaic. However, the lanceolate and relatively large Paleoindian points do disappear and are replaced by smaller notched points. Points such as these small Early Plains Archaic tips appear at an earlier date in both the Great Basin and in the Eastern United States. Given that there is a continuous pattern of eastern influences into the Northeastern Plains in later times, we believe that the appearance of new, notched points styles is the result of a diffusion of cultural influences from the east. This may have been due to the increasing population in the regions east of the Mississippi River where a more abundant resource base gave rise to larger, and over time, more stationary populations. The natural outcome of such demographic pressures is for growing groups to look to unsettled land for pioneering experiments. We believe that the river valleys that were the focus of settlement in the east formed a set of conduits for upstream movements through the Mississippi drainage and into the Northeastern Plains. About 7,000 years ago there is some evidence of more substantial occupation along major rivers in south-central Iowa (Whittaker 2016). This is suggestive of groups expanding out of the eastern US to the north and west toward and into the Northeastern Plains, or of cultural influences spreading from group to group, a process that anthropologists call diffusion. We suppose that any such westward movement from the eastern woodlands of North America would have brought with it the notched and stemmed point technology that was developing there by 10,000 years ago, and would explain the stylistic changes seen in Early Archaic assemblages in the Bend area.

The private artifact collections from the Sheyenne Bend region contain many diagnostic artifacts from the Middle and Late Plains Archaic. These include point types such as Oxbow, McKean, Hanna, Duncan, and Pelican Lake. Most of these types are common throughout the Northern Plains and are especially abundant in the northwestern portions of the Great Plains. Oxbow, with indented bases and side notches that give it an eared appearance, may be the earliest Middle Plains Archaic type to appear on the Northwestern Plains. Some archaeologists believe it moved east from there beginning perhaps before 5,000 years ago (Epp and Dyck 1983:96). Oxbow points overlap with McKean–Duncan–Hanna points, also indented-base points but instead of an ear-like notching at the point base, a lanceolate form for McKean and stemmed forms for Hanna and Duncan (Epp and Dyck 1983:100–105). There are dozens of these Middle Plains Archaic point types in the Bayley collection alone, retrieved on the eastern side of the "elbow" of the Bend area. Reeves (1990:169ff) argues that during Oxbow times evidence for bone grease extraction at Northern Plains archaeological sites appears and is probably related to the use of pemmican to store meat. Also, tipi rings are occasionally present at these sites and, together, tipis and pemmican indicate a set of very effective inventions to make life on the Plains more successful. These innovations persist and remain part of Plains living until past the time of European settlement.

The final portion of the Archaic is characterized by finely made corner-notched points known as Pelican Lake. These are present in private collections from the Bend region, and are found at an Archaic site 32RI785 just south of the Bend region, on the Lake Agassiz beaches near the Wild Rice River. Here, as in other parts of the Northern Plains, Pelican Lake peoples continued the lifestyle of their predecessors.

Some comment is appropriate regarding the variety of projectile points found during the Archaic, and in other time periods as well. Archaeologists define many different types of projectile tips, often on the basis of small differences between forms. For example, Davis and Keyser (1999:260) make a strong case for combining two Middle Plains Archaic point styles, Hanna and Duncan, into a single type. Their argument is that it is often impossible to reliably separate the two styles, and that Duncan is nothing more than a Hanna point that has been sharpened after use by some re-chipping. Another issue with point styles as chronological markers or cultural indicators is that they sometimes re-appear at much later times, or they persist over much or even across culture-historical periods. Oxbow, for instance, although regarded as an Early-Middle Plains Archaic type, has been documented for the Woodland Period (Haug 1976). We can use point styles as general guides to time periods or to prehistoric cultures, but they alone are not dependable indicators in every case.

A Cultural Sequence for the Plains Woodland and Late Prehistoric Periods

The Plains Woodland period that follows the Archaic in time is not well represented in the Bend region. In some ways, we know more about the Archaic in the Sheyenne Valley than we do about the more recent Plains Woodland. The cultural features that characterize Plains Woodland are not exactly the same as the ones found in the Eastern US, where domestic plants, mound building and pottery are either in their beginning stages or are common enough that they are recognizable in the archaeological record. The first of these three features, domestic plants, is poorly attested in the archaeological record of the Woodland in the Bend. There is a squash seed associated with a rough date of AD 900, but little else to suggest the use of domestic plants. The other two Woodland features, ceramics and earthen mounds are present, but since both persist into the Late Prehistoric Period, it is sometimes difficult to assign sites, particularly mound sites, to the Plains Woodland and not to the Late Prehistoric. In any case, as with the Archaic, we believe that the Woodland cultures of our study region were in part a product of influences from the east.

There is some reason to believe that the diffusion of cultural traits was responsible for the movement of eastern cultural traits into the Northeastern Plains during the earlier Woodland. A study of the skeletal remains of prehistoric individuals from Minnesota was carried out by physical anthropologists prior to these remains being reburied under the Native American Graves and Repatriation Act. For the Minnesota region it appears that skeletal evidence of continuity is strong for the Paleoindian through the early portion of the Woodland. It is with the advent of domestic plants and gardening in the later part of the Woodland and in the Late Prehistoric Period that there is good evidence of possible population movements into the region (Myster 2001). Most burial mounds in the Bend region have not been excavated professionally, so it is not clear whether any of them date to the Woodland. The Lisbon burial has a Terminal Woodland date, but no mound was recorded from this burial eroding from the wall of a gravel pit. The Anderson Mound dates to the Late Prehistoric, roughly the fifteenth century, and an Oneota-like vessel was found in one Bend region mound, indicating a similarly late date. However, at Jamestown, not far west of the Bend region, the use of mounds was shown to persist from the Woodland through the Late Prehistoric.

If we turn our attention to the sequence of cultures known from occupation sites, we may identify several phases for the Plains Woodland and Late Prehistoric periods. The phases are based on artifact collections from surface survey and from excavated contexts. We use the term phase to refer to a set of archaeological materials found in a discrete geographic area within the framework of a limited time period (cf. Willey and Phillips 1958:22). The artifacts from sites belonging to a phase will be similar to each other in their stylistic features. A phase might persist for decades, or perhaps for several centuries. Two phases are Plains Woodland, one is transitional, and three phases are Late Prehistoric. A final phase is defined for the very early Historic Period, or Protohistoric.

Plains Woodland Period

Dahnke Phase

The first is an Initial Woodland phase present at the Dahnke–Reinke site at the mouth of the Sheyenne, northeast of the Bend area, and dated to about 2,000 years ago (Thompson 1990: 59). The pottery is not distinguished by any particular form of decoration; however, exterior bosses or punctations are found on some vessels. The pottery is grit tempered and relatively thick-walled, and surfaces are generally cordmarked. Isolated sherds of this type of pottery are found at some sites in the Bend area, but excavated components with this type of pottery have not been found. This ceramic material may be related to the ceramics found at the Naze site on the James River, which bear resemblance to ceramics from southwestern Minnesota and even into the Illinois country to the southeast. There is better evidence of an Initial Plains Woodland presence in the Bend region from surface collections of projectile points. The several private collections, or those housed at the Historical Society Museum in Bismarck, indicate the common occurrence of Besant points, which are normally dated before about AD 500. Unfortunately, excavated contexts for this style of projectile points are rare for eastern North Dakota and for the Sheyenne Bend area. A Besant point was identified at the Lisbon burial, but with a Terminal Woodland radiocarbon date of around AD 900. No ceramics were found in the burial, and it is not classified as part of the Dahnke phase.

The Dahnke phase is contemporaneous with Avonlea on the Northern Plains, and with Elk Lake culture in central Minnesota. Coincident with the Dahnke phase in other parts of the Northern Plains, some archaeologists have noted the high incidence of Knife River flint associated with sites that yield Besant points. It has been suggested that a trade network extended eastward across the Northern Plains transferring the high-quality flint to the forested areas east of the Mississippi (Clark 1984). Others see an Initial Plains Woodland trade involving obsidian from the Rocky Mountains and certain types of sea-shell (Johnson and Johnson 1998:218). There is no evidence of this trade, or of any special association of Besant with Knife River flint in the Sheyenne Bend. Perhaps such conclusions will develop when intact Besant archaeological components are found here.

Farther to the west on the Northern Plains Initial Woodland Besant sites provide good evidence of a complex of cultural features related to highly efficient bison hunting. Corrals for trapping animals and even ceremonial structures believed to be associated with shamanic rituals for attracting bison have been found. Some archaeologists see Besant as a cultural climax for bison hunting on the Northern Plains (Forbis 1998:63). Although such features characterize the Initial Plains Woodland in other regions, the same is not attested in the archaeological materials from the Bend region.

Sand Hills Phase

The second phase for the Plains Woodland in the Bend is the Sand Hills phase, assigned to the Terminal Plains Woodland in our study area (AD 600-1000). Pottery associated with this phase is not as thick as Dahnke phase ceramics, and is often decorated with dentate impressions or stamps and shows similarities to St. Croix pottery from Minnesota. This pottery also evinces some similarities with the Smith site variety of Laurel in northern Minnesota. Ceramics are characterized by the use of wrapped impressions, typically cords, applied horizontally to the jar neck. The lower body is cordmarked. Decorative additions include notching, rows of punctations and sometimes vertical combing of the jar neck. These ceramics were found at the Irwin Johnson site in the southernmost portion of the Bend region. Gibbon and Caine (1980) believe that this extension across the forest-prairie boundary is suggestive of some important adaptive shifts in the life-way of the people who made this ceramic ware. Obviously, the resources of the prairie contrast with those of the forest and lake country to the east. We are not so sure that any such important shift is indicated for this time period. Pottery from earlier times also crosses from the woodlands into the prairie (cf. Anfinson et.al. 1978), nor do we have any real evidence of life-style differences among the people who lived in the Bend region at this time. Also typical of this part of the Plains Woodland are the use of small notched points, including types known as Avonlea and Prairie Side-Notched, that are usually believed to have been used to tip arrows. The Besant projectile points typical in the earlier Initial Woodland are regarded as too large and heavy to have functioned adequately with the Plains Indian bow. Whether the bow and arrow were introduced or invented at this time is not entirely clear, but certainly sometime by Plains Woodland times the bow was introduced, and its use was widespread when the Europeans arrived. The bow and arrow have often been regarded as superior in both hunting and warfare to atlatl and darts, perhaps delivering more accuracy or greater range.

The later part of the Sand Hills phase is equivalent to Blackduck in central and northern Minnesota. Probably dating to the later part of the Sand Hills phase is a site along the Maple River Bend near the Sprunk site, and a private collection obtained by Eldon Johnson. This excavated Maple River site yielded pottery belonging to the type known as Blackduck, common throughout northern Minnesota and extending into the Canadian provinces. Although Blackduck is normally associated with lake-forest resource use, including wild rice, Blackduck sites are known from the prairies of the Red River Valley, and southwestern Manitoba, and in both areas the sites provide good evidence of bison hunting. Certainly, by the Terminal Woodland, the Historic Period pattern of Minnesota peoples of lake-forest country coming into the prairie to hunt bison, usually during the summer, is a common practice.

Late Prehistoric Period

The Late Prehistoric Period is a time of significant cultural changes. The most important is the advent of small-scale farming, maybe better described as gardening or horticulture. Sometime after AD 1000 domestic plants made their appearance on the Northeastern Plains. The precise time for their arrival is not clear. In fact, some native plants such as *Chenopodium* may have been used as a domesticate even earlier, but evidence for this is not well established. The so-called tropical cultigens, maize, beans, and squash, which have their origins in Mexico, were probably being used in some parts of the Plains after AD 900, and some have argued for their use in the far northern part of the Plains after AD 1000 (Boyd et al. 2006). The impetus for this likely came up the valleys of the Mississippi and Missouri rivers and their tributaries, since farming had its beginnings in the eastern forests and riverine environments prior to its appearance in the Plains. Early farming before the use of draft animals and plows usually involved the use of woodlands where trees could be cut down and gardens planted in the new openings. In the Bend area prairies, thick sod prevented farming in the grassland, but in the river-bottom lands where the forests were to be found, gardens were planted, and along these narrow ribbons of arable land, the gallery forests of the prairie rivers, farming moved into the Great Plains.

The time from about AD 950–1250 is sometimes called the "Medieval Warm Period." Climatic conditions were somewhat warmer than previous or subsequent centuries, perhaps favoring the spread of farming. Another factor may simply have been the growth of populations in the eastern woodlands leading to the budding of communities and their spread into the easternmost periphery of the Plains, where the idea of farming and the crops involved in it were picked up by Plains populations. These groups, in turn, began to flourish and spread farther upstream into the interior portions of the river valleys on the Plains.

In the Bend region, we have clear evidence for domestic plants at the Shea, Sprunk, Schultz, and Biesterfeldt sites, but these are dated to about the fifteenth century or later. Whether domesticates were being used prior to this time is an open question, although squash, possibly a cultivar, was found with the Terminal Woodland dated Lisbon burial.

In any case, sometime in the Late Prehistoric Period the communities in the Bend region were engaged in a life-style different in some important ways from that of their predecessors. People lived in more or less stable settlements in upland locales, and these communities probably lasted for a decade or longer. They may have moved during the cold season to protected areas in the lowlands along the rivers. We have direct evidence they grew maize, squash, and tobacco, and more than likely also used sunflower, Chenopodium, and maybe even beans as garden crops. The rest of their food would have come from wild species of plants and animals, bison being the most important.

Anthropologists, historians, and archaeologists have all described the Historic Period and Late Prehistoric peoples of the Northern Plains River valleys as participating in a 'dual economy.' This term is meant to describe the life-style of the Plains Village peoples as reliant on both hunting-gathering, and on farming carried out by individual households. More recently, Hamilton and Nicholson (2006:255) describe the adaptation of the Northeastern Plains Village people in somewhat more detail as involving specialized bison-hunts, generalized foraging for wild plant-resources and small game, and horticulture; perhaps better referred to as a 'triadic economy'. This makes sense. Bison hunts were typical of all Northern Plains groups, but so was the systematic use of wild plants like prairie turnip, ground nuts, and other seeds, roots and herbs. Since farming was also widespread at this time a tri-fold adaptation may be the most accurate description of their life-way.

The Late Prehistoric featured several phases, based largely on distinctive ceramics. Four phases are defined here for the Late Prehistoric Period: Lucas, Matoti, Shea, and Mirror Pool, although Lucas is more accurately described as transitional between the Plains Woodland and the Late Prehistoric. These phases are regarded mostly as part of the Northeastern Plains Village Tradition (NEPV) (Toom 2004; Gregg et al. 2016:42-43). In the sense we use the term here, a tradition consists of a number of phases that persist over a long period of time, and share common features. Sites belonging to the NEPV tradition have been found in the Sheyenne and Maple valleys of southeastern North Dakota, in the Lake Traverse–Big Stone Lake area, in west-central Minnesota, in the Devils Lake basin, in the James River Valley, as well as in the prairie provinces of Canada. The NEPV tradition dates to between AD 1200–1800. It is characterized by small settlements exhibiting evidence of large and small game hunting, use of waterfowl, fish, and shellfish, gathering wild plants, including berries, Chenopodium, amaranth, and other seeds. Maize is found in the form of kernel and cupule fragments. Scapula hoes used for gardening are also found. Stone tools are made from a variety of raw materials, including imported Knife River flint, and locally procured tool stone such as Swan River chert. These tools include scrapers, a variety of bifacial and unifacial cutting, piercing and rubbing tools, and small triangular (Eastern Triangular) and Prairie and Plains Side-Notched points, although in some cases larger notched points are also found at sites (Michlovic and Schneider 1993). Pottery is variable. Vessels are normally globular and relatively small, being around 20-25 cm diameter, although at the Shea site, some larger Sandy Lake vessels were recovered. Pots commonly have out-flaring rims and pronounced necks. Surfaces are often smoothed or cordmarked and sometimes smoothed over the cordmarking. Broad incised line decorations are typical. In some cases, there are ceramic wares from the Missouri Valley mixed in with NEPV ceramics, and in other cases, wares found in the woodlands of Minnesota, particularly Sandy Lake, are found together with the NEPV vessels (Michlovic and Swenson 1998; Michlovic, Holley and Dalan 2020). Mound burial has also been associated with the NEPV throughout the Northeastern Plains (Syms 1979).

Lucas Phase (Transitional Terminal Woodland-Late Prehistoric)

The Lucas phase is transitional between Woodland and Late Prehistoric and thus reflects both traditions. We believe this unit is dated roughly around AD 1000–1200, and it may be considered as a development into the Northeastern Plains Village Tradition, but not fully a part of it. Dating is based on the style of the pottery decorations, not on absolute or radiometric dates. Two collections from sites on the Okiedan Buttes, Lucas, and Heath (32RM230), are identified as part of the Lucas phase. The Lucas site enclosure was excavated by Michlovic (1990a; see also Holley and Kalinowski 2008), while the Heath site and its collection of artifacts derived from unreported testing by Elden Johnson in the 1960s (Holley 2008). Some Lucas phase materials were also found at the Irwin Johnson site.

Ceramics typical of the phase manifest Woodland and Late Prehistoric traits. These include vessels with cordmarked lower bodies and others with smoothed plain, polished plain, and simple stamped vessel surfaces. Decoration on the vessels was made with cordwrapped, plain, or dentate dowels impressed on the upper body of the jar. Incised line decoration and punctation are rare. Only seven discrete vessels were identified in the sample based on rim segments and an equally small number of sherd diagnostics. There is no broad and deep incising, or trailing, symptomatic of Cambria/Silvernale styles (found in the Minnesota River Valley and Red Wing, Minnesota areas). Wall thickness averages 5 mm.

The ceramic diagnostics from the Lucas site appear to fit into two sequential time periods: Terminal Woodland or Initial Middle Missouri Variant (for which we are approximating as AD 900–1250) based on a comparison with collections and descriptions of material from surrounding regions. This broad time span designation is based on the presence of thin-walled vessels, grit temper, and a variety of surface treatments and decorations. The prevalence of the plain surface treatment at the Lucas site suggests that the primary occupation is relatively late, that is, the very last part of the Plains Woodland time span. It would appear that the assemblage lacks the proportional mix of traits for the Northeastern Plains Village Tradition identified by Toom (2004), at least for the James River variant of this complex.

To the south, surface collections from several sites in the Big Stone Lake region (Anfinson 1997; Johnson 1991) compare favorably with the Lucas site collection as regards decorative technique and proportion of surface finishes. The ceramics are also associated with ditched enclosures and mounds. In this part of southwestern Minnesota there is a concentration of modest sized enclosures with burial and linear mounds and similar kinds of ceramics that would correspond to the Lucas site. Testing at one of these sites, Shady Dell, by Lloyd Wilford yielded sparse remains (Anfinson 1997). The Shady Dell enclosure is quite interesting in that it also consists of a completely enclosed ditch along the bluff edge with a possible linear mound nearby (Winchell 1911:303). This site is affiliated with the Shady Dell phase, which is contemporaneous with Lucas, but the ceramics are dominated by cord impressed decorations.

Another Lucas phase site is Heath, discovered about half a mile west of the Lucas site. Heath site ceramics derive from multiple excavations and machine stripping. The ceramics reveal a greater time span than Lucas, reinforcing the notion that the Lucas collection dates to a narrow occupation span. Ceramics that are presumably early include cordmarked jars with thick bases (.7-.9 cm thick) and fabric impressed finishing of the neck reminiscent of Blackduck and Lake Benton Late Woodland wares, from northern and southern Minnesota respectively. Initial Middle Missouri traits comprise the use of simple registers of dentate stamps or tool impressions on plain necks with cordmarked lower bodies. Cambria affiliations are indicated by the broad incising to form parallel curvilinear designs with intaglio impressions on the interior. Small necked jars with polished surfaces and exterior or superior tool impressions are typical of this time period as well.

Matoti Phase

Evidence for the next proposed phase is tenuous, although something with the characteristics enumerated below must exist. We have a date from one site, 32RM60, but have a pitiful sample of grit tempered sherds to document it. A single pure component has been excavated (Michlovic 1993b) at 32RM92 near Fort Ransom. Study at the Rotenberger site has provided the bulk of the data for this phase. Surface collections for this phase are available as well.

The Matoti phase is ensconced in the Northeastern Plains Village Tradition with a distinctly eastern cast that contrasts with the James River examples. Smoothed vessels surfaces are present, with polishing common, although cordmarking lingers. New surface treatments that include simple stamping and check stamping are present. Ceramic diagnostics comprise the notched rim, smoothed plain, high neck NEPV jar associated with the type Riggs Plain. A mix of Cambria and Oneota influenced incising is diagnostic along with unique decorative styles such as broad incising on the interior of the jar rim. Shell temper may be present, but it is a decided minority. There is also a veneer of Extended Middle Missouri traits.

If it were not seemingly pristine at two sites, we would consider the Matoti phase a sampling problem. The two secure sites are an unnamed one at Olson Farm along the Red River near Ft. Abercrombie, and the site 32RM 92, near Bear's Den Hillock in Fort Ransom. The third site was identified during a survey of the Sheyenne River as 32RM30, also near Bear's Den, hence the name for the phase (Matoti = Bear's Den in Dakota).

At 32RM92, all of the sherds were grit tempered and most were smoothed surface. Diagnostics were not numerous but included incised and punctated vessels similar to Oneota examples found at Shea and Sprunk. Two examples include alternating lines and rows of punctations and the punctuates bordered by vertical lines. This design is replicated at other, well dated sites, such as Ithuhu (AD 1300–1400) on the James River and Sprunk (AD 1400–1500) along the Maple River. Appliqué nodes and notching are found on six rims. The rims appear to be unmodified by either thinning or thickening and typical of Northeastern Plains Village pottery rims. The paucity of shell tempering and textured surfaces is strikingly different from what we have along the Maple River and elsewhere at the same time.

Site 32RM30 is located farther south along the Sheyenne; the artifacts from the site derived from a relatively small surface collection. The diagnostics are fascinating in that they are highly suggestive of an AD 1200–1500 timeframe. Only plain surface sherds are evident and all are grit tempered. The diagnostics include a sherd with parallel punctuations bound by trailed, or broad incised lines and vertical parallel lines, both similar to examples from the Sprunk site. Of the two rims, one is incised with a rounded notched lip, unusual for the region and the other has a lip notch, diagnostic of this time span.

The final site, unnumbered and collected by University of Minnesota archaeologist Lloyd Wilford, is near historic Fort Abercrombie on the upper Red River. The collection is small and is from an unnumbered site curated at the Minnesota Historical Society with accession no. 358. The sample consists of grit-tempered plain surface ceramics with examples of curvilinear trailing. This is presumably Cambria-like in affiliation and features possible Oneota-like decorations with fringe punctations. Sixty-three sherds all with identifiable surfaces are either smoothed or incised and all are grit tempered. The sherds reveal curvilinear incising and punctations or elongated jags similar to other Oneota-like material. The rims are not diagnostic, and one is unusual with horizontal deep gouges on the interior. Similar interior decorations of jar necks are found at multiple sites far into Minnesota, and suggest a previously unknown connection.

Shea Phase

Based on excavations at the Shea, Sprunk, and Peterson sites, and on the study of collections from a number of surface sites in the Sheyenne Bend region, Michlovic (2008a) defined the Shea phase. While the Matoti phase appears largely based in the traditions of the NEPV, the Shea phase represents a different mix of eastern influences. At Shea phase sites it is typical to find woodland-like Sandy Lake along with the NEPV pottery. Sandy Lake pottery is usually globular with weak shoulders and often straight rims, although sometimes they are flared. Temper may be grit, but in the Sheyenne Bend it is more often crushed clam shell, and vessel surfaces are cordmarked. Decoration on Sandy Lake is not common, although lip impressions made with a finger or a stick, and stick or cordwrapped stick impressions on the rim or rim interior are perhaps the most common when vessels are decorated. Occasionally Sandy Lake pottery in this region has shallow, broad incisions on the vessel neck or shoulder, reflecting Oneota influence.

If Sandy Lake were the only ceramic ware present at Shea phase sites it would actually be considered a Late Prehistoric culture extruded from the nearby lake-forest country of Minnesota, where Sandy Lake ceramics are most common. However, in addition to the Sandy Lake ceramics, Shea phase sites contain equal amounts of smooth and polished surface pottery with narrow incisions, finger or stick impressions on the lip, and shallow punctations. Sometimes rims have an L- or T-shape, but more often are rounded or flat. This pottery is invariably grit tempered and is quite distinct from the co-occurring Sandy Lake ceramics. Most of this pottery would be assigned to a type known as Buchanan ware in North Dakota (Gregg et al. 2016:B: 42-43), a ceramic style typical at Northeastern Plains Village sites. Usually, Shea phase ceramic collections display characteristics of both cordmarked and plain vessels, suggesting strongly that the sites were occupied by people who used both of these kinds of pottery, sometimes making vessels with the distinctive feature of one or the other type of pottery, and at other times mixing the features of the two ceramic wares.

One problematic site dating to the Shea phase site is the Schultz site (Wood 1963 and see above). This has a single radiocarbon date of about AD 1450. The site exhibits greater ceramic diversity than other Shea phase sites in the region, but typical Shea Phase smooth surfaced, incised ceramics, along with cord marked, shell tempered pottery. There is a notable presence of fine-line incised sherds and braced rims with cord impressions that are anticipatory to decorative practices at the Protohistoric Biesterfeldt site. Even if the Schultz site is coeval with the Shea phase, as indicated by the radiocarbon date from our excavations, the artifact collection from Schultz is different in several ways from Shea and Sprunk. Thus, it is possible that we have markedly different ceramic collections from sites located within a day's walking distance (Maple River and Sheyenne River). We are aware of intense border wars within the Northeastern Plains during historic times between the Dakota and Ojibwa, which may have an antiquity involving different players. The Schultz collections made by Will and Hecker have been identified as a marginal participant in the Coalescent Tradition (Johnson 1998: Figure 10.1), which is significant given the designation of the Biesterfeldt occupation as Post-Contact variant of the Coalescent Tradition. Coalescent pottery has also been identified along the Red River (Breakey 1981: Figure 2). A counter argument by Ahler (1993) holds that the Schultz site is ancestral Hidatsa and thereby related to developments in the Knife–Heart River sections of the Missouri River Trench. Another occupation, the Hintz site (Wheeler 1963) in the nearby James River Valley is also identified as a Coalescent member. If Schultz is classified as Coalescent then it is not part of the Shea phase–NEPV tradition.

Shea phase sites are well dated to the middle of the fifteenth century and into the sixteenth century. The economy has been well documented as focused on hunting and gathering, a heavy reliance on bison, and gardening featuring maize and tobacco, although other domesticates are probably present as well, though not attested at excavated sites. Small triangular projectile points, and occasionally Plains Side-Notched are most common. Many sites are known from artifact scatters in floodplains, but the best known are small, upland enclosures like Shea, Sprunk, and Peterson.

Mirror Pool Phase

Occupations dating after the Shea phase, which we have identified as the Mirror Pool phase, are poorly known. The phase represents an increase in the visibility of Middle Missouri River styles such as Knife River Braced and Le Beau Cord Impressed. Such a trend characterizes other areas of the Northeastern Plains. In keeping with the strong eastern relationships, cordmarking is still present but simple stamping dominates. There is also the occasional shell tempered vessel. Surface treatments of Matoti continue and brushing is introduced.

The Anderson Mound Site (32RM220) excavated by Elden Johnson in the 1960, is the only site in this locality with a radiocarbon date, and that one reflecting an age of AD 1567, calibrated to range from AD 1490–1680. This date derives from a sample taken from a burial mound (Vehik and Vehik 1985:14). Ceramics from the site are meager, however, the mix of grit and shell tempering, the use of simple stamping, decorative cord impressions, and thick vessel walls are consistent with a terminal-to-post-Shea phase span. The nature of the assemblage and date could be construed to represent a transition to Biesterfeldt (Protohistoric) vogues in the valley, although the presence of a burial mound is rooted in long-lived traditions in the valley (Holley 2008). Vague mentions of a burial mound at the Biesterfeldt site exist in the early literature of the site (Gardner 1868) but we are unsure of the veracity or its ties to the village.

Two other sites reveal stronger ties to the Middle Missouri Trench. The Swanson site is a collection derived from Elden's Johnson's 1960s work near the Anderson Mound site. Pottery indicates a late occupation reflected in braced rims, cord impressed decorations, and fine-line incising. Most of the sherds are grit-tempered with smoothed plain or simple stamped surfaces. The Schultz site is nearby and the original work at that site by Hecker and Milligan includes an artifact collection with ceramics that reveal styles similar to Le Beau Cord Impressed and Knife River Braced Rim from the Missouri Valley. These wares are relatively late in the prehistoric sequence. The ceramics exemplify a shift towards styles typical of the Missouri River Trench, although it is important to determine if these connections are with the Mandan strain in central North Dakota (Ahler 1993), or even ancestral Hidatsa, and the Middle Missouri Tradition, or with the Arikara Coalescent Tradition from further south. Throughout the Northeastern Plains we see ceramic collections display greater Plains influence near the end of the sequence (for example, Nicholson et al. 2008; Schneider 1982). This may be due to the attenuation of cultural development (depopulation) in the east, and the florescence of societies along the Missouri River.

Chaiena Phase

This final phase in the sequence presented here is not prehistoric but is based on the finds made at the Protohistoric Biesterfeldt site. The best dates for the Biesterfeldt occupation are from 1720–1780, but certainly dating to after the European incursion farther to the east. The site does provide an immediately post-prehistoric occupation date for the region. Native groups continued to occupy the Sheyenne Bend well into the 1800s (Anonymous 1909; Howard 1966; Thorfinnson 1975). Enigmatic sites identified to the north of the Bend Region on the Sheyenne (Haury and Schneider 1986:196-197) may hold promise for the study of the 19th century.

This phase is named Chaiena after a Dakota term for the Cheyenne who are the presumed occupants of Biesterfeldt. The site and its artifact collection have been classified as Post-Contact Coalescent by Wood (1971). The ceramics are a variation on pottery found at Arikara sites along the Missouri River in South Dakota, a similarity so striking that at least one colleague informally suggested that the site might have been used not by the Cheyenne, but by the Arikara themselves.

Chaiena ceramics feature surface treatments that include smoothed plain necks with simple stamped lower bodies. Brushing is also present. Decorations comprise a variety of impressions using cords or wrapped rods. A unique characteristic of these ceramics is the presence of thin-walled, small jars with fine-line incised designs on the neck that may be further ornamented with punctations.

Discussion of Phase Definitions

The variation in the ceramic assemblages representing these phases is real, but the alignment and assumptions that we present here about this variability is still in question. There are several problems that need to be addressed.

The Shea phase is one we know the most about with dates and excavation of multiple sites revealing dietary patterns, cultural affiliations, and the possibility of housing. The relative paucity of Shea phase sites along the Sheyenne River proper is problematic. It is clear that shell tempering drops out to nothing moving upriver on the Sheyenne. The Peterson site is the most northwesterly site on the Sheyenne River with shell tempered ceramics. Schneider's survey north of the Bend and the brief reports on work upriver all admit to the absence of shell tempering, although some shell tempered Sandy Lake pottery is found at Devils Lake. We can also add the absence of Oneota traits in this area as well, as they do seem to go hand in hand with the Shea phase.

Does the Shea phase represent an intrusion by proto-Dakota into the region, as suggested by Michlovic (1985)? This analysis has shown that stretching back to Woodland times, the Minnesota connection has been strong in the region and we have reason to think of the eastern portion of the Northeastern Plains as the western boundary of developments recognized in the lakes-country and the upper Mississippi River Valley.

The Middle Missouri River cultural developments also have an important role in the Late Prehistoric cultures of the Bend, culminating we believe in the Biesterfeldt site. The Schultz site also reveals the presence of Middle Missouri Coalescent traits prior to the Biesterfeldt occupation. Although present along the Maple River, Middle Missouri traits are far more common on the Sheyenne.

Monument construction was an important factor in the Late Prehistoric of the region as well (Holley 2008). We presume that earthen monuments are mostly associated with the NEPV tradition. This is based on limited archaeology, such as the mounds and artificial embankments at the Lucas site, mounds associated with Peterson, Shea, and Sprunk, an

Oneota-like pot from the Ranes mound group on the Okiedan Buttes, and the sixteenth century date from Anderson site. Even bearing in mind that the Woodland record is potentially obscured by alluvial deposits, there is clearly an explosion in sites in the region with the advent of the Late Prehistoric. Take the Maple River, where an intensive survey recovered about 50 sites in a relatively small area, and of those with pottery nearly all date from the Late Prehistoric. What accounts for this explosion? Climatic changes, population increases, more intensive farming practices, or some other factor: all might be offered as explanations for developments, particularly after AD 1400, but we are unable to certainly identify the causal agents.

The Late Prehistoric Period is the best known of all prehistory. By this time a very successful life-way involving a variety of food sources had been achieved, including the long-established pattern of hunting large and small game, fishing, fowling, and plant gathering, along with the widespread use of domesticated plants, particularly maize. Attendant on this new subsistence routine, the so-called dual economy of the Northern Plains, were settled communities such as Lucas, Shea, Sprunk, and Peterson; sites that leave clear signatures on the surface to draw the attention of the archaeologist. Furthermore, during the Late Prehistoric period there is clear evidence of cultural relationships between the people of the Bend region and groups to the south, east, and west. This may be seen in the ceramic assemblages that reflect connections with the Missouri Valley as well as with the lake-forest region of Minnesota and the village groups of southern Minnesota and northwest Iowa, especially Oneota. Finally, during the Late Prehistoric period we are witnessing the emergence of cultures that will eventually become the known ethnic groupings of the Historic period, including the Cheyenne, Dakota (Yanktonai), and probably the Hidatsa.

Tales Told by Points and Pottery

Distinctive forms of artifacts tell a historical tale. Anywhere archaeology is done, and certainly in the Sheyenne Bend, artifact styles are apparent in collections whether picked up in fields by artifact hunters, or found by archaeologists in surveys and excavations. Both stone and ceramic manufactures were often designed with both functional and stylistic elements. Today, specific design features may be used to distinguish one product of a class from another. Take automobile designs as an example: Fords are styled differently than Chevys. In industrial societies, these distinctions may be part of marketing tactics. In ancient times, we believe that stylistic

Sheyenne Bend Phases, Plains Woodland through Late Prehistoric

Initial Woodland

Dahnke 500/300 BC – AD 600: Thick-walled (avg 7-8 cm) pottery with horizontal and vertical cordmarking, net impressed, and smoothed. Decoration uncommon but includes exterior bossing and punctations; both occur on the upper portion of the vessel.

Terminal Woodland

Sand Hills AD 600 – 1000: The Sand Hills has two units. Early unit has dentate stamped decorations on smoothed plain or cordmarked surfaces. Vessel walls are thinner (averaging 5-6 cm). Affiliations with St. Croix and Laurel. A later unit of this phase is equivalent to Blackduck.

Transitional

Lucas AD 1000-1200: Lucas is transitional between Woodland and Late Prehistoric. Woodland traits include cordmarking, diverse jar neck decorations including smoothed, sometimes with polishing, wrapped rod impressions, and incising. Influences are from Initial Middle Missouri and Cambria. Wall thickness avg. 5 mm.

Late Prehistoric

Matoti AD 1300 – 1500: Matoti is in the Northeastern Plains Village (NEPV) tradition. Smoothed vessel surfaces with polishing are common, but cordmarking lingers. Simple stamping and check stamping are introduced. Notched rim, smoothed plain, and high neck jars associated with the type Riggs Plain. Cambria and Oneota influenced incising are diagnostic along with broad incising on the interior of the jar rim. Shell temper may be present, but it is a decided minority.

Shea AD 1400 – 1550: Shea phase has a different mix of eastern influences than Matoti. Riggs Plain notched rim jars are common, yet, the shell tempered Sandy Lake is a significant member of the phase. Oneota influences are important. There is considerable overlap with the Matoti and Shea phase, yet the Matoti phase lacks appreciable presence of Sandy Lake ceramics. As with Matoti, Middle Missouri traits are present.

Mirror Pool AD 1500 –1700?: Mirror Pool shows an increase in Middle Missouri River styles such as Knife River Braced and Le Beau Cord Impressed. Such a trend characterizes other areas of the Northeastern Plains. Continuing strong eastern relationships, cordmarking is still present but simple stamping dominates. There is occasional shell tempering. Surface treatments of Matoti continue and brushing is introduced.

Historic

Chaiena AD 1700 – 1820: Chaiena is the final ceramic complex best exemplified at Biesterfeldt. Surface treatments include smoothed plain necks with simple stamped lower bodies. Brushing is also present. Decorations include impressions using cords or wrapped rods. A unique characteristic of these ceramics is the presence of thin-walled, small jars with fine-line incised designs on the neck that may be further ornamented with punctations and punctations.

variability in artifact forms was the product of group pressures encouraging people to follow certain templates in certain classes of artifacts for a variety of reasons. To simplify, specific stylistic preferences might be a result of traditions passed down in families, and family traditions in a group, whether a small band or village, would influence other members of the community, all together conforming to certain vogues, or style preferences. In different communities slightly different styles would be used to make artifacts, whether projectile points or ceramic vessels. Furthermore, through time, styles would gradually change as artisans accumulated innovations in design. Thus, archaeologists track time with artifact styles, whether they are projectile points or clay pots.

Stone is much more difficult to fashion into desired shapes than clay, so projectile point forms are less sensitive than pottery as markers of cultural variation across space or through time, and many archaeologists have more confidence in the interpretation of ceramic variability than they do with lithics. Even so, we have shown throughout the past in the Sheyenne Bend that projectile points track the passage of time in a rough way. We have a pretty good idea of Paleoindian point forms and how to differentiate them from Archaic or Woodland forms. We are less able to use them to disaggregate social groups at any one time. Consider that Avonlea or Prairie Side-Notched points from the Plains Woodland are found all over the Northern Plains, not just in the Sheyenne Bend, or even only in the Northeastern Plains. Besides this, these point styles sometimes persist for hundreds of years. It is easier to differentiate cultures, or set up a chronology, using pottery.

For example, during the Lucas phase the ceramic vogues in the Bend area reflect southern and western influences, while the Shea phase is clearly and heavily impacted by some sort of cultural intrusion or stimulus from the east and from the south represented by Sandy Lake pottery and Oneota decorative motifs, respectively. Overall, the major cultural forces impinging on the Bend region in the Late Prehistoric seem to have come from the village cultures along the Missouri and James Rivers, from the Late Prehistoric wild rice harvesters in central Minnesota, and from the Oneota peoples who lived to the south in southern Minnesota, Iowa, and eastern South Dakota. At the present, we see these influences but are not able to describe them in detail or very accurately evaluate their relative importance in the cultural developments of the Sheyenne Valley. What is clear is that pottery types in the traditional sense are less useful in tracing these interconnections than are the individual decorative designs themselves; decorating a vessel with a twisted cord, for instance, rather than with a punctate or boss or using broad incisions rather than stamping with a notched stick. Different decorative motifs can be easily identified; however, the combination of these motifs into pottery "types" is almost endless and leads to a confusion of types at every site, where the motifs are often mixed or matched in slightly different ways, giving rise to a multiplicity of type names. While the tracking of motifs or design elements is most helpful, we still recognize certain broad categories of ceramic production, which are sometimes referred to as wares, such as Sandy Lake, Oneota, or Northeastern Plains Village wares.

We can get an idea of some of what this means from the work done at the Shea and Sprunk sites. Here we have well-dated sites from about AD 1450 on the Maple River bend. The pottery at the two sites was almost identical. Roughly half the pottery at each site was Sandy Lake, very common in the Late Prehistoric lake-forest country of Minnesota. The other half consisted of various Northeastern Plains Village styles. Both kinds of pottery were found together in the same layers, and in some cases, vessels combined features of each of these wares. We know from historical and anthropological study that in many North American Indian societies, women were responsible for making much of the pottery. The pottery at these Shea Phase sites tells us that some people from central Minnesota brought pottery, or their way of designing pottery, to these sites in the Bend region. The Northeastern Plains kind of pottery is common in the James Valley and the Devils Lake basin. This local pottery may represent a more resident population. To us it is obvious that people from different areas have formed a single community, which we define as the Shea Phase.

There is plenty of ethnographic evidence to support the idea that the decorative sharing in ceramic technology reflects social interchanges. We know from many Native American societies that women taught their daughters and granddaughters the craft of making pottery, and it stands to reason that they would take with them their practice of ceramic production to any new home they might move to. Sharing marriage partners across band boundaries was not uncommon, and marriage partners might often be from different villages. Hassrick (1964:110), for instance, recounts a marriage between members of different Teton bands, while Sharrock (1974) documents the widespread merging on the Northern Plains of entire communities of different ethnicities. Her study of inter-ethnic relations on the Northern Plains in the Historic Period shows that sometimes families, or even entire bands from different tribal groups would merge to form a new social grouping. Occasionally, this would be accomplished by people who literally spoke different languages, for example, the joining of groups of Algonquian speaking Cree with Siouan speaking Assiniboine. Quite clearly, this type of social interaction would potentially result in mixing of artifact styles, decorative motifs and even manufacturing techniques. It is easy to understand how women with different instructors in the craft of making pottery—mothers, grandmothers, aunts—would bring new ways of pottery design to their respective homes after marriage, at least in cases where they left their parents' village to live with a man from another community.

Another possible explanation for the mixture of ceramic motifs is related to trade contacts. We know that in the early Historic Period there were large trade fairs on the Northern Plains and in the Upper Midwest (Wood 1980: 98). One probably operated near Red Wing on the Minnesota–Wisconsin border, another near the Minnesota River–Blue Earth confluence, and another may have been near Big Stone and Lake Traverse. One of the largest was the great trade fair on the James River in South Dakota. Besides these there were the large villages of the Arikara, Mandan, and Hidatsa on the Missouri River that served as trade centers into the nineteenth century. These gatherings almost certainly occurred as well in the Late Prehistoric Period and would have brought together peoples from many different groups, where exchanges were made in food, furs, and other products. Ceramic vessels may have traded hands, or at least, people were able to observe the ways their neighbors or trading partners decorated their pottery, taking with them ideas for ornamentation back to their home territories and villages.

Trade and Travel

In the same way that their Historic Period descendants moved widely over the grasslands, so too did the more ancient peoples of the region. Many of us today have little appreciation of the dimensions of long-distance travel prehistoric people on the Plains engaged in. For instance, a 1705 Winter Count records a Teton visit to Hudson Bay to trade for metal kettles (Hanson 1975), and other sources indicate the Yankton sometimes visited the Ute to obtain salt and travelled as far south as the Gulf of Mexico. On occasion a band of people might detach from the larger group and live independently for years at a time. "This ever-searching lifeway produced conflicting accounts of their whereabouts, and caused confusion among early French explorers, such as LeSueur and the family Verendrye." (Samson-Flood 1986:16). Taking this into consideration, the presence in the Sheyenne Valley of Knife River flint, or occasionally obsidian from the Rockies, or black chert from northwestern Ontario, or Gulf of Mexico shell, is eminently understandable. The historian Arnold Toynbee, many years ago, referred to the great steppes of Eurasia as like the sea, not so much barriers, but as mediums for travel. So, it was also for the American grasslands. And the movement across the plains was facilitated not only by the lack of natural barriers, but by the rivers, such as the Missouri, the Minnesota, Des Moines, Big Sioux, James, Red, and of course, the Sheyenne. These arteries served to funnel cultural influences from north to south, west to east, and in the Northeastern Plains, most obviously from east to west. But rivers were not needed for travel. Crossing the open plains from one valley to the next was routine for pedestrian Indian groups. Consider that the Sheyenne Bend near Fort Ransom is only about 25 miles from the James River, and the James about 100 miles from the Missouri. These are very reasonable distances for foot-travel among groups that were accustomed to long journeys. We assume that people from the Sheyenne Bend could have travelled to the Missouri River within a week or so, or to the headwaters of the Minnesota River in two or three days.

Mobility among hunter-gatherers was more than a matter of occasional long-distance travel. For most of prehistoric times the people of the Sheyenne Bend lived off the wild resources of the land that they could find on the prairie or in the gallery woodlands and river. Even after the introduction of domestic plants these people would still have depended heavily on wild food sources. These resources, even when abundant, did not last for long. People had to move regularly to new hunting grounds or gathering patches. The Historic Period peoples of the Western Plains are well-known to have been nomadic. The Cheyenne moved about 33 times each year for a distance of about 10 miles or more. The Crow moved 38 times per year. This is about one move every 10 days or so (Kelly 1995:125). Of course, in the Historic Period the horse facilitated travel, making it a much less onerous undertaking. And finding pasture for horses required more frequent moves. Still, this gives an idea of the mobility of people who do not depend on farming. We can only make an educated guess about how to translate this into a calculation of mobility in pre-horse days, but it is highly likely that a group of families would not be able to survive in one location unless they were farming.

Warfare, Ceremonialism, and Earthworks

The relations between peoples in the larger Northeastern Plains region were not always peaceful. The obvious fortification of some sites, such as Shea, Sprunk, and Peterson, is indicative of more volatile interaction and probably raiding. Ditches at these sites were originally up to ten feet wide and five to six feet deep, and they were clearly meant for defensive purposes. In the Historic Period warfare was common among peoples of the Great Plains, and there is good evidence for inter-tribal violence in the Late Prehistoric Period as well, especially among agricultural groups. Bamforth (1994) argues that deteriorating climatic conditions beginning around AD 1250 made farming on the Plains more difficult, and consequently there was a more intensive competition for scarce agricultural land. Archaeological evidence in the Missouri Valley of the Dakotas, including heavily fortified communities and in some cases, even human remains showing traumatic and violent deaths, is found increasingly through the fourteenth century. Since native farming was restricted to the fertile river bottom land, shifts in weather patterns that made growing crops difficult would have ramified up the narrow stream valleys in rapid fashion. By the fifteenth century Shea and Sprunk were occupied on the Maple River, and Peterson and Nelson on the Sheyenne, with obvious defensive features. Similar settlements are present about 60 miles to the southeast around Lake Traverse and Big Stone Lake at the Minnesota River headwaters.

We find archaeological evidence of inter-group warfare common among farmers from many parts of the world. Farming communities are generally larger than those of hunter-gatherers and tend to grow faster. This leads inevitably to conflicts over territory. Furthermore, farmers need arable land, and in the Bend region this would have been river-bottom land. Once heavy timber had been removed from a plot of land, it became especially useful and perhaps a more attractive target for interlopers. In any case, for the archaeologist, it is not surprising to find evidence of farming and warfare hand in hand.

Finally, the great ceremonies of the Plains peoples, such as the Sun Dance, while not specifically reflected in the archaeological remains, might be compared to the type of ceremonies that surrounded the construction of the numerous mounds at Bear's Den Hill, or on the Okiedan Buttes, or in the construction of some of the circular enclosures like the Lucas site. Indeed, the large number of burial mounds, linear embankments, petroglyphs, and Native-named localities in the Bend region, all are evidence of the ceremonial significance of this part of the Sheyenne

Valley. That indicators of population interaction, trade, war, and ceremonialism are all present here is a strong reflection of the prehistoric significance of the region as a whole.

Bison and the Plains Adaptation

Many features of Plains Indian life known from the Historic Period had substantial antiquity. Bison hunting, the staple of historic Plains peoples' livelihood, dates back to the earliest inhabitants we know about in the Bend region. At the Rustad site the bison represent an extinct chronospecies of bison, and bison are found in every excavated context, including the Protohistoric Period represented at Biesterfeldt. Another typical Plains cultural trait is the tipi. Although these have not been excavated in the Bend, tipi rings were once visible near Bear's Den Hillock, and in other parts of the Plains these are believed to date to as early as 3,000–4,000 years ago. The tipi was a structure designed for easy set-up and dismantling, a characteristic that would have made hunting the roaming bison much more successful. Native people on the Plains during the Archaic learned to make pemmican, dried meat pounded with berries and stored in grease. Luther Standing Bear (1975:22) said his people called it *wasna*, and often used it on long journeys. Frison (2004:224) explains that an adult travelling over the Plains might need about eight pounds of bison meat each day, but only one and a half pounds of high-energy content pemmican. Although we do not find pemmican preserved at any of the archaeological sites in the region, pemmican required strips of dried meat (usually bison), grease from bone, and berries. Bone grease extraction is something that is inferred from large quantities of fragmented bone occasionally documented in site deposits. At Sprunk, we found bison grease adhering to the interior of every ceramic vessel tested.

From earliest times the bison formed a foundation for Indian life in the Sheyenne Bend. At some sites the incidence of bison remains dwarfs any other artifactual or ecofactual find. Bison were a staple of Plains Indian life as anyone who has read or studied the peoples of the Great Plains knows. Yet bison were never domesticated in prehistoric times; they were hunted, not bred. Even so, the bison was apparently not overhunted and when the first Europeans arrived and left written accounts of the Plains region, all were deeply impressed with the innumerable animals that made up the herds. Euro-Americans estimates of bison numbers in the nineteenth century in the range of forty to sixty million were not uncommon. Clearly, American Indians and the bison had developed a special kind of relationship, and in spite of high levels of human predation, the herds persisted and even flourished. How is it that the Plains peoples hunted bison for over ten thousand years yet never hunted them prior to the Euro-American intrusion in any manner that seems to have made a difference in their numbers?

Any reading of Plains ethnography clarifies in short order that the bison was central to peoples' subsistence. The bison was a major, perhaps the major, source of food for most groups, and it was also a source for clothing and shelter (tipi covers), and for tools and utensils (horns and bone). Many essays and books have been written describing the manifold uses to which the Indian put the Plains buffalo. But beyond its practical uses, the bison figured importantly into Plains Indian ceremony, and was sometimes even interred in mound burials. It was a major figure in Native religion and was related in some myths to the origin of people. Bison were revered, and ritual performances were often related to bison hunting and kills. We mentioned earlier that at one site in Wyoming during Besant times a bison corral with a central post and possible shamanic structure was found. Oetelaar (2014) explains how Plains people such as the Blackfoot regarded bison on a par with themselves, that is, as part of the same cosmos, not as part of a different, natural world. The Plains people incorporated the bison into not only their economy, but into their social life, and into their rituals and ceremonies. We believe that the incorporation of bison into the totality of Plains Indian culture contributed to the measured use of the bison herds, which were not seen as a resource to be merely exploited, but as one to be husbanded.

Concluding Comment

Such, then, is the authors' present state of knowledge regarding the archaeology and prehistory of the Sheyenne Bend region. Although we can see the outline of a distinctive sequence of cultures the entire story is yet to be unraveled. The Yanktonai people lived here in the Historic Period, but how long before the eighteenth century they may have occupied this region is an open question. The presence of Sandy Lake pottery, often associated with Siouan peoples, suggests that they, or perhaps some or another Dakota group was in the Bend region by the fifteenth century. There are stories told by the Dakota of a feud between two groups of Yanktonai leading to a schism, with one group splitting from the other and moving to the north. These northerners became the Assiniboine who lived in northwestern Ontario and southern Manitoba in the Early Historic Period. We know now that the Assiniboine and their relatives, the Stoney, are linguistically distinct and form a group equally related to the

Yanktonai and Santee Dakota. Could one or both of these peoples have previously lived in the Bend area? From the historical accounts we also know that the Cheyenne once lived in the Sheyenne Bend, and we have an identified village site at Biesterfeldt that stands as testimony to this narrative. The question that remains is whether the Cheyenne at Biesterfeldt came to this place from the Minnesota River Valley to the southeast, or whether they arrived here from the west, perhaps after they were already in communication with people such as the Arikara who used similar ceramics and architecture as that found at Biesterfeldt. There are also claims that the Hidatsa lived in the Sheyenne Bend region in the later portion of the prehistoric period. This claim comes in part from Hidatsa origin stories, and from pottery collected at some sites in the Bend—Schultz, for example—that show commonalities with Hidatsa ceramics.

For earlier periods, identifying ethnic groups known from later times becomes more speculative. In fact, as we move back in time for a millennium or more prior to the earliest historical records, there is no real consensus among scholars that our modern ethnic groups existed as recognizable cultures. For the Woodland Period, and more certainly for the Archaic and Paleoindian Periods, there is not even much speculation among archaeologists about the ethnicity of people who lived in the Bend area.

We do know that over thousands of years there were cultural influences from other areas pulsing into the Sheyenne Valley. Fragments of copper from the western Great Lakes area, sea shell from the Gulf of Mexico, obsidian from the Rockies, pipestone from southwestern Minnesota, and large amounts of Knife River flint from west of the Missouri, all found their way into this region. We can detect influences from the same parts of the continent in pottery designs, or in the architecture of burial mounds and earthworks, and from earlier periods, influence can be traced in the stylistic features of stone spear and arrow points. While some of these outside cultural impacts might be regarded as trivial, others revolutionized the life-way of the people in eastern North Dakota. Maize, for instance, a plant known to have its origin in Mexico, had a major impact on the economic foundation of everyday life in the Bend.

So, with this we end our account of the ancient Sheyenne Bend. Our narrative has been spotty in many ways, not because we wished to highlight one or another period in time, but because the archeological record itself is incomplete and does not provide adequate coverage for every century, or even each millennium. Today, more than ever, we need robust efforts to recover the dwindling archaeological record from prehistoric times. Sites are being destroyed by natural events such as floods and river bank erosion, by rodents tunneling through sites, by natural decay of some archaeological remains, and of course, by land and resource development. Plowing, tiling, ditching, dams, bridges, roads, and the like all have a damaging impact on the record of the past. At the same time, we realize that some of our neighbors in the Native American community are hostile to the archaeological work that goes on all around the country. They often feel that archaeologists are trying to mandate the history of North America's native peoples. Our intention is not to tell anyone what they have to believe about their past. We only wish here to offer the archaeological evidence that has been uncovered and present it for fair review. Naturally, the reader is free to accept it or not. There are also some who feel that archaeologists have no right to dig in the ground and disturb ancient sites. To those critics we must simply express our regret and disagreement. The archaeological past is a gift from the earth; something that has been preserved for a time in the soil so that we might come to know about past times. We can turn away from this if we choose. Eventually, the ground will absorb the evidence from the past as it cycles everything in it into something new. The archaeologist accepts this gift of knowledge with the understanding that to do otherwise is to waste an opportunity to learn and to know about our collective history. It's a choice we do not justify but can only lay out for fair debate.

Finally, we call for a vigilant public that is aware of the potential archaeology holds for learning about the past. We need concerned public officials, and we need archaeologists willing to devote themselves to the study of places like the Sheyenne Bend. Archaeologists invest vast resources in the study of the lands of the Bible, the pyramids of Egypt, the glories of Greece, and other celebrated and great monuments of the past. But the archaeologist who is also an anthropologist understands that it is our mission to learn about *all* people, not only the ones who are celebrated in history books, or came first, or made the biggest monuments. It is our duty to shed light on the fascinating record of the lands all around us: lands without pyramids, or Parthenons, places lacking in gold or gems—lands, in fact, like the Sheyenne Bend. Accepting this duty, we will someday come at last to the fuller understanding of the past of all people in every place.

References

Ahler, S.A.

1993 Plains Village Cultural Taxonomy for the Upper Knife-Heart Region. *The Phase 1 Archaeological Research Program for the Knife River Indian Villages National Historic Site, Part IV, Interpretation of the Archaeological Record*, edited by T.D. Theissen. Midwest Archaeological Center, Lincoln.

Ahler, S.A. and A.A. Swenson

1993 KNRI and Upper Knife-Heart Region Pottery Analysis. In *The Phase I Archaeological Research Program for the Knife River Indian Villages National Historic Site, Part III*, edited by T.D. Theissen, pp. 1-171. Midwest Archaeological Center, Lincoln.

Anfinson, S.F.

1997 *Southwestern Minnesota Archaeology*. Minnesota Historical Society, St. Paul.

Anfinson, S.F., M.G. Michlovic and J. Stein

1978 *The Lake Bronson Site (21KT1): A Multicomponent Prehistoric Site on the Prairie-Woodland Border in Northwestern Minnesota*. Minnesota Archaeological Society, St. Paul.

Anonymous

1909 *History of the Red River Valley: Past and Present*. Volume II. Herald Printing Company, Grand Forks.

Anonymous

2012 Vegetation, North Dakota Fish and Game Department. Internet resource at http://gf.nd.gov/wildlife/plants-habitat/habitats/vegetation. Accessed September 9, 2015.

Arnold, H.V.

1918 *The Early History of Ransom County*. H.V. Arnold, Larimore.

Artz, J.A.

1995 Geological Contexts of the Early and Middle Holocene Archaeological Record in North Dakota and Adjoining Areas of the Northern Plains. In *Archaeological Geology of the Archaic Period in North America,* edited by E.A. Bettis, III, pp. 67-86. Geological Society of America, Boulder.

Ashworth, A.C.

1999 Climate Change in North Dakota Since the Last Glaciation—Review of the Paleontological Record. *Proceedings of the North Dakota Academy of Science* 53:171-176.

Bailey, V.

1926 *A Biological Survey of North Dakota.* North American Fauna, No. 49. Government Printing Office, Washington.

Bamforth, D.

1994 Indigenous People, Indigenous Violence: Precontact Warfare on the North American Great Plains. *Man* 29 (1):95-115.

Barker, W.T. and W.C. Nelson

1974 *Lower Sheyenne River Basin: Water, Land, People.* North Dakota State University, Fargo.

Bettinger, R.L.

2001 Holocene Hunter-Gatherers. In *Archaeology at the Millennium,* edited by G.M. Feinman and T.D. Price, pp. 137-195. Kluwer Academic/Plenum Publishers, New York.

Boyd, M.

2007 Paleoindian Geochronology of the Assiniboine Delta of Glacial Lake Agassiz. *Canadian Journal of Archaeology* 31(3):198-221.

Boyd, M. C. Surette and B.A. Nicholson

2006 Archaeobotanical Evidence of Prehistoric Maize (Zea mays) Consumption at the Northern Edge of the Great Plains. *Journal of Archaeological Science*:1-12.

Bluemle, J.P.
1979 *Geology of Ransom and Sargent Counties, North Dakota.* North Dakota Geological Survey, Bulletin 69, Part 1. Grand Forks.
1988 *Guide to the Geology of Southeastern North Dakota.* North Dakota Geological Survey, Associated Printers, Grafton.

Bluemle, J. and S.B. Anderson, J.A. Andrews, D.W. Fisher and J.A. LaFever
1986 *North Dakota Stratigraphic Column.* North Dakota Geological Survey, Grand Forks.

Bowers, A.W.
1965 *Hidatsa Social and Ceremonial Organization.* Smithsonian Institution, Bureau of American Ethnology, Bulletin 194. U.S. Government Printing Office, Washington, D.C.

Bray, E.C. and M.C. Bray
1976 *Jospeh N.Nicolett on the Plains and Prairies: Expeditions of 1838-39 with Journals, Letters, and Notes on the Dakota Indians.* Minnesota Historical Society, St. Paul.

Breakey, K.C.
1981 Description of Some Ceramics from the Middle Red River Valley, Minnesota - North Dakota. *The Minnesota Archaeologist* 40(1, March):33-41.

Brink, J.W.
2008 *Imagining Head-Smashed-In: Aboriginal Buffalo Hunting on the Northern Plains.* AU Press, Edmonton.

Bryce, G.
1884 The Mound Builders: A Lost Race Described. *The Historical and Scientific Society of Manitoba, Transactions 18.* Winnipeg.
1904 Among the Mound Builders' Remains. *Manitoba Historical Society Transactions.* Series 1, No. 66.

Bushnell, D.I.

1927 Burials of the Algonquian, Siouan and Caddoan Tribes West of the Mississippi. *Bureau of American Ethnology, Bulletin 83*. Government Printing Office, Washington D.C.

Callahan, K.

1999 The Fort Ransom Writing Rock and Other Cupmarked Boulders at Fort Ransom, North Dakota. Available at the University of Minnesota Library, Minneapolis.

Chapman, K.A., A. Fischer and M.K. Ziegenhagen

1998 *Valley of Grass*. North Star Press, St. Cloud.

Chomko, S. and W.R. Wood

1973 Linear Mounds in the Northeastern Plains. *Archaeology in Montana* 14(2):1-19.

Clark, F.

1984 Knife River Flint and Interregional Exchange. *Midcontinental Journal of Archaeology*. Vol. 9, No. 2:173-198.

Cooper, L.R and E. Johnson

1964 Sandy Lake Ware and Its Distribution. *American Antiquity* 29(4):474-479.

Coues, E.

1897 *New Light on the Early History of the Greater Northwest: The Manuscript Journals of Alexander Henry and of David Thompson, 1799-1814*. Francis P. Harper, New York.

Dahlheimer, T.I.

2003 The Coldwater Spring Deception. Electronic resource, http://www.towahkon.org/Coldwater.html Accessed September 19, 2020

Davis, C.M. and J.D. Keyser

1999 McKean Complex Projectile Point Typology and Function in the Pine Parklands. *Plains Anthropologist* 44(169): 251-270.

Deloria, E.C.
2007 *The Dakota Way of Life*. Mariah Press, Rapid City.

DeMallie, R.J.
2001 Yankton and Yanktonai. In *Handbook of North American Indians*, v.13 (2), edited by R.J. DeMaille, pp 777-793. Smithsonian Institution, Washington, D.C.

Dobbs, C.A. ed.
2000 *Alliance Pipeline L.P.: Excavations at 32RI785, Richland County, North Dakota.* Hemisphere Field Services, Minneapolis.

Dyck, I. and R. Morlan
2001 Hunting and Gathering Tradition: Canadian Plains. In *Handbook of North American Indians*, v.13 (1), edited by R.J. DeMaille, pp 115-130. Smithsonian Institution, Washington, D.C.

Epp, H.T. and I. Dyck
1983 *Tracking Ancient Hunters*. Saskatchewan Archaeological Society, Regina.

Fagan, B.
2005 *Ancient North America*. Thames and Hudson, London.

Fenn, E.
2015 *Encounters at the Heart of the World: A History of the Mandan People*. Hill and Wang, New York.

Forbis, R.G.
1992 The Mesoindian (Archaic) Period in the Northern Plains. *Revista de Arqueologia Americana* 5:27-69.

1998 Besant Phase. In, *Archaeology of Prehistoric Native America: An Encyclopedia*, edited by G. Gibbon, pp. 63-64. Garland Publishing, New York.

Frison, G. C.
1971 The Buffalo Pound in Northwestern Plains Prehistory: Site 48CA302, Wyoming. *American Antiquity* 36(1):77-91.

1998 The Northwestern and Northern Plains Archaic. In *Archaeology on the Great Plains*, edited by W.R. Wood, pp. 140–172. University of Kansas, Lawrence.

2004 *Survival by Hunting*. University of California, Berkeley, Los Angeles/London.

Galler, R.W. Jr.

2008 Sustaining the Sioux Confederation: Yanktonai Initiatives and Influence on the Northern Plains. *Western Historical Quarterly* 39(4):467–490.

Gardner, W.H.

1868 Letter. Smithsonian Institution Collections, Washington, D.C.

Gibbon, G.E.

2012 *Archaeology of Minnesota*. University of Minnesota, Minneapolis.

Gibbon, G.E. and C. Caine

1980 The Middle to Late Woodland Transition in Eastern Minnesota. *Midcontinental Journal of Archaeology* 5(1):57–72.

Gregg, M.L.

1985 *An Overview of the Prehistory of Western and Central North Dakota*. Bureau of Land Management, Billings.

Gregg, M.L. (ed)

1987 *Archaeological Excavation at the Naze Site (32SN246)*. Report submitted to the Bureau of Reclamation, Billings.

Gregg, M.L., P.R. Picha, F.E. Swenson, and A.Bleier

2016 Archaeological Component of the State Plan. State Historical Society, Bismarck.

Grinnell, G.B.

1918 Early Cheyenne Villages. *American Anthropologist* 20 (4):359–380.

Hamilton, S. and B.A. Nicholson

2006 Aboriginal Seasonal Subsistence and Land Use on the Northeastern Plains: Insight from Ethnohistoric Sources. *Plains Anthropologist* 51(199):253–280.

Hanson, J.A.
1975 *Metal Weapons, Tools, and Ornaments of the Teton Dakota Indians.* University of Nebraska, Lincoln.

Hassrick, R.B.
1964 *The Sioux.* University of Oklahoma, Norman.

Harris, K.L.
1987 *Surface Geology of the Sheyenne River Map Area.* North Dakota Geological Survey. AS-15-A1.

Hauer, G.
n.d. Expected Meat Yield from a Bison Bull Carcass. https://www.canadianbison.ca/download_file/view/128/611. Accessed December 8, 2017.

Haug, J.K.
1976 *The 1974-1975 Excavations at the Cherry Point Site (DkMe-10): A Stratified Archaic Site in Southeast Manitoba.* Manitoba Department of Tourism, Recreation and Cultural Affairs, Winnipeg.

Haug, J.K. and M.R. Fosha
2008 Hartford Beach Village: Twenty-Five Years Later. *North Dakota Archaeology* 8: 69-86.

Haury, C.E.
1990 *In the Footsteps of T.H. Lewis: Retracing of the Northwestern Archaeological Survey in North Dakota.* Department of Anthropology Contribution 256, University of North Dakota, Grand Forks.

2005 Analysis of Fauna from the Rustad Site. In, *Archaeology and Paleoenvironment at the Rustad Site (32RI775).* Plains Anthropologist Memoir 37:91-134. Augustums Printing, Lincoln.

Haury, C.E. and F.E. Schneider
1986 *Cultural Resources Survey in the Sheyenne River Drainage.* Department of Anthropology, University of North Dakota, Grand Forks.

Helzer, C.
2010 *The Ecology and Management of Prairies*. University of Iowa, Iowa City.

2014 Bison Good, Cattle Bad? *The Prairie Ecologist*. Electronic Resource at http://prairieecologist.com/2014/01/21/bison-good-cattle-bad/ Accessed September 22, 2015.

Hewes, G.W.
1949 Burial Mounds in the Baldhill Area, North Dakota. *American Antiquity* 14(4):322-328.

Henning, D.R.
2005 The Evolution of the Plains Village Tradition. In *North American Archaeology*, edited by T.R. Pauketat and D.DiPaolo Loren, pp. 161-186. Blackwell, Malden.

Henning, D.R. and D.L. Toom
2003 Cambria and the Initial Middle Missouri Variant Revisited. *The Wisconsin Archaeologist* 84:197-218.

Hofman, J.L. and R.W. Graham
1998 The Paleo-Indian Cultures of the Great Plains. In *Archaeology on the Great Plains*, edited by W.R. Wood, pp. 87-139. University of Kansas, Lawrence.

Holley, G.R.
2008 Place Names, Mounds, and Landscape: An Interpretation of the Late Prehistoric Occupation of the Northeastern Plains. *North Dakota Archaeology* 8:53-67.

Holley, G.R. and M.G. Michlovic
2013 *Archaeology at the Irwin Johnson Site (32RM172)*. Archaeology Lab, Minnesota State University, Moorhead.

Holley, G.R., M.G. Michlovic and R.A. Dalan
2011 *Report on 2008 Archaeology at the Biesterfeldt Site (32RM1), Ransom County, North Dakota*. Department of Anthropology and Earth Science, Minnesota State University Moorhead, Moorhead.

Holley, G.R. and E.M. Kalinowski
2008 The Lucas Site: Enclosures, Military Camps and the Terminal Late Woodland of the Northeastern Plains. *North Dakota Archaeology* 8:127-138.

Howard, J.H.
1966 *The Dakota or Sioux Indians*. J&L Reprints in Anthropology, Lincoln.
1984 *The Canadian Sioux*. University of Nebraska, Lincoln.

Innes, R.J.
2011 Cervus elaphus. In *Fire Effects Information System*, U.S. Department of Agriculture Forest Service. Electronic resource at http://www.fs.fed.us/database/feis. Accessed August 30, 2015.

Irwin, H.T. and H. M. Wormington
1970 Paleo-Indian Tool Types in the Great Plains. *American Antiquity* 35(1):24-34.

Isenberg, A.C.
2000 *The Destruction of the Bison*. Cambridge University, Cambridge.

Jackson, M.A. and D.L. Toom
2004 Bivouac site (32RY189) Evaluative Test Excavations within the Gilbert C. Grafton State Military Reservation, Ramsey County, North Dakota: Final Report. Department of Anthropology, University of North Dakota, Grand Forks.

Johnson, A.M. and A.E. Johnson
1998 The Plains Woodland. In *Archaeology on the Great Plains*, edited by W.R. Wood, pp. 201-234. University of Kansas, Lawrence.

Johnson, C.M.
1991 *Archaeological Reconnaissance in Traverse County, Minnesota*. Reports of Investigations, Institute for Minnesota Archaeology, Minneapolis.
1998 The Coalescent Tradition. In *Archaeology on the Great Plains*, edited by W.R. Wood, pp. 308-344. University of Kansas, Lawrence.

2007 *A Chronology of Middle Missouri Plains Village Sites*. Smithsonian Institution Scholarly Press, Washington D.C.

Johnson, E.

1962 The Prehistory of the Red River Valley. *Minnesota History* 38:157-165.

Kay, M.

1998 The Great Plains Setting. In *Archaeology on the Great Plains*, edited by W.R. Wood, pp. 16-47. University of Kansas, Lawrence.

Kelly, R.L.

1995 *The Foraging Spectrum*. Smithsonian Institution, Washington, D.C.

Kindscher, K.

1987 *Edible Wild Plants of the Prairie*. University of Kansas Press, Lawrence.

Knapp, A.K., J.M. Blair, J.M. Briggs, S.L. Collins, D.C. Hartnett, L.C. Johnson, and E.G. Towne

1999 The Keystone Role of Bison in North American Tallgrass Prairie. *Bioscience* 48(1):1-39.

Kordecki, C. and M.L. Gregg

1986 James River Valley Archaeological Survey 1985. Report submitted to the Bureau of Reclamation, Billlings.

Kroeber, A.L.

1939 *Cultural and Natural Areas of Native North America*. University of California, Berkeley.

Landes, R.

1968 *The Mystic Lake Sioux*. University of Wisconsin, Madison.

Layton, R.

1995 Relating to the Country in the Western Desert. In *The Anthropology of Landscape: Perspectives of Place and Space*, edited by E. Hirsch and M. O'Hanlon, pp. 210-231. Clarendon Press, Oxford.

Lewis, T.H.

1891 Cup-Stones Near Old Fort Ransom, N.D. *The American Naturalist* 25 (293):455-461.

Little Wolf, S.

Nd Precolumbian Tribal Dogs in the Americas. Electronic Resource at http://www.native-languages.org/dogs.htm. Accessed September 25, 2015.

Lowie, R.H.

1982 *Indians of the Plains*. University of Nebraska Press, Lincoln.

McElrath, D.L., A.C. Fortier and T.E. Emerson

2009 An Introduction to Archaic Societies of the Midcontinent. In *Archaic Societies*, edited by T.E. Emerson, D.L. McElrath and A.C. Fortier, pp. 2-22. State University of New York Press, Albany.

McHugh, T.

1972 *The Time of the Buffalo*. Alfred A. Knopf, New York.

Meyer, D. and D. Walde

2009 Rethinking Avonlea: Pottery Wares and Cultural Phases. *Plains Anthropologist* 54(209):49-73.

Meyer, D., A.B. Beaudoin and L.J. Amundson

2011 Human Ecology of the Canadian Prairie Ecozone ca. 9000 BP: The Paleo-Indian Period. In *Human Ecology of the Canadian Prairie Ecozone: 11,000-300 BP*, edited by B.A. Nicholson, pp. 5-41. Canadian Plains Research Center, Saskatchewan.

Michlovic, M.G.

1985 The Problem of the Teton Migration. In *Archaeology, Ecology and Ethnohistory of the Prairie-Forest Border Zone in Minnesota and Manitoba*, edited by J. Spector and E. Johnson, pp 131-145. Reprints in Anthropology 31. J&L Reprint, Lincoln.

1990a The Lucas Site (32RM225): A Fortified Prehistoric Site in the Sheyenne Valley, Ransom County, ND. Minnesota State University Archaeology Lab, Moorhead.

1990b Northern Plains-Woodland Interaction in Prehistory. In *The Woodland Tradition in the Western Great Lakes: Papers Presented to Elden Johnson*, edited by G.E. Gibbon, pp. 45-54. Publications in Anthropology No. 4. University of Minnesota, Minneapolis.

1993a *Cultural Resources Survey in the Floodpool Area of the Proposed Maple River Dam*. Cass County Joint Water Resources District, Fargo.

1993b Archaeological Test Excavations at 32RM92, Ransom County, North Dakota. Archaeology Lab, Moorhead State University, Moorhead.

1996a Archaeological Test Excavations at the Solhjem Site (32RI718), Richland County, North Dakota. Archaeology Lab, Moorhead State University, Moorhead.

1996b Archaeological Investigations at the Rustad Site. In, *Quaternary Geology of the Southern Lake Agassiz Basin*, edited by K.L. Harris, M.R. Luther, and J.R. Reid, pp. 127-135. Bismarck: North Dakota Geological Survey Miscellaneous Series 82.

2005 Excavations at 21CY39: A Blackduck Component on the Northeastern Plains. *The Minnesota Archaeologist* 64:49-84.

2008a The Shea Phase of the Northeastern Plains Village Culture. *North Dakota Archaeology* 8:35-51.

2008b Archaeological Test Excavations at the Peterson Site (32RM401), Ransom County, North Dakota. Archaeology Lab, Minnesota State University, Moorhead.

Michlovic, M.G. and D. McMaster
1982 Preliminary Report on the Sprunk Site (32CS13), Cass County, North Dakota. *Newsletter of the North Dakota Archaeological Association* 3(3):9-15.

Michlovic, M.G. and F.E. Schneider
1993 The Shea Site: A Prehistoric Fortified Village on the Northeastern Plains. *Plains Anthropologist* 38:117-137.

Michlovic, M.G. and F.E. Swenson
1998 Northeastern Plains Village Pottery. *North Dakota History* 65 (2-3):11-25.

Michlovic, M.G. and G.L. Running IV eds.
2005 *Archaeology and Paleoenvironment at the Rustad Site (32RI775).* Plains Anthropologist Memoir 37. Augustums Printing, Lincoln.

Michlovic, M.G. and G.R. Holley and R.A. Dalan
2012 Archaeological Testing at the Schultz Site (32RM215), Ransom County, North Dakota, 2009-2010. Archaeology Lab, Minnesota State University, Moorhead.

2019 Archaeology of the Sprunk Site (32CS4478). *North Dakota Archaeology* 9:1-26.

Montgomery, H.
1906 Remains of Prehistoric Man in the Dakotas. *American Anthropologist* 8(4):640-651.

Moore, J.H., M.P. Liberty and A.T. Straus
2001 Cheyenne. In *Handbook of North American Indians*, v.13 (2), edited by R.J. DeMaille, pp 863-885. Smithsonian Institution, Washington, D.C.

Mussulman, J.
2011 Blackbird Hill, Nebraska. Electronic resource, http://www.lewis-clark.org/article/1052, Accessed February 2018.

Myster, S.M.
2001 *Ten Thousand Years of Population Relationships at the Prairie-Woodland Interface: Cranial Morphology in the Upper Midwest and Contiguous Areas of Manitoba and Ontario*. Ph.D. Dissertation, University of Tennessee, Knoxville.

National Park Service
2006 Sacred Site and Traditional Cultural Property Analysis. Bureau of Mines Twin Cities Research Center, Main Campus, Hennepin County, MN. Electronic resource, https://www.nps.gov/miss/learn/management/upload/TCPCommentsFinal.pdf. Accessed December 6, 2017.

Neuman, R.W.
1975 *The Sonota Complex and Associated Sites on the Northern Great Plains*. Nebraska State Historical Society, Lincoln.

Nicholson, B.A.
1990 Ceramic Affiliations and the Case for Incipient Horticulture in Southwestern Manitoba. *Canadian Journal of Archaeology* 14:33-60.

Nicholson, B.A., S. Hamilton, M. Boyd and S. Nicholson
2008 A Late Plains Woodland Adaptive Strategy in the Northern Parkands: The Vickers Focus Forager-Horticulturalists. *North Dakota Archaeology* 8:19-34.

Olsen, S.J.
1974 Early Domestic Dogs in North America and Their Origins. *Journal of Field Archaeology* 1 (3/4):343-345

Omodt, H.W., G.A. Johnsgard, D.D. Patterson and O.P. Olson
1968 *The Major Soils of North Dakota*. Agricultural Experiment Station, North Dakota State University, Fargo.

Oneroad, A.E. and A.B. Skinner
2003 *Being Dakota,* edited by L.L. Anderson. Minnesota Historical Society, St. Paul.

Oetelaar, G.A.
2014 Worldviews and human–animal relations: Critical Perspectives on Bison–Human Relations among the Euro-Canadians and Blackfoot. *Critique of Anthropology* 34(1):94-112.

Pearsall, D.M.
2012 People, Plants, and Culinary Traditions. In *The Oxford Handbook of North American Archaeology*, edited by T. Pauketat, pp. 73-85. Oxford University Press, Oxford and New York.

Peck, T.R. and J.W. Ives
2001 Late Side-Notched Projectile Points on the Northwestern Plains. *Plains Anthropologist* 46 (176):163-193.

Reeves, B.O.K.
1990 Communal Bison Hunters of the Northern Plains. In, *Hunters of the Recent Past*, edited by L.B. Davis and B.O.K. Reeves, pp. 168-194. Unwin Hyman, London.

Running, G.L. IV
2005 Geoarchaeological Investigations. In *Archaeology and Paleoenvironment at the Rustad Site (32RI775)*. Plains Anthropologist Memoir 37, edited by M.G. Michlovic and G.L. Running IV, pp. 11-62. Augustums Printing, Lincoln.

Samson-Flood, R.
1986 *Lessons from Chouteau Creek*. Crescent Publishing, Hills, MN.

Schnieder, F.
1982 A Model of Prehistoric Cultural Developments in the James River Valley of North Dakota. *Journal of the North Dakota Archaeological Association* 1:113-130.
2002 Prehistoric Horticulture in the Northeastern Plains. *Plains Anthropologist* 47:33-50.
2005 The Lisbon Burial (32RM201). *North Dakota Archaeological Association Newsletter* 26 (4):1-12.
2008 A Long Time Ago in the James River Valley. *North Dakota Archaeology* 8:1-17.

Sedivec, K.K. And J.L. Printz
2012 *Ecological Sites of North Dakota*. Natural Resources Conservation Service, North Dakota State University, Fargo.

Severson, K.E. and C.H. Sieg
2006 *The Nature of Eastern North Dakota:Pre-1880 Historical Ecology*. North Dakota Institute for Regional Studies, Fargo.

Sharrock, S.
1974 Cree, Cree-Assiniboines and Assiniboines: Interethnic Social Organization on the Far Northern Plains. *Ethnohistory* 21(2):95-122.

Sheldon, A.E.
1919 *Histories and Stories of Nebraska*. University Publishing, Lincoln.

Skinner, A.
1915 Associations and Ceremonies of the Menomini Indians. *Anthropological Papers of the American Museum of Natural History*, 13 (2).

Snortland, J.S.
1994 Northern Plains Woodland Mortuary Practices. In *Skeletal Biology in the Great Plains: Migration, Warfare, Health and Subsistence*, edited by D.W. Owsley and R.L. Jantz, pp. 51-70. Smithsonian Institution, Washington, D.C.

Spector, J.D.
1993 *What This Awl Means: Feminist Archaeology at a Wahpeton Dakota Village*. Minnesota Historical Society, St. Paul.

Standing Bear, L.
1975 *My People the Sioux*. University of Nebraska, Lincoln.

Steuter, A. and L. Hindinger
1999 Comparative Ecology of Bison and Cattle on Mixed-Grass Prairie. *Great Plains Research* 9:329-342.

Strong, W.D.
1940 From History to Prehistory in the Northern Great Plains. *Essays in Historical Anthropology in North America*, 100. Smithsonian Institution, Washington, D.C.

Stubbs, D., D. Sather and A. Ollendorf
2001 *Twenty-Nine Archaeological Sites and Site Leads, Proposed Flood Control Dam and Associated Features along the Maple River, North Dakota*. HDR Engineering, Inc.

Syms, E.L.
1979 The Devils Lake-Sourisford Burial Complex on the Northeastern Plains. *Plains Anthropologist* 24(86): 283-308.
1982 The Arvilla Complex: A Reassessment. *Journal of the North Dakota Archaeological Association*. 1:135-166

Tesky, Julie L.
1995 Bos bison. In: Fire Effects Information System, [Online]. U.S. Department of Agriculture, Forest Service, Rocky Mountain Research Station, Fire Sciences Laboratory (Producer). Electronic resource at https://www.fs.fed.us/database/feis/animals/mammal/bobi/all.html Accessed December 4, 2020.

Thomas, C.
1894 *Report on the Mound Explorations of the Bureau of Ethnology*. Smithsonian Institution, Washington, D.C.

Thompson, R.S.
1983 The Edgar L. Bayley Collection. *Newsletter of the North Dakota Archaeological Association* 4(3):3-10.

Thompson, R.G.
1990 *The Archaeology of the Dahnke-Reinke Site (32CS29)*. University of Iowa, Iowa City.

Thorfinnson, S.M.
1975 *Ransom County History*. Ransom County Historical Society, Fort Ransom.

Toom, D.L.
2004 Northeastern Plains Village Complex Timelines and Relationships. *Plains Anthropologist* 49:281-297.

Toom, D.L., editor
2014 *Akata Site (32SN121) 1996 Excavations, Stutsman County, North Dakota.* University of North Dakota Anthropology Research Contribution 450. Grand Forks.

Tucker, S.J.
1942 *Indian Villages of the Illinois Country, v.2.* Scientific Papers of the Illinois State Museum, Part 1, Atlas. Springfield.

United States Geological Survey (USGS)
2017 USGS 05058700 Sheyenne River at Lisbon, ND. Electronic resource, https://waterdata.usgs.gov/nwis/uv?05058700. Accessed December 8, 2017.

Valero-Garces, B.L., K.R. Laird, S.C. Fritz, K. Kelts, E Ito and E.C. Grimm
1997 Holocene Climate in the Northern Great Plains Inferred from Sediment Stratigraphy, Stable Isotopes, Carbonate Geochemistry, Diatoms, and Pollen at Moon Lake, North Dakota. *Quaternary Research* 48:359-369.

Vehik, R.
1979 *An Archaeological Survey of Selected Portions of the Lower and Middle Sheyenne River Basin in North Dakota.* U.S. Army Corps of Engineers, St. Paul.

Vehik, S.C. and R. Vehik
1985 Anderson Mound: A Late Prehistoric Burial Mound in Eastern North Dakota. *The Minnesota Archaeologist* 44(1):3-17.

Wedel, W.R.
1961 *Prehistoric Man on the Great Plains.* University of Oklahoma, Norman.

Wheeler, R.

1963 *The Stutsman Focus:An Aboriginal Culture Complex in the Jamestown Reservoir Area, North Dakota.* Smithsonian Institution Bureau of American Ethnology Bulletin 185. U.S. Government Printing Office, Washington, D.C.

Whittaker, W.

2016 The Palace Site and the Appearance of House Basins in the Middle Archaic. *Plains Anthropologist* 61(239):250-272.

Widga, C.C.

2006 *Bison, Bogs, and Big Bluestem: The Subsistence Ecology of Middle Holocene Hunter-Gatherers in the Eastern Great Plains.* Ph.D. Dissertation, University of Kansas, Lawrence.

Willey, G. and P. Phillips

1958 *Method and Theory in American Archaeology.* University of Chicago, Chicago and London.

Winchell, N.H.

1911 *The Aborigines of Minnesota.* Minnesota Historical Society, St. Paul.

Wood, W.R.

1959 Two Woodland Vessels from North Dakota. *American Antiquity* 25(1):123-125.

1963 Lisbon Flared Rim and Owego Flared Rim Wares. In *The Stutsman Focus:An Aboriginal Culture Complex in the Jamestown Reservoir Area, North Dakota*, by R.P. Wheeler, River Basin Survey Papers, no. 30. Bureau of American Ethnology Bulletin, 185: 231-232.

1971 *Biesterfeldt:A Post Contact Coalescent Village on the Northeastern Plains.* U.S. Government Printing Office, Washington, D.C.

1980 Plains Trade in Prehistoric and Protohistoric Intertribal Relations. In *Anthropology on the Great Plains*, edited by W.R. Wood and M. Liberty, pp. 98-109. University of Nebraska, London and Lincoln.

1993 *Joseph N. Nicollet's 1839 Manuscript Maps of the Missouri and Upper Mississippi Basin.* Illinois State Museum, Springfield.

1998 Introduction. In *Archaeology on the Great Plains*, edited by W.R. Wood, pp. 1-15. University of Kansas, Lawrence.

About the Authors

Michael Michlovic is Emeritus Professor of Anthropology, Minnesota State University Moorhead, where he taught from 1975-2015, and served as chair of the Department of Anthropology and Earth Science. He studied anthropology at the University of Pittsburgh and received a Ph.D. from the University of Illinois. Michlovic conducted fieldwork in the Eastern and Midwestern US, as well as the Northeastern Great Plains. His research interests include the archaeology of the Northeastern Plains, popular uses of the past, and the Archaic period. He is a former editor of the *Minnesota Archaeologist* and past president of the Council for Minnesota Archaeology.

George R. Holley is currently Emeritus Professor, Minnesota State University Moorhead. He earned his PhD in Anthropology from Southern Illinois University Carbondale. Holley has been practicing archaeology since 1973 across the United States in the Southeast, Midwest, Plains, and Southwest, and in Mesoamerica. Prehistoric ceramics are his specialty and he has created ceramic sequences for Tchefuncte ceramics in Louisiana, the Cahokia site and Middle Silver Creek in Illinois, the Sheyenne Bend region in North Dakota, and for the Classic Maya city of Piedras Negras, Guatemala. He is presently working on a Handbook for Minnesota Precontact Ceramics.

www.ingramcontent.com/pod-product-compliance
Lightning Source LLC
LaVergne TN
LVHW010612100826
845148LV00014B/2939

* 9 7 8 1 7 3 6 4 9 8 6 7 5 *